Matt Griggs was born in 1976. Growing up in the beachside suburb of Cronulla in the south of Sydney, Griggs was raised in a beach-loving family alongside sporty brothers, a PE-teaching father and an ever-supportive mother. Sport consumed his life, but it was surfing that swallowed him whole. Griggs reached the top ten of Australia in the junior and open ranks, competing around the world as a professional surfer for six years. He retired in 1999 to work for *Tracks* magazine as a full-time writer and remains a committed surfer.

SEBASTIAN ROJAS

surfers

A line-up of surfing's most inspirational characters

matt griggs

Harper*Sports*
An imprint of HarperCollins*Publishers*

Harper*Sports*

An imprint of HarperCollins*Publishers*, Australia

First published in Australia in 2002
by HarperCollins*Publishers* Pty Limited
ABN 36 009 913 517
A member of the HarperCollins*Publishers* (Australia) Pty Limited Group
www.harpercollins.com.au

HarperCollins*Publishers*

25 Ryde Road, Pymble, Sydney NSW 2073, Australia
31 View Road, Glenfield, Auckland 10, New Zealand
77–85 Fulham Palace Road, London W6 8JB, United Kingdom
2 Bloor Street East, 20th floor, Toronto, Ontario M4W 1A8, Canada
10 East 53rd Street, New York NY 10022, USA

National Library of Australia Cataloguing-in-Publication data:

Griggs, Matt.
  Surfers: a line-up of surfing's most
  inspirational characters.
  ISBN 0 7322 7485 0.
  1. Surfers – Biography. 2. Surfers – Anecdotes.
  3. Surfing. I. Title.
797.320922

Every effort has been made by the author to contact copyright owners of images
contained herein. Any copyright holders who have not been contacted are welcome
to contact the publishers.

Front cover photograph: Andrew Buckley
Back cover main photograph: Andrew Buckley
Back cover portrait photographs: Sarge
Cover and internal design by Luke Causby, HarperCollins Design Studio
Printed and bound in Australia by Griffin Press on 79gsm Bulky Paperback

8 7 6 5   04 05 06

Dedication

To inscribe or address (a book, piece of music, etc.) to a patron, friend, etc., as in testimony of respect or affection.

Nah, just joking.

This book is dedicated to the ocean, because no matter what mood it's in, it always waves at you.

THE LINE-UP

INTRODUCTION

About a week before red-pen-wielding warrior-cum-editor Patrick Mangan took to the final chapters of this book with one last flourish, I had an encounter. A moment a poet might describe as one of clarity. As usual, it was in the surf. While Patrick was suffering, trying to correct my spelling mistakes, even entertaining the idea of plugging his red pen into an ink drip, I was surfing a reef break in Cronulla and having a great old time.

I had just finished every interview and written every profile. The writing process was a painful though rewarding experience and I was grateful to all the guys interviewed in *Surfers* for showing me their true selves. Of the 26 surfers who ended up in this book, all have a special story of unique significance. Their anecdotes — or anecdotes about them — have travelled like waves through thousands of line-ups all around the world and I feel privileged to have been in some of those line-ups to catch them. What a journey it has been, I thought to myself, sitting silently out the back of my home break.

After a year-long assignment, I was back where this whole thing had started — the ocean. Home. The water was chilled by winter and marked by a clean groundswell. I paddled into a wave, comfortable with the predictability of local knowledge, and pulled into a barrel. Relaxed and excited, I looked up at the lip to check out the view as I sped out of the tube, playing with it like an old toy. Then it happened. I saw something I wanted to show you, the reader. Frozen in that millisecond of simplicity was the cover of this book — the shape, the colours, everything. It transfixed me. Locked inside that tube, time froze and I saw the photo that had been pinned on my mental noticeboard for months with the message, 'Share the stories of all the freaks you've ever met, or wanted to meet, call it *Surfers* and take the reader inside their lives. But hurry up, Patrick's freaking.' In the end, the ocean had showed me what I wanted to show you. Scientists say waves never stop and now I think I know why.

The first guy I told about my experience was my work and surf buddy Ben Mondy. Ben's the deputy editor at *Tracks* and spends more time at my house than I do. 'You're off ya head Griggsy,' he told me as I paddled toward his laughter.

To be honest, that's exactly how I felt — dosed up and a little tipsy from the pit. It made me realise that sometimes you have to stop, take a good look around, and smell those salt-scented roses.

In writing this book I wanted to tell the stories of surfers who inspire; to show surfers from every angle; to give you a new reason to go surfing, no matter who you are, where you are, or where you want to be. I wanted to invite you inside the barrel that is life and, more than most, the life of the surfer, so I looked far and wide for surfers whose stories deserved to be told. What's more, I had Patrick scent the book with salt, so please — exhale calmly and read each chapter with your nose. But don't forget to go surfing afterwards; it will clear the airways.

Dean

MORRISON

M ost people have diaries to keep themselves organised. I'm not sure what, if anything, Dean Morrison does. He is one of the most exciting young surfers in the world today, but no matter how much his popularity increases, he seems oblivious to responsibility. It's the way he was and the way he is. We call him 'Tricky', because you never know where the prankster is, or what he's going to do next — and I don't just mean on a wave. He's a street kid, a disciple of the points of Coolangatta, brought up by one of its best champions, former world number one Wayne 'Rabbit' Bartholomew.

'Hi, you've reached Dean, ummm, please leave a message.' Beep. A computerised voice came on the answering machine on his mobile. 'This mailbox is full.' It had been full for a couple of months. Sometimes I wonder why Dean even has a phone; he never uses it. Though I'm sure he knows the games inside out.

So I did what everyone has to do — I rang his girlfriend, Elady. Elady has been with Dean for a couple of years now. And the two Gold Coast kids are great together. 'She grounds me,' Dean told me once. 'It's unreal.'

'Hello.' Her voice was soothing and friendly.

'Hi Elady,' I said, introducing myself, 'I'm trying to track down your boyfriend.'

She was in Brisbane, studying for an exam when I called. 'Oh, OK, he's probably surfing.' No surprise there. 'He was supposed to be ringing me this arvo though,' she said. 'Can I get him to call you back? On this number?'

Of course he forgot to call back but it gave me time to reflect. The first time I'd really hung out with Dean was in Indonesia, when he decided at the last minute that he'd come on a boat trip with Andy King, Mick Cain, me and a few others through Lombok and Sumbawa. We were in West Oz at the time and he bought a new ticket for double the price and landed in Bali with winter clothes. The next day we went down to Volcom (his major sponsor at the time) in Kuta, so Dean could get some boardies to surf in the Balinese heat. He turned up at the Volcom store and introduced himself to the Balinese lady behind the counter. His mumbled and barely audible street talk confused the poor lady. She was probably petrified of giving out free clothes to someone whose dark skin looked like her own. His Maori genes, combined with the Queensland sun, make him feel at home in most tropical islands.

A little shy at first, Dean finally pointed to a life-size poster of himself on the wall behind her. '... Ummmm, that's me there.' She looked embarrassed. Dean giggled. 'Nah, just joking. That's me over there,' he said, pointing to another poster of someone else. 'Nah, just joking ... That's me.' The lady's head just about exploded and she ushered her assistant over to accommodate this confusing man, as quickly as possible.

We boarded the boat. Though he was sick for the first week of the trip, Dean didn't complain once. When he had enough energy to get up for a piss, he decided he could surf again and didn't get out of the water during daylight hours. If you think you're a keen surfer, spend a couple of weeks with this guy and he will rock your world.

'Hi, you've reached Dean...' The next day he was still not answering his phone. A bit more time to reflect. We were on a flight about to land in Los Angeles. When Andy King, who was sitting next to us, went to the dunny, Dean thought it would be a good idea to cut out a portrait-size porno photo and slot it in Kingy's passport. Of course he had my permission. 'Will he freak, will he care?' he asked, giggling.

When Kingy arrived at the most security-conscious airport in the world, he looked confused when the immigration official said, 'Is this some kind of joke, Mr King?'

'What? What?'

He had no idea that a lovely looking lass, with pierced nipples and her legs spread, was looking out at a US immigration official saying, 'Cum inside me!'

Beep, still his answering machine. Deadline approaching. Come on Deano. Where are you? More time to reflect. Hawaii, season 2001/02.

DEAN MORRISON

Deano was at Pipeline, sitting out the front of a house he has stayed at for years. This day was huge and onshore — it looked nothing like Pipelines — and Deano and the boys were settling in for the arvo with some beers. 'I'll give you US$100 if you paddle out to third reef and catch a set,' said Joel Parkinson to Dean. 'Yeah, me too,' chimed in Mick Fanning. 'Righto,' said Deano, putting down his fourth beer, and paddled straight through the frothy onshore 20-foot mess — and straight to third reef. He took off on the first set, and rode it all the way in to the cheers of his Aussie compatriots. Unfortunately for Dean, he already owed Parko and Mick US$100 each anyway, but at least he got to pay off his debts.

Beep, beep, beep. Still no answer. Time for more reflections. This time we were at his home on the Gold Coast. I was admiring Dean's new Holden HSV ClubSport as we got out of the surf at Duranbah during the 2002 Aussie leg of the World Qualifying Semis (WQS) tour. Of course, he had just qualified for the WCT and had also just signed a healthy six-figure sponsorship with Oakley. Life was good.

He had his car parked at the top of the little hill sandwiched between the clubhouse and the Tweed Bar. I didn't even know this car park existed. Jay Phillips was towelling off after a surf, Jevon Harvey was packing up his video gear and talking to Joel Parkinson and Mick Fanning. His mates had similar cars. 'They're just me mates I hang out and get pissed with,' Deano said.

'Is it the same model as Joel's?' I asked, as he revved the engine. It roared and cracked and Dean giggled with excitement at his new toy.

'Nah,' he said, jumping at the chance. 'It's one better. Jump in, we'll go for a drive. Hang on,' he added, picking a disc from his CD stacker, 'listen to this...' *DOOOOF!* He giggled again. What a noise factory; it was like a compressed concert. Inside it was how I remembered

'Kitt' on the TV show *Night Rider*. It was black and sleek. But on the outside it was muscly and beautifully scary. We drove over past the Tweed Bar and turned right on the street that goes up to the D-Bah lookout. My stomach dropped with the accelerator. I hoped the kid knew what he was doing. The wheels spun and he hit second gear and the wheels spun again at third. He giggled. I freaked. This was no ordinary car. We raced up to the very top where a huge compass looks over the beach Dean has surfed a million times, before finishing the time trial back at the club house.

'Wow!' I thought out aloud.

He smiled at what was perhaps his fastest lap to date. 'Pretty good eh?'

Only two years ago, Dean was driving a rusty Toyota Tarago that he bought for $500. A car he used to have to push-start. 'I always had to park it up the top of this hill,' he said, 'so I could get home.'

Deano was born on 22 December 1980 at Tweed Heads. His mother was a Maori who had married his Australian father to come and live in Australia. His upbringing was a little different to most. He became a street kid, a delinquent of sorts, who spent most of his time surfing. He won events and sponsors early in his life, which fuelled his dream to surf all day every day. He didn't have much money and would do whatever it took to stay in the water. There was an uncanny resemblance here to former world champion Wayne 'Rabbit' Bartholomew. And it was Bugs who would change Deano's life.

'I first met Deano at D-Bah in 1991,' said Bartholomew. 'He was this little guy who had enough guts to put it on me that he wanted to join Snapper [the star-studded surfing club]. I initially waved him off and told him to come back when he was 11 or 12. Half an hour later he was back, basically tugging on my boardshorts for my attention.

He asked for a try-out and I gave him a shot in an Under–14 heat. There was about 4–5 foot of swell running, at least twice overhead, and Deano strategised by sitting off the wall and plucking wedges. He flogged our best cadets, and they gave him some respect. At the end of the day he was still hanging around and I gave him a ride home. Next minute he's got me picking him up before school and dropping him off on my way to work, then he'd fly into my office at 4 p.m. and talk me into a latey.'

Bugs and Dean formed a tight relationship that was mutually necessary. Bugs didn't have a son, yet — and Deano needed some kind of guidance. He couldn't have picked a better person. 'At the time I was happily living in a great house that Wayne Dean had built me up at Bilambil Heights at the back of Tweed,' said Rabbit. 'I'd bought the land with my winnings from the 1982 Coke Surfabout and sat on it for 19 years, then had Deany build me a modest but very comfortable and stylish dream house. That was me, done and dusted — until Deano worked his magic. They were building these cool-looking apartments on Kirra Point and every morning after I'd picked him up in the backstreets of Kirra we'd drive around the point and he'd go, "You should buy one of them" or "C'mon Bugs, you should live here". I'd respond with a "Shut up kid, I'm happy on the hill", but he was so persistent. Then one day I'd had enough of his propaganda and I pulled in and checked out the front middle apartment. That was nine years ago and it was the best thing I ever did. The little bugger was right, but the funny thing is that he had his bedroom sussed out while I was still checking the kitchen. A month later he moved in and the rest is history.'

They surfed every day. You'd see them together cracking each other up, laughing and surfing all the time. Being a world champion, Bugs captured Dean's respect. But more so by being a character that he could have fun with and learn all those things that you're too proud to learn off your own dad.

'We have a special relationship,' said Bugs. 'Part father/son, part mentor/student, part old buddy/little mate. I took him under my wing because I could see my efforts would be rewarded with dedication and commitment. Plus I liked the kid's style, humour and street savvy. I saw a lot of the young Bugs in Deano, and I know that people helped me, especially during those formative years when it was easy to go off the rails and end up a juvenile delinquent. Just like me, there was a ratbag element to Dean's makeup, and if guided, this could be harnessed and transformed into an athletic pursuit. The rest of the maturity thing would just fall into place; the most important goal was to fill the mantelpiece with first-place trophies. And that's exactly what he did.'

With Rabbit as his coach and mentor, Dean became the best junior surfer in Australia. He won the Gold Coast, Queensland, Australian and world titles all in one year. He won the Hot Buttered/Ocean & Earth Pro Junior and finally qualified for the World Championship Tour (WCT) in 2002. That's when things changed. Dean bought his own house with all the money that was coming in just as Bugs had done — and Rabbit became the president of the ASP. Despite still being the best of pranksters when together, it was as if they'd both suddenly matured.

'These days it is a lot different,' said Bugs. 'I don't coach or manage Deano any more. I guided him into suitable management and he trains with various coaches as the need arrives. When I was gearing myself for the ASP job I understood that the neutrality of the position meant the end of the Bugs/Deano era. And it was really hard to tell him that when he was old enough to go out on a serious campaign to

DEAN MORRISON

qualify for the WCT, he would have to move on. I thought about that a lot and while it kind of tore me up it also worked out naturally, because the sponsors came through and with it the opportunity [for Deano] to be financially independent. Dean flew the Kirra coop in February 2001, bought his own house, got a girlfriend, bought a hot car, qualified for the WCT and set his career up.

'Of course I'm proud of him. He is his own man and a fine young Australian he has turned out to be. I last coached Dean in October 1998. We ended the era with him winning the 1998 Gold Coast, Queensland, Australian and World Under–18 Junior Titles. Now he walks his own walk and is learning the ropes at WCT level. He has his mates, his manager, his coaches, but at the end of the day, he's on his own path because the bottom line is that when Dean is in the line-up at Teahupoo, Pipe and Cloudbreak, there is nobody holding his hand. Deano Morrison is running his own race and good luck to him. I hope he realises his dream.'

'Deano!' He was at the airport, about to leave for a promotional surf trip to Indonesia. He called me reverse charge because he had no money on him. He'd learnt a lot of things from Bugs. 'Sorry Griggsy, I almost forgot. I just remembered then.' He laughed at his own irresponsibility. Deano cracks himself up a lot. He might seem the quietest of the three Coolangatta kids, himself, Joel Parkinson and Mick Fanning, but he is always the one lurking in the background, giggling at some prank he has just played on someone. He doesn't need other people to keep himself occupied and entertained. In fact he does his own thing more than anybody. It's like he's the only one who understands his humour in its entirety, so he's happy to keep himself entertained. Just this year, during the Quiksilver Pro, a time when Deano had his first WCT event at his home at Kirra, you'd

DEAN MORRISON

think he would have been the main guy hanging around, soaking it up. But he was down the coast surfing with his mates, or on the golf course. In fact, most of the time he was by himself.

'I need to get away,' he said, 'to play golf or just go and surf by myself. It's the release that I get and what I enjoy the most in surfing — just being on an uncrowded beach, somewhere, looking for waves.'

As a surfer, Dean started very young. 'My first memorable moment in the surf was when I got a barrel at Kirra. I was about seven. It was probably a two-second barrel,' he laughed as a last call rang out for a Qantas flight. 'But I thought I was in it forever — like I was going to have to walk back from Tugun or something. The barrel was in front of my mate when I took off. Then when I came out, I was pretty much in the same spot ...'

These days, Dean is the best surfer at Kirra. The beneficiary of the views out the window of Rabbit's apartment, he has got to know the wave inside and out. He knows when to pull in and when to turn. When he rides the tube, he sits tight to the wall of the wave, toying with it. He drops his shoulder in the wall to slow down, not just his hand. When it's pumping, you'll see him on more waves than anyone, the ultimate standout. He surfs all day, constantly running back around the point and jumping in the water at the big groyne. I'm sure he's sneaked a wave off us all out there at some stage. But it doesn't have to be pumping for Deano to surf all day. He is so motivated. That's his training, surfing four times a day, every day. That's all he does, and he explains it simply: 'It's just so much fun surfing. I can never go in, because your next wave can always be better than your last. Why would you want to be doing anything else?'

Growing up, Dean didn't do anything else but surf. While his mates were in the classroom, he was learning his trade in the water. I asked

DEAN MORRISON

him when he had left school, trying to hurry as I heard more boarding calls in the background. He wouldn't have noticed them. 'I don't think I ever went,' he laughed. 'Officially, I left halfway through year 12, but I probably only went for one year all up.'

Deano's life in solitude has somewhat dissipated. As one of the highest-paid and most marketable surfers today, he is expected to do a lot more promo work. He is also expected to perform. 'I do love to do all that stuff,' he said. 'I love the video stuff because watching good footage is so good for your confidence. The only pressure is that I personally want to do really well. But more so, I want people to look at me as a really good surfer. The rest of the media stuff doesn't really matter to me.'

When Deano won the Surf Cult Pro, the last WQS event of the Australian leg, he won it with an aerial 360. Tricky. As he talked on his mobile in the competitors' area to an interviewer, still wet from the final, his mate Troy Brooks came over to tell him a story about the casino the night before. Deano erupted into giggles and forgot all about the interview. When he realised he was holding the phone, about a minute or two later, he had this look, like, 'How did that get in my hand?' He hung up and collected his trophy. The commentator asked him if he had any words to say. 'Not really,' he giggled. 'Nah!'

Deano never does have much to say. So how does he want to be perceived? I gave him the opportunity before he boarded his flight.

'I don't know,' he said. 'Just as a hunk ... Nah! Tough guy! Nah. I like long walks along the beach,' he laughed again. 'Nah, seriously ... just a down-to-earth guy who just wants to go surfing and be known as a good surfer.'

Go get 'em 'Tricky'.

DEAN MORRISON

David

GUINEY

I n 1986 David Guiney paddled out to a new break for the first time with Mark Jackson in Tasmania's deep south, a place where giant cliffs drop deep into an ocean that runs all the way to Antarctica. What they stumbled upon was a new realm in surfing that would forever change their perception of ocean power. A secret wave that had been plugged to the wall of the Southern Ocean for too long and that needed to release some of its seemingly limitless energy. It was a test where two surfers probably learnt more about themselves in one surf than in the rest of their surfing lifetime. Mark, a very competent surfer, feared the death-defying abnormalities of this break — he never wanted to come back. Guiney did. For over a decade in fact, by himself, he travelled back to this place two-and-a-half hours of bushwalking away from any civilisation and medical help. It is perhaps one of the greatest pioneering surf stories of the modern era.

Surrounded by giant cliffs and endless ocean is a wave called Shipsterns, originally named over a century ago after the distinctive shape of the headland that stands guard over the break. 'The first guy that took me down there was Johnno Rhodes,' recalls Guiney. 'He lives there and was taking tourists down there in the '80s just to look at the waves smash on the rocks. It's an intense piece of coastline. Massive cliffs that drop into the ocean. No access other than by boat. He was saying, "David, you've got to come down and check it out". I looked at it and nowhere was breaking because the water just drops straight off from the cliffs into such deep water and waves don't break. Then there was this one spot, that stuck out on its own. I saw it and just went "WOW!"'

Guiney, now 46, lived out many surfing adventures through the '70s and '80s around the world, but all this came to an end when he found what he was looking for in his own backyard. 'I'd surfed G-Land, Padang, Desert Point, Outside Corner, rah rah rah ... and there was still more to come. But when I saw one wave that day it solved everything. I knew I never had to travel for waves again. For me I had entered a whole new realm and it became my passion. It was like hunting big game and I spent a lot of time there.'

What Guiney found was one of the most intimidating waves ever seen and he describes it as if it were a part of his family. 'It's got this perfect triangular edge that drops out into the water and that's what

DAVID GUINEY

makes it so good. It's the only break on that entire piece of coastline. In the blink of an eye the waves hit the shallow ledge and transform from a lump in the ocean into a 20-foot face.'

To get the true scope of the intensity of the waves, imagine a 120-foot-high cliff that stands before the break. According to Guiney, 'The waves break at least 150 to 200 metres in front of the cliff.' There is seaweed and bits of driftwood sitting at the top of that cliff. Swells from the south have had probably 30 seconds to slow down before hitting the cliff, but it isn't enough. One of the most intense reef set-ups in the world spits bits of seaweed and driftwood up the top of the cliff like pieces of unwanted meat stuck in its teeth.

Although it has only recently entered mainstream press under the name Fluffies, the wave has flirted with the limelight for years, but still remained in the shadow of waves like Teahupoo and Mavericks, simply because no one went there. 'Everyone was caught up chasing waves in Indo, the Maldives, Tahiti. They were just following each other,' says Guiney. 'They were all sheep!'

It was then that Guiney introduced another local, Andrew Campbell, to his discovery (Campbell named it 'Fluffies' in newspaper interviews after a *Tracks* feature brought it much media attention Australia-wide). In a sense Campbell took over the reins from an ageing Guiney. It was like Guiney wrote him into his surfing will so that the wave would live on in guarded succession. But there were no rules, no clauses and what followed was a massive tug-of-war that continues to this day. They both realised the wave was dead as they knew it and are now competing for their name on its gravestone.

'There was almost going to be a contest on out there a few years back,' says Guiney. 'When Andrew found out and he wasn't invited he

DAVID GUINEY

was a little upset. At that stage he hadn't surfed it yet so I just told him, "Hey, go and surf it, forget everything else, just go and surf it." But he needed someone to push him and he needed photo evidence, so he invited Rasta [David Rastovich], who has since spent a lot of time there, and Justin Gane down there for the videoing of *Pulse 2000.'* I could hear a vague sigh over the phone. 'That was the beginning of the end basically.'

While their efforts brought it to the edge of mainstream attention, the article in *Tracks* rocked the whole surfing world — and Guiney. Kieren Perrow, Drew Courtney and Mark Matthews subsequently made one of the most memorable surf trips in history. Shipsterns hit the main stage everywhere and ended Tasmania's divine isolation from world surfing forever. There have since been many attempts to go down there and the wave is now a common topic of conversation for most surfers.

Guiney believes its new exposure is a reflection of two different eras. 'It's almost like the old surfer/new surfer thing. Especially here in Tasmania, where the mentality is to reject the spotlight. As far as Andrew goes, I gave it to him. I said, "You can surf this wave for the next 20 years by yourself, or you can sell your soul and pay the price for that." He now regrets it. Me personally, I wouldn't have done it. I just sit back and watch.'

It must have been weird for Guiney, talking to me about a wave he wouldn't let a camera near for so long. But I was beginning to understand that neither he, nor Andrew Campbell, nor *Tracks*, had the power to decide who would grace the line-up. The wave itself would. His voice remained calm, content. If one big wave can satisfy someone for a while, imagine what 15 years of it can do.

DAVID GUINEY

It takes time and energy to get to know a new break — tides, winds, swell direction. According to Guiney, the bigger the wave is, the better it gets, and he is always eager to tell stories of wipeouts that left him breathless for days. 'This one time I bounced off the reef, the cliff wall and the bottom again in such short succession. I wasn't even down for that long but [the wave] just threw me around like a rag doll. The take-off is right in front of this big rock that sticks up out of the water and if you come off, it's all over. After that wipeout I didn't go back for months. It really freaked me out. On some big days I didn't even catch a wave. The loss of life is really only one step away. It's a choice. It wasn't a wave you felt like surfing all the time. One wipeout out there and you just go in.' It was a routine that Guiney got used to — going in after every wipeout. 'It takes everything. It takes your energy, it takes your confidence, it takes your ego, it takes it all so that you've got nothing left.'

While Guiney, a goofyfooter, admits coming in waveless, he was less than impressed with the overall performance of the surfers on the *Tracks* trip of July 2001. 'Kieren got one epic wave, the kind of wave I've never seen anyone take off on out there, ever. If he hadn't caught that wave, the whole feature would have been a little bit depressing. As for the other guys, I can't even remember them being out there. After a few waves each, and a few wipeouts each, they went in. It really annoyed me because it actually was starting to pick up. It was double the size and I was just like, "Where are they all?" I'm not saying I would have done better, it's just that we are dealing with a new level of surfing.'

I could feel the punchline coming and his point was clear. 'The fact is that the wave dealt it to them and I think that's worth reporting. If you look at that massive wave that Kieren gets, everyone is going crazy

DAVID GUINEY

about it. But if you actually look at it closely, he's about 10 feet in front of the barrel. It's such a visual wave that everyone is still getting excited about it. The wave is a new level and it's gunna take a little while to get used to it and surf it well.'

This response brought much ridicule, not only from the surfers of the trip, but other surfers. 'What's he thinking?' said Kieren, who had the cover shot. 'The boys were charging — and I didn't see him anywhere.'

Kieren thought about replying to him in a letter. He actually sat in the *Tracks* office and started typing, but thought it was not worth the energy. Mark Matthews, however, did. People were wondering who this guy was. 'Let them talk,' Guiney told me in one of his many calls. 'It's healthy for everyone, including the wave. This is not your usual wave.'

Guiney, who's donated plenty of skin and blood to the cliffs of the wave, believes, 'It's the biggest surfer trap out there. It's gunna bring so many surfers in and there are going to be very few people who will actually cope with it. They will go and their egos will get nailed and it will only be the smart ones who will turn their back on it. It's a good leveller and there are enough waves to level everybody. It really is something that Australian surfing and professional surfing needed.'

Guiney told me more about how the wave improves as it gets bigger. 'It takes the step out of it,' says Guiney. 'It's actually more dangerous on smaller swells. I wouldn't surf it unless it was at least 12 foot.'

I could barely contain myself. So how big does it get? 'Recently we had the biggest forecast ever — eight-metre predictions. People were saying it was 30 foot from the top of the cliff. What they don't realise is that 30 foot from the cliff is about 50 to 60 foot when you're out there. To put that into perspective — four or five times bigger than when Kieren and the boys had it, that was only an eight-foot swell everywhere else. Koby Abberton and a few other boys were down here but Andrew took them to the wrong spot. They blew it. All you would have needed is someone in the water not even catching waves and you would have had the best surf shots ever taken in Australia, stuck in everyone's brains forever.'

Since the early days of this wave's discovery I've had many in-depth conversations with David Guiney about the wave. He was always quick to tell me the latest story. One, in August last year, was when a navy frigate, HMAS *Sydney*, tested the waters off Tasmania. In southwest waters it ran into a massive swell, up to eight metres high, and took aboard 120 tonnes of water, sinking everything but the superstructure. At one stage the boat was thought to be lost. The force of the impact caused a 600-kilogram plate that protects the propulsion unit to buckle. Guiney tells me these stories with pride, but with slight apprehension. Like Campbell, he is competing for attention down there in a race that is splitting the otherwise tight surfing community apart.

While Guiney remains somewhat disillusioned over the wave's exposure, he knows that ultimately it will be the wave that decides who surfs it and who doesn't, once again reminding me of his surfer's trap analogy and the 'ego leveller'. 'I sort of care about what I've lost,' says Guiney. 'But I was smart enough and lucky enough to be there when I was and to have kept it quiet for as long as I did.' Guiney doesn't surf it too much any more. 'I still enjoy surfing but I just pick my days now when I know it's on and I can surf it by myself,' he says. He would hear a story from someone about the wave and search them out and put it straight. He really considers it his baby and feels responsible for its development.

DAVID GUINEY

One guy told me a story about a secret spot, not too far away from Shipsterns. 'We rocked up there in our boat and there was this guy already there, surfing in a pair of Speedos and going mad on these huge waves. He was yelling at us, demanding how we found out about this wave and telling us to go in.'

'If I could take it all back, I wish I hadn't taken anyone down there,' says Guiney, 'but I have a few other secret spots. The thing is, a wave like that was needed in professional surfing. All these new big waves that we are finding are making everything else look pretty depressing and it's about time they were tested properly.'

He is also quick to bring up the lack of adventure in today's surfers, as opposed to his own era of expressive freedom and discovery, when guys like Rabbit, Terry Fitzgerald, Wayne Lynch and Co. scraped together the most shoestring of shoestring budgets and went looking for waves. 'These kids don't know how to find waves any more,' says Guiney. 'I think that's what's lost in surfing. Unless they see photos in a magazine or hear about it, they're all a bit lost really.'

Though Guiney is starting to pull back from Shipsterns, the adventure lives on in him. In between personal expeditions up and down the Tasmanian coast looking for new waves, he is eager to see people have a go at the wave he called his own for 15 years. He is even helping the local government in its quest to use it as a tourist attraction, which seems to contradict his earlier philosophy, but everyone evolves at some stage. Like an overcompensating parent, he just can't let his baby go.

Every surfer has at least once in their life stumbled upon a secret wave or been told about one. And everyone has the choice of what to do with that knowledge — that secret code. Guiney's story taught me a good lesson about human nature. I realised those early years were probably the best of his life, being exposed to the purity of simply discovering and riding such a monumental wave.

In any case, the future of Shipsterns seems certain. It will attract people, it will intrigue people and it will test people, just like it did David Guiney 15 years ago when he first paddled out with Mark Jackson. But while one per cent of the surfing population will vaguely contemplate the thought of slapping on a steamer and tackling the beast, the other 99 per cent will be content to stay at home, opt for postcard equatorial waters, or just sit back and enjoy the pictures. 'Time will tell,' says Guiney.

There's a confronting pause over the phone. 'So when are you coming down, cobber?'

DAVID GUINEY

Taj
BURROW

T he bank next to the contest was ripe with excitement. Taj seemed very anxious as he watched on. He had a heat in 10 minutes and the magnetism of free surfing commanded his attention. The heat was a mere formality, a slight hurdle, mingling with other thoughts in his mindspace. 'Oh my God, did you see that!' His mate Damon Nichols pointed to Corey Lopez who was surfing on the bank next to the contest. He had just landed a four-foot-high aerial in front of the photo gallery ... or was he talking about the

SARGE

thousands of nude women (yes, nude women) on the French beach? Distractions.

'Taj Burrow check in for your heat,' boomed a voice over the PA. Taj looked tense. Nude woman, aerial and photo possibilities ... heat. Focus. Bang! Another huge air by Andy Irons. 'Shit!' Taj was entertaining too many thoughts as he paced around the contest area. He hated not being the one doing those aerials and knew he could have done better. He put his straightjacket on and ran down for his heat. He absolutely annihilated it, came in early and ran down the beach to beat the rest of the free surfers as well. It was a good, perhaps standard day in the life of Taj Burrow.

Taj would have to be one of the most motivated guys around and his energy stretches far beyond his burning enjoyment of the sport. The fire in the belly is fuelled by an intense competitive nature that feels extinguished by anything less than first place. All you have to do is watch him in the water, or watch him watch somebody else surfing well, and you get a taste of how competitive he is. 'I just can't help it,' says Taj. 'I hate losing and I hate seeing other people win. It's heavy!'

From a very young age Taj fuelled this fire into a talent that raged out of control. But he wasn't just stoking surfers. The highest-profiled, most competitive surfer in Australia has also attracted a few ladies on his travels around the world. Far from sleazy and an arm's length from boring, Taj is more than a world-class surfer. He's a lady killer of the highest order.

Though he resembled a garden rake in his early teens, Taj was already Western Australia's best surfer and winning national titles out of his age division, turning heads wherever he went. People were talking early about this young talent from West Oz and they were never disappointed. If anything they were struggling to comprehend what this tiny little guy could do. 'The first time I saw TB,' says good mate and tour professional Damon Nichols, 'we were about 13 or something, down at the Aussie titles at South Australia. I had heard all about how hot this kid was from WA. He ended up losing the first heat and I was like, "Fuck, what's all this shit about?" Anyway, he went free surfing next to the contest and was ripping, full tail slides and reverses and shit. That shit was crazy back then.'

Taj would rock up to events with surfboards more akin to a small wooden instrument that removes pieces of food from your teeth. The gallery was screaming for answers. Was his shaper onto something? He was riding boards that had shrunk to 14" in width. Or did his wiry frame and tight progressive surfing have more to do with it? Or was he just doing it to impress the chicks? At 13, Taj was doing manoeuvres only seen by Slater and a select group of other surfers.

His light package may have lacked the power of the Sunny Garcias, Mark Occhilupos and Luke Egans, but he was beginning to make up for it by where he surfed in the wave — tight, critical and always going for big turns in the steepest, most difficult section. But there was another element to his makeup that enabled Taj to dissolve lips, take to the air, and get into positions most couldn't imagine. An element that led him to a win in Australia's professional Junior Series at age 17 (four years below the cut-off age) and into a rumoured $65 000 contract with his now major sponsor, Billabong. An element that saw him rise to number two in the world at age 22, behind six-time world champion Kelly Slater. An element that has him currently producing a healthy six-figure sum as Australia's highest-paid surfer and has his peers labelling him as a definite world title contender for years to come. The element? Speed.

TAJ BURROW

'The kid's lightning fast man,' says tour rival American Tim Curran.

'Yeah, I guess I always have enjoyed going fast,' admits Taj. 'It wasn't the fact that I just wanted to go fast, though. It was more that I wanted to do airs, and to do airs you need speed.'

This has been Taj Burrow's niche. He's quick and he is the leader of a leading futuristic manoeuvre, the aerial. Taj goes fast due to an overload of energy complemented by where and how he surfs in the wave, reaching speeds that usually require a motor and landing aerials from heights at which most people develop phobias. It is this styled individualism that has enabled Taj to headline an era of huge advancements in the sport. He is at the forefront of modern surfing and nobody explains it better than Rabbit Bartholomew. 'I am quite certain that the surfing Taj does over the next few years will be totally groundbreaking. He has also been the beneficiary of a great rivalry with Andy Irons. The unspoken struggle for supremacy between these two gladiators is one of the most stimulating aspects of the ASP World Tour. Between them they have raised the performance bar to outrageous heights and in time this will be a measurable cog in the evolution of surfing.'

Former world champions Mark Occhilupo and Sunny Garcia (both over 30), both confirm Taj's star status and marketability. Even Kelly Slater predicted Taj would take his crown after his retirement. He now sees him as one of the biggest threats, if not the biggest threat, in his comeback year. Though he still hasn't attained a world title, it seems fate is steering Taj in the right direction. Had it not been for a fateful tangent early in his life, he could have been selling hot dogs outside Yankee Stadium.

When Californians Vance and Nancy Burrow wanted a change in their lives, back when their only son was just out of toilet training, they simply gave the globe a spin. Where their fingers stopped, a whole

TAJ BURROW

new beginning awaited, and no one benefited more than Taj. As fate would have it, the Burrows came to one of the best wave venues in the world, Yallingup in the Margaret River region of southern West Oz. It was this breeding ground that fostered the perfect training wheels for Taj's ride to the top.

Sometimes surfers from rural areas lack motivation and drive because there are no other surfers to push them. Not Taj; he had the likes of Jake Patterson and James Catto, as well as a constant stream of airline tickets from sponsors eager to send him away on photo shoots with some of the world's best surfers. Taj always had someone to try and beat.

For Taj, the country lifestyle of Margaret River allowed him to work not only on his surfing, but on a look that screamed sensitivity — with a touch of rugged manhood derived from living in the bush — and the chicks were screaming for it. So began his life as a bachelor, and stories about Taj were running wild. 'It's unreal for us married guys,' says Nathan Webster. 'He gives us the best stories.' 'The guy's a freak,' says Damon Nichols.

Taj had already nailed the art of seduction and another difficult art, surfing in small waves. Taj surfs with an energy and spark most people can't ignite until the surf is at least three or four feet. While most people fight the middle of a small wave, where the power is, to stay afloat, Taj carves complete top to bottom lines as if it were a perfect wave. 'Because I'm always trying to do aerials, I seem to ride pretty far up on my board, looking for speed', Taj says. 'I just want to go fast.'

I remember being at Durban once for the Gunston 500, the world's longest-running professional event. The swell was so small that we could barely catch the waves, let alone surf them. 'Don't worry,' said Luke Hitchings. 'They'll call it off for sure ... hang on, oh no, Taj is

TAJ BURROW

coming out. No Taj. Go in. Go IN!' The line-up sighed collectively. We all knew Taj would make it look more than contestable and that the first heat would be starting on schedule. This happened quite a bit when he first joined the tour and jealous tongues wagged, 'Sure, the skinny little bloke might be able to surf small waves, but how does he go in the big stuff?' They didn't know him too well. The scary part is Taj surfs with the same creativity and commitment no matter how big the surf is. It's all part of his competitive nature.

Taj often seems genuinely confused when he loses. As humble and down to earth as he is, this 'How did I lose?' attitude is the best indicator of someone who is used to winning. But like anyone else, there is a flaw. 'I always seem to win the hard heats and lose in the easier ones,' admits Taj. For the first time in our interview he was starting to look uncomfortable and began scratching his head nervously and fidgeting as if before a heat. 'I don't know why, I just seem to wig out. I know there are a lot of heats that I should have won, but I just didn't give it my best tactically.'

Always respected for his free surfing, Taj is still struggling for that perfect blend of go-for-it surfing whilst wearing the straightjacket of a competition singlet. 'I usually tone it down in heats, especially against easier guys and it's just not the way I surf. I usually try and surf radical. Twenty-five minutes isn't a long time for a heat and anything can happen in the ocean in that time, so I've got to learn not to make mistakes. Sometimes I just froth around too much and make mistakes because I think the heat is going to be easy, but you just can't do that any more. I've just got to step up and,' he laughs, 'kick their arse.'

For such an incredible talent Taj seems to rely a lot on feedback. In his bid for the '99 world title, he employed the services of former Western Australian professional and top 16 competitor Mitch Thorson as

TAJ BURROW

his coach. 'Yeah, that was good,' Taj reflects, 'to have someone there to help me out with my heats. Sometimes I've just got too much energy and I make mistakes. I'm always asking people for help, whether it be how my boards are looking or other stuff, especially Jake [Patterson]. He helps me out a lot.'

It's a two-sided coin the 1999 Pipe Master is more than willing to toss. Jake Patterson, who has been in the top six in 2000 and 2001, sees Taj's potential and feeds off him in a *Star Wars*-like apprenticeship — developing his maturity whilst expanding his own repertoire. 'He's always had a better car than me,' says Jake in an appreciative shade of green. 'But he did teach me how to punt [do an aerial].'

Jake, also from Yallingup, has benefited greatly from Taj and is the first to write his mentor a reference. 'I remember this one trip we did up north (WA) in '94. We had some hell waves and he was ripping. He was only 15 and he was pushing me so much in the big stuff. Taj rips in anything from one to 20 foot and it's only a matter of time before he gets the world title.'

Current head judge on the ASP World Tour Perry Hatchett says, 'Taj is one of the leading exponents in the newly designed ASP criteria and is always one to watch for an array of new moves not seen at many local breaks.' There is no doubt Taj's futuristic surfing is at the forefront of the sport today, at any level. Taj has phalanxes of photographers putting their hands up to join him on maiden voyages into new heights of aerial surfing. He always has a plan and will predict his next turn before the wave comes. 'He's unbelievable,' says Rick Jakovich. 'When I want to try a new shot or he wants me in a new angle he nails the turn every time. He does air like people do floaters.'

Taj's surfing is literally worth millions. 'Every time you video him you can make a couple of grand,' says Patterson. When it comes to making

TAJ BURROW

movies and shooting photographs, Taj is a very professional outfit. At 23, he's made two videos, *Sabotaj* in '99, and *Montaj*, which he reached into his own industrial-sized pockets to produce himself late in 2001.

There are not many surfers or administrators who'd say a bad word about Taj. But when talking about him they all seem to lead to one of two things. His ability to innovate on a wave or his success with women. 'He surfs really well,' says Beau Emerton. 'I could say a lot more, but I won't!'

Taj's fellow surfers are all green with envy about his knack with the opposite sex. But are women water to his competitive fire? It seems to be his only real distraction. *Tracks* writer and tour guru Paul Sargeant reckons, 'If he could believe in himself as much as he believes in his libido, he'd be a world champion.' Taj steers away from this, even hinting at the prospect of a girlfriend. 'I'd like to travel with a girlfriend on tour,' he says, imagining the competitive possibilities without the distraction of single women. 'I think it would make me do better. At the moment I lose focus from events, I swear. Maybe in the future I'll start travelling with a girlfriend. I mean I couldn't have a girlfriend at home and not travel with her, but it's hard to find a girl who would just drop everything and come and do the tour with me, especially one that you're comfortable with, so we'll see how we go.'

Indeed we will. But while the ladies line up for their respective auditions, the rest of the surfing world is eagerly awaiting a world title. In '99 Taj was runner-up. In 2000, he finished seventh after what he would call a bad year, while the September 11 disaster cut short the 2001 campaign. He might not have lived up to the world's expectations yet, but if Taj gets his own way, as he usually does, that title will soon be sitting in his lap faster than a French groupie. And that's more important to Taj in the long run.

Layne

BEACHLEY

'Who won?' I asked three female surfers, as I headed up a hotel elevator in Durban, South Africa. The girls, still red-faced from exertion and defeat in a just-completed event, cussed and jerked into an uncomfortable, though familiar spasm — I shouldn't have asked. 'Fucking Layne ... again! I wish someone else would win, it's getting so boring.'

The three finalists picked Layne Beachley to pieces with words as sharp as an ice pick. 'She was ripped on, she was so lucky. The judges love her ...

and her hair! ... oh her hair!' I felt as comfortable in that lift as a male Tupperware dealer at a hen's night.

Women's surfing has always struggled to put sand under the crotches of spectators. For a long time it lacked identity and unlike many other sports, such as tennis and golf, women simply couldn't come close to the talent of the men. But now that is starting to change and as the women's market for surfing explodes, the lady who lit the wick seems to have also bridged that gap. Does Layne really warrant a comparison with her male counterparts? Tradition says no. Previously, when women's surfing heats came on, it was time for lunch. But the winds of change are evident in more than Layne's pay packet and the jealous cat scratch in my ear from that horrible elevator ride.

'Being a world champion, you are a target,' admits Layne, who now owns four titles. 'But it's not a personal vendetta. It's like we are all out there to win. I've got to draw on my experiences and remember what it was like being the underdog and how it felt as the number two trying to take out the number one, and how I used to put shit on the number one to lift my confidence.

'I don't take it personally. It's very easy to take it personally because when you're number two, no one's going to tell you you're number one. The minute you're there no one wants to see you win, everyone wants to see you lose and everyone wants to take you out. You're a target and people go from saying, "You can do it" to "Who gives a shit, we'd hate to see you win, can you lose already". You've got to take the emotional aspect out of it and treat it as a profession.'

Layne's confidence and maturity is what has elevated her to where she is today. She doesn't fall for the bitchiness or the stereotypes that characterise her sport. She just gets on with the job. 'When I first started, all the boys at Manly told me, "Don't you dare become a lesbian."' She laughs. 'It was pretty frightening for a 17-year-old girl who wanted to make a career out of professional surfing and be a world champion.'

Layne got over it quickly. While other girls complained about the stereotypes, she collected world titles like best-and-fairest awards. Instead of being worried about what boys thought about her, she gave them something to worry about — she was beating them, and she earned respect quickly.

Upon meeting Layne, you see that driven, focused side of her straight away. There's something in her eyes — an agenda, a purpose. In the early days, however, frustrated with women's surfing which, at the time, was still a ship without a captain, she didn't know what route to take.

'At one stage I was ready to give it all away,' she admits. 'I was second in the world and could hardly get a decent contract from Quiksilver. Now there's Roxy and other women's labels popping up everywhere, as well as magazines.'

Layne, who had got her teeth into just about every sport as a tomboy growing up at Manly Beach, is one of those headstrong people who could have pursued anything and succeeded. While she procrastinated for a few years, her motivation came from an unlikely source — one of the sport's strongest critics, a man who once challenged Pam Burridge to a surfing contest because he thought women surfers were all kooks, and lost: Channel Nine commentator Darrell Eastlake.

'Darrell Eastlake was the one guy who was instrumental in me continuing on, because I wanted to retire in '95 and '97. Both years I was ready to quit, and he said if you win a world title you'll have the credibility to do anything you wish to do. I thought that should make life easier in the long run. I'll keep working harder and see what happens.'

LAYNE BEACHLEY

Layne made a decision: she wanted to be a world champion. Making more sacrifices than a satanic cult, she sharpened her sword and came out swinging in '98. I vividly remember watching her in an event on the Gold Coast. There had been a transformation. Not only was I looking at the future world champion, but I became acutely aware that I could perhaps be looking at one of the sport's greatest. Her surfing, despite its raw energy, didn't seem as polished as Lisa Andersen's, who also owns four world titles and an eye for style. But all of a sudden, Layne turned into a winner. It was as simple as that. She made it happen. Layne had been to seminars on how to make money in the off-season, as well as motivational seminars and she developed the look of determination often associated with a tiger.

The media, especially the Australian media who love their world champions as if they were their own family, took her on in her infancy and nurtured her like an only child. She was also cultivating quite a healthy image for herself. 'There were a few very positive role models out there at the time like Wendy [Botha], Pam and those girls. As the typical surf media did at the time though, they tended to focus more on the negative aspects of it. They tended to try to find all the ugly goths or try and fish out how many lesbians there were on tour.'

The one thing that surfing lacked was femininity. What was needed was a style in the water and on the wave that stood up and said, 'I am a girl and this is how we do it!' Physically, anatomically, women have much better balance than men. But the girls ignored their natural calling and continually banged their heads up against the wall by trying to surf like men. What ensued in this futile pursuit was a look akin to a supermodel trying to do the wild thing in a pair of King Gee overalls.

'It's a tough discussion and a debate that we've always had. Even though we should never be compared we tend to compare ourselves anyway, just solely out of searching for respect and recognition by them [men]. But what we should do is be proud of who we are and what we are and support each other and each other's quest to be stronger and more powerful and still maintain grace and style. Something that Pam did. She has such grace and style and flow and is someone who has a lot of feminine quality in her surfing. And Lisa Andersen, she's a classic example of that, too. She really broke down so many barriers for women in regards to style and performance. Once she became world champion over and over again, she really brought a lot of attention to women's surfing.'

Layne pretty much took the baton that Lisa dropped when she decided to retire and make little Lisas in '97. Layne, who was already starting to dominate, had set herself goals to break Lisa's records. Such is her competitive nature. Previous platforms are her first step. She has now equalled Andersen's tally and is on her way for world title number five. 'I can't retire until I get it,' she says.

But one thing's going to be different. The former number one chick is coming home to roost. It seems Quiksilver, unhappy with the last bunch of world champions, needed to fill a void on tour and they have sent in their biggest artillery, Andersen and Kelly Slater, to lay a couple of world title eggs in the Quiksilver kitchen. The pair have 10 world championships between them. Only time will tell, but the battle between Layne and Lisa promises to assume titanic proportions. A record awaits either one.

When Layne won her fourth world title in 2001 at Maui in Hawaii, it had 'meant-to-be' written all over it, not unlike when MR won his fourth crown title. Layne lost her quarter-final heat and there were three or four other girls behind her on the ratings, within a goosebump of taking it from her. Layne, who says, 'I have proved in the past that I perform well under pressure', somehow snapped like a carrot. Actually, she was as cool as a cucumber. The waves just didn't come to her. The rest of the girls only needed to get through their heats. But in an unlikely scenario, they all lost in their quarter-finals too. Press releases came back that afternoon of Layne not coming in after her shock loss. They said she paddled down the beach to console herself. Rumour has it, though, she stayed in the water and psyched her opponents out. Watching, lurking. Not getting in the way, but still getting in the way. Layne seems to have this positive energy around her. She makes things happen.

Layne also possesses an uncanny gift in big waves. This is the main thing that sets her apart from other girls, gives her an advantage over Lisa and has men all over the world nervously cupping the weight of their own testicles and asking the question. 'How the frick does she charge so hard?'

'I surfed a 30-foot wave last season in Hawaii,' says Layne, as if talking about buttering her toast. 'It was the biggest wave a girl's surfed, yeah.' The amount of times I've heard someone tell a story of how they caught the biggest wave they've ever caught in Hawaii, then looked to their inside and seen Layne calling them off! How's that for the ultimate in demoralisation? But she works hard for it. 'Ken [Bradshaw, big-wave legend and Layne's boyfriend] used to make me swim out the back on massive onshore days and bodysurf Sunset. It used to scare the shit out of me but after a while you get used to it — and now we just do it for fun.'

Layne's starting to hunt down big waves like some of the Hawaiian veterans, and has set herself no limits. 'I'd love to be at least on the ultimate list for the Eddie [Eddie Aikau Memorial at Waimea Bay, the most prestigious big-wave event in the world].

'I used to love surfing Waimea,' she continues, 'but now it's got so crowded and more dangerous than it's ever been. There's a whole lot of idiots out there that shouldn't be there and they don't look around, they're not concerned about anyone else in the water but themselves. It makes it incredibly dangerous, life threatening, so I don't go out there any more. But I'd love to surf 20-foot Waimea with only a few other people. It's a pretty gnarly wave. After that I'd just love to continue my tow-ins and see how far I could take that. I really haven't set any goals for the moment for big-wave surfing.'

Not having a goal for Layne is so out of character that it clearly demonstrates her willingness to go for just about anything. She trains hard, but her confidence to surf big waves is self-generated. 'We'll see what happens. I'll just get myself ready and go. This is what happened last year. It got 30-foot and I had the opportunity to go towing with Ken's tow-in partner. Ken was in Florida calling my cell every 10 minutes telling me to go somewhere else, don't go towing, you're not ready for it. And I said, "Well, I'm here and you're in Florida, and I think I am. Bye." I had a great time. It's just a matter of being mentally and physically prepared for the biggest wipeout of your life.'

That's where big Ken comes into it. He has been at the forefront of big-wave surfing seemingly for the last century. Perhaps better known amongst the masses for taking off on maybe the biggest wave ever ridden (a 66-foot monster) on the *Biggest Wednesday* video, Ken and Layne have been a formidable force for the better part of four years. More than just boyfriend and girlfriend. 'You can push each other and that's what I find with Ken and me. I really push his way of surfing and he really pushes me.'

LAYNE BEACHLEY

This professionalism surrounds Layne like an aura. You can almost see it. She is confident, though down to earth. As far as being a role model goes — which is her biggest achievement — Layne learnt a very important lesson early on. 'A classic example was at Bells in '98. I lost to Pam on a paddling interference and I wanted to just come in real angry, slam the board down near the judges, blame everyone except yourself. That's what people tend to do. I was walking up the car park and I was so upset with myself. I just wanted to scream and punch and kick. I put my board in the car and sat there and just started to contain myself. Steve Robertson's wife walked up with his kids and one of the kids was chucking the biggest tantrums and I thought, "That's how I feel, I wish I could get away with that."

'It sort of cracks it up and releases it for me and then five minutes later I finished getting changed and about 10 girls walked up and said "Layne! Layne! We've been looking for you all day. We've been waiting here to get your autograph." Can you imagine if I'd chucked a tantrum what those girls would have thought of me? What kind of inspirational role model is that, that can't handle losing? It was a really good lesson. I guess that's why I tell it. It taught me a lot about how you don't know who's watching and who's drawing inspiration from you. It would have been horrible for them if I'd clicked out. Then I look at people that I used to draw inspiration from and wonder how they would have reacted. It has since really made me want to stay grounded.'

Layne is now an icon. The daughter you always wanted and the competitor you always feared. If you pick up a copy of the latest dictionary in three years' time don't be surprised if her name lies next to 'women's surfing'. She typifies it better than anyone.

LAYNE BEACHLEY

Oscar
WRIGHT

O scar Wright has always been fascinated by his own reflection. I remember rooming with him at the world amateur titles in Brazil in '94 as juniors. He would spend entire journeys up eight floors of the hotel lift above Barra Da Tijuca Beach looking deeply into the mirror, playing with his hair, checking out his newly formed facial growth. But there was at least one thing Oscar was interested in more than his own image — creating images himself. While the rest of us fussed over boards and worried about having imported

BUCKLEY

enough of our favourite wax, Oscar sat quietly in the corner of our room, contemplating what pictures to draw on the bottom of his board and whether he'd imported enough Posca pens to cater for his creativity.

'He's been drawing ever since he was two,' says Oscar's mum, Cathie, who gave birth to him at Ingleside on the northern side of Sydney in July 1976. 'It's all he did. He was into drawing jungle animals, palm trees, anything really, and he would draw pretty much every day. Birds too, he especially liked birds.'

Oscar jumped on a fibreglass surfboard nine years after he drew his first feather in flight. At the time Damien Hardman had just won his first world title and Pottz [Martin Potter], Archie [Matt Archibald], [Christian] Fletcher and [Bud] Llamas were starting to do functional aerials. At 11, Oscar had already entertained the imagery of flight himself, both as an artist and as a surfer. 'I was always fascinated with flying, I guess,' he says. 'I didn't start surfing till late but once I did, I didn't stop. Surfing for me was just so much fun. It had everything I needed.'

He became competitive at an early age. Not with winning, but with performance, and he had an incredible pack of talent circling him like sharks. He didn't get caught up in trying to beat them, being more interested in trying to do better turns than them — in the air. And he was sharing quality air space.

Every five years or so, the hotbed of talent shifts like a realignment of the stars. A freakish group of friends push each other to new limits. Right now the stars are aligned to the Gold Coast: Mick Fanning, Joel Parkinson and Dean Morrison. All friends. It is a mirror image of what Ozzie enjoyed at North Narrabeen during the mid-'90s with the likes of Hardman, Chris 'Davo' Davidson, Nathan 'Noodles' Webster and Steve Clements.

OSCAR WRIGHT

'Friends were so important to Ozzie,' recalls Cathie. 'When he was seven he used to say, 'Mum, I've only got seven friends.' And he would cry when they went home. He also had an imaginary friend called Harold, a bad kid with long hair who we used to invite for dinner before his sister Annie was born.'

'I went to the same school as Davo, Steve Clements, Noodles, Denny Shallis [1990 Australian Under–16 champ],' says Ozzie. 'So many good surfers.' Though he chose to surf at South Narrabeen ('I was too scared of all those older fuckwits') his surfing compared favourably with almost anyone's, and like now, it was because he had something different to offer.

'I remember sitting at the carpark one day with Matt Cattle and seeing this guy fly across a northy wall and pop two airs on the one wave,' says photographer Andrew Buckley, otherwise known as Shorty, who took the cover photo for this book. 'There were two or three industry people sitting there that day and all of a sudden because of that wave, he just took off. Truth is he'd been doing it every day down at southy, but now he was noticed. Big time!'

While his peers evolved in competition, Oscar, despite finals berths in state and Aussie titles, couldn't seem to match up. As a surfer he was complete: style, carves and airs. He owned as many manoeuvres as textas, but he just couldn't seem to colour in between the competitive lines. 'I don't know why,' says Ozzie. 'I mean, I used to like contests, but I never went that good.' He just never seemed to have the patience. For Oscar, 'it's all about fun'. While everyone was trying to get through heats and make Aussie titles, Oscar was simply trying to do the biggest turns.

I remember coming out of a heat with him in a semi-final of a pro junior at Newcastle in '95. He had just got his arse kicked by Mitch Dawkins and Shaun Brooks. Nothing new. But he got the crowd on their

OSCAR WRIGHT

feet with one huge air that went seemingly from Main Beach to Merewether. It was the highlight of the event, but as usual, not enough to progress through the heat. When we all came in, photographers and important people with notepads were coming up to him from nowhere. 'Haven't you got a wettie sponsor?' I heard Bosko, a prominent photographer, ask. 'Can we speak about sponsorship next week?' asked another representative.

While other competitors were out the back ripping turns all the way to shore, Oscar would hunt down a left shorey where he could get his board out of the water and show everybody his latest drawing. 'He has always done what he wants,' says Luke Hitchings. 'That's what I respect him for the most, apart from his surfing. He doesn't care what anyone else is doing or saying, he just does whatever he wants, goes wherever he wants, surfs however he wants. He would go all the way to Europe and miss his heat because there was a sick shorey for doing airs somewhere else.'

And so Oscar was born. While he was starting to get a lot of attention, surfing didn't quite cater for him yet. Here was this freak that did three massive airs a wave, that dressed like who knows what, acted like who knows how and painted like who knows why? Companies just didn't know how to market that yet. He was ahead of his time — and not through meticulous planning. Just by being himself. Or trying to discover himself.

All of a sudden Ozzie was a household name as surfing began to break off into factions in the late '90s. His surfing, his art and his personality took off all around the world as he offered a package nobody had seen before, especially in America where he exploded on to front covers everywhere and took off in domestic air shows. 'I went in one air show over there and did alright, but that's kinda it.' He

OSCAR WRIGHT

probably just went there to check out some galleries and find a few left shories. 'The exposure's . . . kinda cool, I guess,' he continues, unsure.

It's really hard to get into Ozzie's head, no matter how long you spend with him. He honestly couldn't care less if anyone else saw those covers. To most surfers, a cover shot is like a hole in one in golf. Ozzie's had more holes in one than Tiger Woods, but it doesn't affect him. His cover of *Surfing* magazine actually sat in the newsagencies for weeks before he wandered out of his home studio to check it out.

He was now earning massive dollars, but nothing had changed. He was still wearing the ripped shirts he would turn up to school in. Clothes he would have slept in the night before, according to school friends. Just last year on his return home from the States soon after the September 11 catastrophe, he was sidelined by airline staff because of his bizarre look, and asked if he was going to cause any trouble. He turns up to movie premieres and surfing functions with long dark cloaks and aviation goggles, but dresses the same when he's painting in a room by himself. People have written it off as smart marketing, but the simple truth is that's Ozzie. To him, everything is a blank canvas.

'I think everyone gets creative in their own way,' says Oscar. 'It's just everyone chooses a different line.' I think Ozzie is in a dynamic state of change. So much so that he cannot even sum himself up. His personality is like a series of artistic reactions to fleeting encounters. He can, however, describe his surfing. 'The lines I've come to doing now in surfing, I think they've come from just surfing South Narrabeen all the time. It's such a closeout and to get anywhere on that wave you have to go so fast. I'd always get to the closeout with all this speed and the natural thing to do was just jump.'

OSCAR WRIGHT

Oscar's technique for aerials was based on horizontal drive from surfing in the middle of the wave, but in doing this he lost a lot of the carving style he showed in his formative years, especially with the 5'5" fishes he was riding. 'Sometimes I get addicted to the feel of them and I can't get off them for months,' he says. 'They feel so good in the air, and are so easy to stick the landing.' The extra width meant he was doing a lot more airs and variations. But is he still at the top of his field? It seems the deep bottom turns of Joel Parkinson and the full rotations and double grabs of Taj Burrow on the standard boards have eclipsed this one-time high-flyer.

'I've never done airs that high,' he admits. 'I'm not sure if I've gone six-foot high and made it. They're so hard to make when you're that high. I've made some really long ones, though. Riding those short stubby things makes your surfing feel fresher; you surf in different parts of the wave and it's easier to try shove-its and stuff like that.' He's also been trying acid drops, running off a reef or a pier and jumping off his board straight onto the wave. 'I want to make a kick flip,' he continues. 'I don't think anyone has made one of them yet.' The latest innovative manoeuvres by Taj and Parko seem to outfly Ozzie's more skate-influenced surfing. Despite this, Oscar remains a source of fascination, which poses the question: is it his surfing that people have been intrigued by or is it his character?

'I am sickly disgusted with the sold-out American magazines,' said a letter to *Tracks* last October by an American named Paul DeBaets. 'Barney Barron and Ozzie Wright are the most covered surfers here. I called and asked *Transworld Surf* why there's so much Barney in the mag and they said it's because "he hangs out at the mag a lot!". The American mags all sit on their asses and wait for the advertisers to bring them the stories. The American companies' marketing campaigns aren't working on the public but they are working on the magazine writers. I am fucking sorry but there's 10 guys in America that blow Ozzie sideways. There's probably even more in Australia! Artist?!!!!? He couldn't get a third-place ribbon at the eighth grade art contest. I am a little disturbed that you even included Ozzie Wright among the aerial pioneers in your vault article. I understand that he set out and did it with no real sponsor help and that's inspirational, but not worth creating a false idol. I am just not one pissed-off seppo. I am curious to know what guys like Taj or Greg Webber feel. If in agreement with my letter, you have a duty to surfing to rid the world of lazy surfing journalism that can be bought with free clothing and a blowjob.' When he read DeBaets's letter, Ozzie was so rapt at the constructive criticism that he made 100 photocopies of the letter and used them as wallpaper at the launch of his *156 Tricks* video.

So what do we aspire to when we pick up a surf mag? What do we want to read about? Ability or character, individuality, or both? Steve Waugh versus Merv Hughes? Sampras versus McEnroe, Lleyton Hewitt, or any one of the three Goran Ivanisevics?'

Oscar is telling his own story: who else on the circuit would write a poem saying simply, 'I love you but you live in Japan'? Or brand his surfboards and paintings with slogans like 'bunny girl sux', paying tribute to his girlfriend (who he calls bunny girl), and '156 tricks sux', taking the piss out of his own *156 Tricks* video?

Oscar singlehandedly set the trend for turning surfboards into canvases and look how many sheep are doing it now. But what has he got that makes people, including journalists, flock to him? On recent trips he was made acutely aware that he was no longer the king of his

OSCAR WRIGHT

field. He has something else — and it's not money, fame or an ability to excel in a chosen endeavour: it's freedom. He does what he wants.

'I remember one day my dad told me all I had to do was paint and surf. That was the coolest thing anyone has ever said to me.' Six years ago, when Ozzie was 19, his dad took his own life. It was on Christmas Day and he has grasped that message ever since. Like it was the last gift he gave to him. 'My dad was a pretty whacky character. He was a great poet and a really good writer. He was stoked when I started surfing and was always telling me to just surf and paint, just to go for it, ya know. That if I did whatever I wanted everything would work out. I think he was so creative and the whole time he was just a landscape gardener. He didn't want me to do that. He wanted me to make a living from my creativity, which was cool.'

'His dad was a radical man,' remembers Ozzie's mum. 'That's where Ozzie gets it from, but he always seemed to have a lot more common sense than his dad.' She laughs at the idea. 'He would always try and calm his dad down. But now he's the one living his own life. Following his dreams like his father told him to, probably even more radically, and it's probably what his father should have done himself.'

Oscar went through some tough times that year and he didn't have his surfing as a release. 'I got ligament and tendon damage in my left ankle not long after, which put me out for three months. It was such a heavy time for me. Then in my second week back I blew my knee out and spent six months out with knee reconstruction surgery. I realised how much I loved surfing and when I got back into it, I just didn't stop. I surfed all day every day, and still do.' With that as his foundation stone, a conscious choice was made to live, and live the way he wanted to. To paint and surf, just like his father wished him to do.

He has both these endeavours firmly in his sights. He won three events in the inaugural Quiksilver Air Show series and won the overall point score as well. You'd think if he has a responsibility to anything, that's it. 'I'm not basing my year around them,' Oscar says. 'If I'm home I'll go in one, but usually there's somewhere else I want to be.' As for his longer-term future, he declares, 'I just want to keep surfing for now, try some new turns, but eventually fade off into my art. Right now, surfing takes up all my time, but my plan is to soon be making more money from my art and start doing it full-time.'

In one of his many books, the surrealist painter Salvador Dali wrote, 'The world does not need another great painter. What it needs is a good moustache.' Perhaps Oscar Pippin Billy Wright (yes, that's his real name) can carry that message on in surfing. One of freedom and creativity. To follow your own road, even if it is uncharted or unfunded. Sure, there are plenty of surfers around these days, like artists. But not one of them is like Ozzie Wright — not even close.

OSCAR WRIGHT

OCCY

'I don't mind doing it anywhere. But shit, not here. Not in Cronulla.' Mark Occhilupo had been on the Billabong Freeway Tour for over a week when he arrived in Cronulla from Coolangatta, a journey from his new home back to his old one. He was signing autographs as part of the new 11-year contract he'd recently signed with his long-term sponsor, Billabong. He had been at the beach all day, and although he wasn't tired — he never is — signing autographs where he grew up made him feel uncomfortable.

'It just didn't feel right,' he said. I

remember Paul Sargeant or Sarge, his long-time friend, telling me once that on one of their early trips down the coast in the '80s, they stopped at a set of lights and someone was looking at Occy. 'What are you looking at?' was Occy's uneasy reaction. According to Sarge, 'He just didn't realise how famous he was and that people tend to stare. Sometimes he still doesn't.'

After 21 years of inspirational surfing and storytelling that would capture the imagination of every surfer — and a slight intermission halfway — Occy was back where he started: Cronulla. A place where being both a friend and a hero makes things awkward. Occy just wanted to be a friend again.

'How does he keep going?' I asked Occy's lifelong best mate, Richie Maurer. His career started at 15, a 'raging bull' armed with a fast style that gored hornless try-hards. He stormed to number three in the world with a style ahead of his time, went walkabout for a few years, returned and captivated everyone again with his free surfing and his comeback attempt, left the tour a second time, got fat, got fit — then won a world title at 33. He's broken every known law of physics and athletic longevity. His surfing is as powerful and sharp as ever, yet faster. It just didn't make sense. Richie's answer was simple: 'He had a break.'

Occy lives on the Gold Coast now and after a big preparation for the start of the 2002 season, and a long bus ride down, the 36-year-old was back in Cronulla, signing autographs in Dunningham Park.

The park is directly in from The Alley where the main road coming into Cronulla finishes. Mark did a lot of surfing there as a grommet, his mum dropping him off from their home in the neighbouring peninsula of Kurnell, where Occy began life as a small kid in a big Italian family. Now his former home sits under a big block of units and he currently owns the penthouse in the building.

The Alley is also a place where, as crazed 12-year-old fans, my best mate, Andy King, and I used to fight over whose turn it was to retrieve his unleashed board. He didn't lose it much, but when he did we'd wrestle all the way to it as it washed to shore. 'Here ya go Occy,' we'd say. 'Thanks grommets,' he'd reply. It would make our day. Yep, the place held a lot of significance for us.

Kingy and I wondered if he remembered us retrieving his board. It was something we talked about all the time. We were talking about it now as we arrived at Richard 'Dog' Marsh's house, before going to watch the football with Occy. The excitement of being around our hero is never lost on us.

'How does it feel to be home, Occ?' I asked as the footy started at Shark Park. He was hiding under the Sharks hat he had borrowed from one of his old mates. The local dutifully copped the sun for the next two halves of football so that his idol wouldn't get that famous jaw sunburnt.

He paused and I thought he was going to say, I'm from the Gold Coast now. 'I'm from Kurnell,' was his answer. All around him a cheer went up as spirited as if the Sharks had just scored.

Surrounding the former world champ were all his old Kurnell mates as well, including Maurer, Barry 'Fanga' Tyte and Marsh. Dog was there during the early days too. 'His mum used to drive us down to Pipe [Aussie Pipe] all the time. Fuck we were keen. We'd travel the three hours just for an arvo surf. We had some epic sessions.'

'This is so good,' said Occy, soaking up the atmosphere. 'I can't remember the last time I was at the footy. I miss it. I haven't been to the footy in ... look! Oh no! They knocked Preston [Campbell] out.'

OCCY

Occy talks with a peculiar lisp. It was worse when he was younger, so much so that Sarge encouraged him to take speech therapy classes. He knew he needed to make victory speeches and it seems now, after 21 years of practice, his voice is still breaking. But no matter how it sounds, or sounded, it is always entertaining, flowing from a jaw stacked with stories.

People were coming from everywhere when they heard he was in town. Some stood back, wondering if it was appropriate to come and meet their hero, or perhaps if he remembered them. All the old faces were there: Mark Henderson, Smurf, Richard 'Spike' James, Dean Whiteman. A reunion nobody dared miss, as they don't happen as often as they used to.

Occy's phone rang. It was Beau Emerton. He had just lost in the one-star WQS that was being held in small waves at Manly Beach. Beau's a magnet for footy and beers and he was hunting his new Gold Coast mate for some sustenance — he knew we'd be here. 'I've been trying to get to Shark Park for ages,' Beau later told me.

'We're over here. Come on, can't you see us, near the sign?' Occy was ducking as he spoke to Beau, looking for a quiet pocket in the noisy crowd and not realising his already short tree trunks were lowering his torso and head out of view. What a perfect surfing build: a long torso for maximum rotation through turns — that's where he gets his power from, not his legs — and short, stocky legs for a low centre of gravity. In one of the hardest sports to master, Occy is still one of only two people in history to look completely comfortable on a surfboard. Tom Curren ('86, '87, '91 world champion) got close and I guess that's why their battles were so intense. Neither of them ever looked like falling.

'Those guys were freaks,' says Gary Green, another pro and former number two from Cronulla. The first man to free surf for a job couldn't make the footy, but he had plenty to say about the Curren/Occy rivalry. 'Curren was so poised and mechanical, but Occy just had this animal in him. You never knew what he was going to do.'

'That's why he's so clumsy on land,' Shane Dorian once said. 'It's God's way of making things even.' He has been known to trip over his own feet once or twice, or swing a cricket bat through more air than ball. It's all part of his package as an entertainer.

Occy kept looking around the ground for Beau, then Dog jumped on the phone. He would find him and Occy settled back into the game. Someone else was in control now. Occy puts all his eggs in the one basket when it comes to making things happen — and after 15 years of people organising him, he was comfortable with that role. He knows what he can do — and he knows what other people can do. He surfs, other people organise.

He focused again. He does that. It's like he's always searching for a better story and doesn't want to risk losing your attention. 'How gnarly is this sign?' he said, as we turned away from the sunlight only to find a billboard behind us reflecting the rays straight back. 'It like, magnifies the sun.' Occy's jaw has seen plenty of ultraviolet in its time. It protruded from his peaked cap like a downhill slope. Everything about Occy is definite: his Italian nose, his father's jawline, his thick stocky frame, his surfing. I thought how weird he would look if he wasn't our hero.

Beau arrived. He was thirsty as usual. He came with the maximum beer count allowable, and a hamburger. He quickly discarded the tomato and lettuce and swallowed the meat and bread down with generous portions of beer and tomato sauce. It's amazing the guy stays alive with his strict carnivorous diet. 'G'day boys, who

OCCY

needs a beer?' It was only the older crew who hadn't met him and they were quickly accommodated. 'Who's winning?'

'We are!' Occy smiled. 'I always bring them luck.' A minute later the Sharks went in for a try. 'I told you,' he chuckled.

'Why weren't you invited as the game caller?' asked Hendo. There was no doubt Occy was the most famous person at the ground.

'Yeah, or at least a celebrity kickoff,' laughed Fanga.

It was always Occy's dream to entertain, so he jumped in immediately. 'Nah, I'm a singer!' Don't be surprised to see an album of Occy's karaoke favourites one day. The man really can sing.

The phone rang again. It was his girlfriend, May. 'Hi babe...' The night was starting to organise itself. 'He needs someone,' said Richie Maurer. 'When he's got the right people around him, he's unstoppable. He just needs someone there to cook for him and get him in bed early.'

Occy hung up the phone with the rest of his night planned. The sun was getting lower, burning straight into our eyes, and it wasn't the only thing staring at the former world champ. He lowered his hat a little further, deflecting the sun and the stares from gathering fans.

'Don't leave without giving my hat back,' said its owner. He thought twice when Occy exposed his head, perhaps feeling guilty, perhaps seeing the surfer's wild hair become even wilder. 'Actually, you keep it. But you have to wear it at Bells [the next event on the tour], because it'll give you luck, and when you win the world title as well.' The owner of the hat smiled at the thought of becoming a small part of history, that somewhere in Occy's extravagant life was his little hat. Maybe he'd see it on a video one time and be able to tell the story to his mates.

OCCY

'Nah, you keep it,' said Occ, giving the hat back. 'I've already won the world title. Cronulla haven't won a premiership yet. They need it more than me. This will bring them luck.'

Before that I'd always thought that Occ was superstitious. Maybe a world title under his belt has eased the pressure. Maybe at 36 he's a little more confident and mature. As far as comebacks go, Occy's has got to be the most successful and inspirational of all time. In the four years he has been back, he's had a world title and two runners-up, and he remains without question the most explosive surfer on tour. It really is hard to know when he'll stop. Surprised, by his own admission, that he's still on the circuit, Occy doesn't know either, but the new contract has made him more comfortable with things.

The footy had finished and we decided to go via Dog's house to the pub. On the way we drove over the crest of the hill at Wanda Beach and got our first sight of the surf. Fifteen years ago, it was blocked by endless sand dunes, but they have been raped and pillaged and turned into red brick units to cater for the urban sprawl. Cronulla has changed a lot and new cafés are a synthetic makeover for a place struggling to maintain its identity. At least they can't change the waves.

The surf was small and a sense of relief wafted over us. Half pissed and still daylight, at least we weren't missing out on waves. 'I remember coming over this hill once and seeing Tom Curren out there,' said Occy. 'It was big and howling on shore. We were all going, "Wow! There's Tom Curren." MR was out there too. He came in and said "G'day grommets" to us. We were like, "Wow, he just said hello to us."'

I looked at Kingy. Now was our chance. 'Hey Occ, do you remember when me and Griggsy used to fetch your board when we were grommets?' Kingy asked, seizing the opportunity. It was like he had just given away our childhood secret.

'Really?'

'Yeah, we used to fight and kick and punch each other all the way to your board. Fuck, we'd run halfway out the back in our pants to get it. See this scar, we had a proper fight one day.'

'No way.' He often feels uncomfortable in these moments. He is so lost in the now that he forgets so many grommets have spent hours studying his surfing, including natural-footers like myself.

We arrived at Dog's house, had a few beers, woke his babies and decided to move on to the pub. Dog's place is a halfway house for close friends with a good story and a full beer. 'When I first moved in,' he said, 'I had a big party and the neighbours complained to the coppers about the noise. I said, "Yeah, no worries." Then the next morning, I went next door and introduced myself. I said, "Hi, I'm Richard, your new next-door neighbour."'

I imagined his long hair and metal studs and rings in his eyebrow, nose, lip and ears and how he would have rocked this lady's comfortable world. '"I don't have many parties, maybe a couple a year, but when I do, I like to make a bit of noise. I own this house, I make a lot of money and I ain't moving out ... let's catch up soon, eh?" She never bothered me again.'

He laughed and I enjoyed his cowboy politics. Dog makes things happen. He's a great friend to all and his social skills are contagiously confident. We walked past two trophies on the way out. They sat near the entrance to his house. One was for runner-up at the Hot Buttered/Ocean & Earth Pro Junior (when he lost to Occy), the other was the winner's. Occy and Dog both noticed them and smiled at their being part of history.

Koby Abberton charging The Box, Western Australia.

Six-time world champ **Kelly Slater** enjoying a secret reef in Tahiti. Imagine the noise this wave made.

David Guiney at G-Land, 1983, before he discovered Shipsterns in his own backyard. It was his last trip to Indonesia.

Brazilian **Neco Padaratz**. A wipeout that nearly cost him his life.

Layne Beachley at Todos Santos, Mexico. The biggest wave ever ridden by a female.

Oscar Wright flying high over Racetracks at Uluwatu, Bali.

Occy carving the barrel inside out at the Quiksilver Pro, 2002.

The current world champ, **CJ Hobgood**. Life's good at the top and in the tube at Cloudbreak, Fiji. He described this barrel during the Quiksilver Pro as 'the best barrel of my life'.

Luke Munro. This kid has a big future.

Silent assassin **Luke Hitchings** showing a Clovelly bommie set the kind of commitment for which he is renowned.

Dean Morrison putting in the time at Pipeline. Here at Backdoor during the 2001/02 season.

While **Rasta** is in perfect rhythm with Chicama, Peru, he's in even better rhythm with life.

On their first trip to Hawaii, photographer/surfer **Jon Frank** and charger **Rusty Moran** took it in turns to catch waves and shoot each other from the impact zone — just to try a different angle.

'Occy's in town,' said one of the local grommets, peering into the pub like it was a high-powered computer game he couldn't play. We had just arrived and heads were turning everywhere. People were checking his framed portrait on the wall (that he'd donated the year before) to make the comparison.

'That's Occy, isn't it?' Nathan Brown, the former rugby league star, was awestruck. He looked nervous when I introduced them, though they already knew each other's work. The Autumn Racing Carnival was on and they swapped tips like stories. It's funny when you see two sports stars come together. They always get along because they share the same lifestyle, but they are always unsure of each other.

Occy has been known to have a flutter. Like many of his peers, cash literally comes and goes in waves. They live on the edge of luck and are confident in its waters. The same applies to Occy's surfing; he doesn't hold back. He goes after it like it's the only thing he knows. It's not, and sometimes you get blown away by how smart he actually is. He just chooses to surf full-on and leave everything else to everyone else.

'Gee, Kirk's surfing good lately,' Occy said to Dog about Kirk Flintoff, the young goofyfooter who Occy placed third in last year's world junior, and who had just arrived at the venue. It was cool that Occy was taking an interest in the up-and-comers. But with gambling on his mind as much as the new wave of Australian surfing, he joined Flintoff at the table. In five more minutes they would pull out a couple of hundred bucks each.

'OK,' declared Occy after filling his pockets with the pub's money, 'what's everyone doing for dinner? Let's go across the road to that seafood restaurant. They've been asking me to come there for a while. I can invite my mum and then I've seen everybody I need to see.' He gave the phone to May, who'd just arrived. 'May, can you please ring mum?' It didn't happen, and it had nothing to do with May's secretarial skills. The night started and finished as a boys' night out.

Occ was supposed to leave early the next day for Bells, but when I saw him the following morning out at The Alley, something seemed odd. 'Still here, Occ?' I asked.

'I can't leave mate,' he said, stirred up by an approaching wave. 'We had the biggest night. I missed my flight — and then missed it again. There's no waves at Bells yet anyway, so I'll be right.'

He turned around and swung into an Alley rip bowl, flying across the wave with jet-like thrust and energy. He hit the last section and took to the air in a crazy controlled upside-down 360 air. He almost pulled it. His board was lost to shore and I thought, how fucking good is this guy to go through all these eras as the best in the world and still, at 36, be going out and partying and ripping the next day? He's the only one left that can do it. As he swam towards shore to collect his board, Andy King had just entered the line-up. It was just like 15 years ago. Andy grabbed his board and paddled it out to him like a dog returning a stick. 'Here ya go Occy . . .'

'Yeah, I do remember now,' he said.

Fifteen years on, it still made our day.

OCCY

Jon

FRANK

I t was a little darker than usual this morning. Thick cloud crowded the horizon and the sun's arrival was delayed as if stuck in traffic. We had to wait. The night before had been pumping and our favourite big-wave spot glistened under failing moonlight. The ocean seemed big, very big. You could hear its roar and feel its energy. We waited in the carpark for more light as wet wetsuits enveloped our bodies, finding warmth in anticipation. The explosion of perhaps a 12-foot set hitting the shallow reef stole our attention. Through squinted eyes we

GRIGGS

could make out a surfer. The take-off was late and he flew to the bottom for what seemed an eternity, somehow making it. Then he became lost in the darkness of the rising face. It was so big, so huge that ... hang on. Somewhere between the moon and the sun he reappeared, riding 12-foot thick ledges at one of the most powerful waves in Australia, if not the world, in the dark—Voodoo. His name? Jon Frank.

'It's so obvious,' said Franky, a surfer, photographer and waterman — often in the same day. 'There's your everyday things, and then there's really good stuff. Just raw emotion where, for one split second, you experience something. You become a part of it — and it's just like ... wow!'

Jon Frank is unique. Like his photography, there is something different about him. He lives life on the extremities of sheer power and emotion, putting himself in positions that mediocre minds would not even think of. Through this, he has become not only a waterman, but also perhaps one of the greatest and most creative photographers of our time.

Jon Frank moved to Australia from England when he was 10. Like anyone different, he was ridiculed. But through this trauma, the individual was born. 'I think it's good at some stage of your life when you're growing up to be an adult, to not be part of the gang, to be given shit, to be ridiculed, to be an outsider ... to feel bad. I don't think that's a bad thing.' He has a knack for saying things you wouldn't have heard before and a skill to bring sense to it. 'After we migrated to Australia I went straight to school and I was the freak for a few years I guess. I was beaten up.' He paused for a second, unperturbed. 'I think it gives you a slant on things ... you learn about people and who they are. I think there's still a part of me that likes being that person that nobody knows or wants to talk to. There's something comforting about that.'

JON FRANK

He looked to the ocean. We were on a balcony overlooking the longest lefthander in the world, Chicama in Peru. There aren't many places he hasn't been. It was only two foot, but the most perfect two-foot line-up you could ever hope for. David Rastovich, who was along for the trip, was also mesmerised as they counted 17 consecutive waves in perfect symmetry. The sun — and *cervazas* — were going down beautifully. Rasta, one of the best free-surfing talents in the world right now and widely known and respected for his spiritual side, threw an observation to the resident offshore wind. (Yes, the wind is offshore every single day in Chicama. All day.)

'I read recently that when you are in the gang, or whatever you want to call it, you flow with that energy. You do what they do. You think how they think.' Rasta is not unlike Frank in many ways and the two get along really well. 'When you get out of the pack,' he continued, 'you can observe more clearly. So through separation, you get individuality.'

They looked at each other like they'd been separated at birth, and then quickly and nervously back at the ocean. 'I never did like people that much,' said Frank. 'Just shooting them.' The pelicans laughed as they flew by.

Jon Frank was a surfer before he was a photographer. He grew up in the suburban outskirts of Cronulla on the south side of Sydney, a place known for little else in the surfing world other than producing powerful reef breaks — and Occy. 'I was lucky to have a couple of key friends who were interested in surfing the same waves as me,' said Frank. 'I left school when I was 14 and started surfing the reef breaks around Cronulla. The Point, Voodoo, they were all we used to surf. We never spent much time at the beach.'

When Franky surfs and shoots, he looks beyond the common denominator. 'There's a difference, ya know. There's surfing and there's surfing, where every wave is different. It bends and contorts off the reef with so much power and energy. The beach just wasn't that interesting to look at, or to surf. And that was lucky because we pushed each other. We surfed some pretty big waves. We started surfing together and then when they became committed to university or whatever, I began surfing it alone. I guess it's not really a solo thing to do, but they say that about a lot of things.' Solitude was where he was most comfortable. 'I don't know why; people go off on tangents. A lot of the time my friends were at uni so I'd just surf it by myself.'

There's a wave in Cronulla that myself and two other mates, Jeremy Hrbac and Andy King, only discovered recently by accident. A wave you would have never imagined; it was like it broke upside down. Elated with our discovery, we relayed the story to Franky one night at the pub. 'Fuck!' he said. 'I've been surfing that by myself for three years.'

'We used to call him the "hair bear", or the "hair farmer", says Jeremy, another who only surfs the reef breaks and is generally considered the best, especially at Voodoo. "We'd be surfing the reefs or the island [Shark Island] when it was big, and he'd always just show up, by himself. He had this massive Afro and he looked so weird. Everyone knew of him, but nobody knew him."'

As in his school life, Franky was never part of the gang in Cronulla, but it was by choice. He was 'comfortable in it'. We would see him out at the breaks all the time, but he was this mysterious character who gave nothing away. Just another quiet guy in the line-up. Shy in character, but not in his willingness to have a serious look at an approaching set. He never talked much, still doesn't, but when he does, he says a lot. He speaks in a soft but confident monotone, and the impact comes from the depth of his analysis.

JON FRANK

A perfectly paced wave ran through its second kilometre at Chicama. It was about half-finished. 'Just standing on the beach having to do a million duck-dives and having waves come in all over the joint never appealed to me. Look at that thing,' he said pointing to the wave. 'I enjoyed the reefs, where there was some kind of reason why the waves were breaking and why it breaks with more colour and power and precision. I like looking at the shapes the waves make and the way they catch the light. That's what came through in my photography, I think.'

Frank was 19 when he first picked up a camera. 'I didn't go to uni or anything,' he admitted. 'I was playing in a few bands at the time, on the bass, and didn't really know what to do. We tried to write a few songs but after a few years it wasn't really working. I realised it wasn't what I was supposed to do. For me surfing was it, but I ended up enrolling in a film and television school, which was really hard to get in to. There were 500 applicants and I was one of the 12 applicants to get accepted on a written test. One of the subjects was photography and as soon as I did that I quit the course. I wanted to do stills photography and wasn't interested in TV.' He rose from his stool and smiled to himself. 'I wanted to be a photographer, so I bought a camera and started shooting photos. I studied for a few years at the Sydney Institute of Technology, which is a really good course, read books, got help from guys like Tony Nolan [legendary *Tracks* photographer], learnt from my mistakes, and just got into it. I took some shots into *Waves* [the surfing magazine] and they just said, "Shit, give us more".'

'When Franky first came along, I knew he was like no other photographer,' says Nolan. 'He is so left of field. When I send his photos to the lab, they spin out at his exposures and colours because they've never seen it before. They think it's out of focus or something.'

JON FRANK

He cracks up. 'That's just Franky for ya, mate. He captures photos that nobody else has even thought of. There's images that flick by your average photographer without them realising, but with Franky, he always seems to capture the things the rest of the boys don't even think of.'

Peru was my first trip with Franky. It felt weird that I didn't know him so well, but I don't think there are many people who do. When we arrived at the first wave, after what seemed like weeks of travelling, he just sat there and watched. Stuck in the mindset of most photographers, I was expecting him to just race out there and haphazardly shoot some action and see what eventuated. But that's not the way he works. He studied the wave, his subject, and the colours in the sky, how they affected the wave face; the whole scene in relation to landscape and seascape. Then he set up his 600mm manual camera way down the beach in an attempt to nail one photograph that summed up all the elements of the surfing experience.

There's a certain confidence that goes with that technique. He knows his ability, and a lot of photographers admire him, including Andrew 'Shorty' Buckley, who calls him 'the best in the world, without doubt. Not just technically, it's what he sees, and the positions he gets himself into.'

'I think what works for me is a cross between cynicism and sensitivity,' said Frank. 'You've got to feel something or notice something, and have the ability to be able to portray it, like painting or whatever. There's normal things, and then there's really amazing stuff. It's black and white. That's just me, though. I think there's got to be some kind of craftsmanship involved as well, some kind of knowledge of what the light's doing, and for me, the best way to communicate that is on film.'

JON FRANK

'He's one of the true photographers,' says Sarge, the best-known of all surfing photojournalists. 'He learnt the right way, before all this automatic crap came in, where all you need is the money to afford a camera and you are in. Jon Frank is a great photographer.'

With his experience as a photographer restricted to the Cronulla reef breaks and odd sojourns down the south coast of New South Wales, Franky's real talent lay in shooting big waves. In 1994, he had an opportunity to go where it all happens, where waves make and break people like boards — Pipeline. I went and retrieved a new beer, and we talked about Hawaii. David Rastovich, who doesn't drink, was sitting behind us playing empty beer bottles with a scary, child-like rhythm.

'I was really lucky that when I first went to Hawaii it was with these two Christian guys from Cronulla — and they just loved big waves: Rusty Moran and Darryl 'Boogs' Van de Polder. I met Rusty out at Shark Island one day and he was telling me he was going to Hawaii and that I should come. I'd been before and I was like, "Yeah, I'll come this season for two months". So we went and just went surfing. Fuck, we had some good days.'

These guys are lunatics. When their names are mentioned images spring to mind of cover shots at Shark Island, of how, during the first trip to Hawaii, they both paddled straight to the inside — and metres deeper than anyone — and got smashed on every wave until they made a couple. I've been in low tide line-ups with these guys and when an unrideable wave comes through, they are first to put their hands up. They are not good surfers, but through sheer grit and guts, are among the best big-wave surfers I know. When the three of them got together, something was going to happen.

'The best thing Frank brought with him to Hawaii,' says Rusty Moran, 'was a fresh mind. He had no influences. He didn't look at other

JON FRANK

photos, he looked at waves. We would surf big Bay [Waimea] and Phantoms [a notorious big-wave bombora outside of Sunset Beach] together all the time that year. It was a good season. We would take turns with the board and the camera.' He laughs, the same way he does when he comes up from a 10-foot closeout after getting smashed on the reef. It's an almost docile laugh, but when he does it, he's either done, or is about to do, something crazy. 'We used to take off deep at the Bay and I, or Franky, would sit in the impact zone on top of a bodyboard to try and get a different straight-on angle. We'd get totally cleaned up because we'd be sitting about 15 metres in front of the explosion.' He laughs again. 'We had some fun, especially at Phantoms, because we used to surf it by ourselves a lot.'

One story in particular remained with me. It was of Franky getting cleaned up by a 20-foot set at Phantoms. It was told to me by Boogs. After retrieving his board and getting back out there, another huge set exploded in front of him. Without a leg rope — and unwilling to swim all the way to shore again to retrieve it (a good half-hour through treacherous waters) — he decided to do an eskimo roll. This old-school manoeuvre entails rolling upside down, holding your board tightly so you're not penetrating the water and letting the wave pass overhead. 'Yeah, I got smashed,' said Franky. 'I'd just got back out the back, so I didn't want to go through all that foamy shit again, so I thought I'd give the old eskimo roll a go.' He laughed, the same way as Rusty and Boogs. It's the only time he sounds goofy. 'I got cleaned up and washed into shore again and I remember the lifeguard looking at me, just shaking his head, going, "I thought it was you again."'

When Franky shoots, you don't know what the hell he's doing half the time. I swam out with him one day when he was shooting Rasta

JON FRANK

down the coast at San Bartolo, just south of Lima, just to get an idea of what goes through his head. It was about four foot but everywhere rocks were sticking up out of the reef like land mines. For him, it's just part of surfing. Everyone can relate to rocks and coming to grief on them. Franky wants to capture these images and it's often at his body's expense. I swam around for about 30 minutes and all I did was get in Rasta's way and come to grief with my new amigo, el reefo.

This whole trip with Franky was one of rediscovery, actually. Being out there reminded me of the early days, surfing out Shark Island with photographers everywhere. I'd see him do the craziest stuff, floating precariously on the reef known as 'Surge', and getting sucked over it every time. We'd laugh and appreciate his bravery, but the other photographers didn't know what to do. How do you compete with that?

The sun was done now at Chicama. We were on our third or fourth beer and Rasta had retreated to his daily ritual of yoga and meditation. We wouldn't see him for at least another hour. Under the silent sky I asked Franky about his photography and the advantage a huge ticker has when he's in Hawaii, or in any big waves.

'Yeah, it helps, I guess. This one time at the Pipe Masters, the year Kelly won his sixth world title, he was going right and nobody was shooting it. Nobody had put their name down to get in the water; every single person was shooting from the beach, I couldn't believe it. I went out and shot that classic semi-final with Kelly and Rob Machado. Kelly was just flying past me in the hugest barrels. I ended up getting the cover shot of *Surfer*.'

Franky is in a minority, a man who appreciates the finer things in life. He watches a lot of old films, reads classic literature and he appreciates great artists, musical and otherwise. He drives a BMW, even if it is old and rusted, and listens to rock 'n' roll music in the dark with a glass full of vodka. 'It's the best way to listen to rock 'n' roll,' he maintains. Just when you think you're starting to get to know him you rock up to his house and he's drinking a vodka in the dark, by himself, listening to Led Zeppelin. But it's not what he's doing, it's how he comes to doing it. You get the feeling it comes from his solitude, watching people do things, say things and make things. When Franky sees things, he also sees how they can become better.

The Pipe Masters that year was one of the last times Franky shot Hawaii with a stills camera only. Though his ability and reputation were climbing unexplored peaks, Franky was getting a little bored. He was starting to get an itch for making movies.

'I remember ringing the editor of *Waves* from Hawaii. It was my third year there ...'94. I rang him at his office in Sydney and I was just like, "I'm off this shit." I used to stay there for two months every year and it was a long haul. I just didn't want to do it any more and he said, "Yeah, well, I've got this idea. I want to make a surf movie." And I was like, "Fuck, I've been thinking about that too. Come home and we'll talk about it — and we'll do it." He wanted to start off with Derek Hynd, Wayne Lynch and a few others, so we got a couple of cameras and off we went.'

Rasta had been meditating to our right for the last hour and when the word *Litmus* came up, he rose instantly: 'Fuck, that movie was good. I remember being so bored with surfing and the way it was portrayed. When I saw that movie — all the people on it as well as all the different equipment they were riding — it gave me energy to keep going. The surfing world really needed it, I reckon. I know I did.'

Frank just about blushed. He was stoked with the recognition, because it was exactly what he was aiming for in the video. 'There wasn't much out there at the time that we thought was reflective of surfing,' he said. 'So we put together the best we could all these places and people that summed it up — and that was *Litmus*.

'We went to Vicco, J-Bay, Ireland, and I ended up in California. I'd been given Tom Curren's phone number and I had a one-night layover in LA. I just thought fuck, I'll give it a go, you know. I'll give this number a try and see if we can get some footage of Tom Curren. I rang it and Tom answered the phone and I went, "Ah hi, you don't know me, but we're making this video and I'd love to get some footage, can I come up and hang out?" He was like, "Yeah, come up." So I went up to Santa Barbara and spent two weeks with him and his family. I met Pat [his father, a famous big-wave surfer]. They hadn't seen each other for a while and I shot some good photos of those guys together. After that, I went to Hawaii. And that was it, that was *Litmus*.'

A few years later, Franky started doing some work for Rip Curl, including *Super Computer*, a movie he shot and directed himself, on film. It won best extreme video of the year at the prestigious NEA awards [the Oscars of extreme sports] in Germany. It was a big achievement. In between, Frank continued to shoot a lot of stills, mainly empty waves, his real passion — and his work was being noticed beyond the surfing world. He produced a book called *Waves of the Sea* — no surfers, just waves — in '98 and had his work in art galleries soon after. 'I think that came about because I shot a lot of empty waves,' he said.

What made you go after empty waves in the first place? I asked. 'Nothing made me want to do it specifically,' he replied. 'I'd just be swimming and these waves were coming through, and they were beautiful. So I'd always shoot them. Why are we compelled to grab our

JON FRANK

camera when we see something? Often it just grabs you and you think, shit, I've got to capture this — right now! So you fumble around for your camera, fiddle with your exposure and try and pull focus as best as you can and hope you've got it, and you never know. But that moment's gone and you start thinking about the next one.'

Frank's exhibitions have been to Bondi and Cronulla and were very successful. 'People are stoked to see that stuff, ya know. Especially on a wall, big, framed. I don't think people realise that the world can look like that, without special effects. I don't think people understand how beautiful things are until you take the time to look at the details. When it's frozen up there in front of you, big, they're like, oh my God! But if they were standing on the beach watching that wave, they wouldn't have even noticed it. Different perspectives, I guess.'

There was a pause for a while as we regathered our thoughts. It was a really cool interview. Just candid conversation. He looked up at me and said with a little bit of a lisp: 'I want to talk more about photography, and how it makes me feel.' Please! 'When I look at a photograph that someone's taken, or watch a movie, see something someone's painted or written where it has affected you personally, it's like they've hard-wired the juice of what it's like to be alive. The best and the worst of everything that is. It's just raw emotion and it's straight into you and there's nothing you can do about it except soak it in. That to me is what good anything is.' He paused. 'Fuck, that's clumsy the way I've put it, but ...'

It's moments like these you realise what a perfectionist Franky is, and that he doesn't just see things, he feels things. 'If you don't feel anything when you are reading a book, or when you go to an art gallery, or whatever it is that you are doing, then what's the point? You may as well be at home watching TV. And you can feel something watching TV too, you know. But sometimes people, they just ... they really get it right.'

On the eve of the millennium, Frank packed his bags and headed on an around-the-world trip on a solo mission of discovery. 'I went to five major cities that interested me. Calcutta, Jerusalem, Moscow, Lagos in Nigeria, Bogota in Colombia. And ended up at Times Square in New York for the millennium.'

It summed up everything Jon Frank is about, as a person and as a photographer. 'It's just what I'm interested in as a photographer, little bits of the world, seeing different people and how they live. To me it's about communicating, seeing the world and depicting it through my photos. It's selfish in a way, because I'm shooting what I see and what I want to shoot.'

I asked him about his trip and his adventures along the way. But it's not something you can talk about with Franky. It's like he's found a new surfing break; he doesn't need to share it. But through his camera lens he can, and it's through these moments of clarity and inspiration that he communicates his unique visions of life, the way he sees it, and in a way very few can. 'It's hard to talk about all that sort of stuff sometimes, because it's so personal. I'd love people to see the photos, though.'

JON FRANK

Trent
MUNRO

'I GUESS the city boys have got to look cooler and be cooler,' chuckled Trent Munro, changing out of a pair of khaki overalls and into a pair of boardies.

While admittedly we'd put him in the overalls for a *Tracks* photo shoot, the favourite surfing son of sleepy Scotts Head looked disturbingly natural in them. Hell, he admits to having milked a cow before, 'but only with one of them machines'. Like most country folk, his wardrobe bespeaks practicality and mirrors his approach to surfing — substance over style, all the

SARGE

way. He's felt the warmth of an ugh boot on cold sand in winter, as well as the freedom of a double plugger in summer. He's different from his city slickin' counterparts who might be seen wearing designer overalls and white leather loafers. 'Too many fuckers care too much about how they look these days,' he said in his slow country twang. 'We ain't got to do nothin'. Ha! We just gotta surf and do it our way.'

After a few lazy, empty waves earlier in the day, Trent, Sarge and I continued on to the Scotts Head Bowling Club for cheap schooners and a chat.

There were no cigarettes or drugs here. No doof, doof. Just a few lawn-bowling 'seagulls' ambling between the bowling green and the pokies with the ubiquitous schooner in hand. We grabbed a table in the corner and Trent began talkin' story. 'I'm not boring you faaarkers, am I?'

As usual, Trent stood out. His pathological confidence, tell-it-like-it-is honesty and uncomplicated demeanour make him the all-Australian heir of Matt Hoy. He's even inherited Hoyo's favourite expletive, which he directed at me straight after I mentioned the comparison.

'Faaark that,' he answered, wiping the first sip of beer from his beard. 'There's only one Matt Hoy ... and there's only one Munro. Deeeal with it. Ha!'

Trent is not a pretty surfer. He doesn't waste time trying to perfect his style, time that would be much better spent 'smashing waves to pieces'. His surfing is raw, fast, powerful and beautifully ugly in that Aussie kind of way. It's uniquely organic. And with the judging system increasingly being geared towards substance over style, big turns over bum wiggles, 'Knackers' is a prototype of the surfer of the future. But getting himself to where he is now was more complicated than milking a cow. When he qualified for the WCT in 2001 he thought he was ready. He wasn't.

Bells Beach, Easter 2001: the waves were pumping and it was fucking freezing.

'Who have you got?' I asked Trent as he ran for a warm-up surf at Winki Pop before the first heat of his WCT career. He let out his usual laugh, and his fluffy head tilted back to allow an explosion of disdain from his 5'4" frame. 'Ha!'

'Who have you got?' I pressed, drawn in with a shivered smirk.

'Some bloke who's gonna finish second. Guilherme [Herdy] I think...' He looked over his shoulders towards the pros gathering in the car park to make sure Guilherme wasn't there; not that he really gave a fuck. 'Ha!'

Trent paddled out at Winki and went crazy. I was as confident of his chances as he was. A few hours later he lost.

'I kinda do that,' Trent reflected, taking another generous mouthful of beer. 'I did get kinda cocky. But I didn't know much about the 'CT then. But you know what? I do now.' It was after that first-up loss that Trent swallowed his pride and decided to reinvent himself. He came back to Scotts Head with a goal.

It's quiet up here at Scotts. Perfect beachbreaks and an awesome point flow year-round for a population the size of a large family. About the most exciting thing that ever happened here was in April '97, when a rusty refugee boat ran aground on the main beach and delivered 58 illegal Chinese immigrants into the surrounding bushland. 'The waves were pumping ... but I didn't see any of them in the line-up,' chuckled Knackers at the time. Empty line-ups is what he likes to see around home, and the waves and solitude of Scotts have become an important sanctuary for him, the perfect foil to his hectic life on tour. Here he can recharge the batteries and fine tune his surfing, most of the time on his Pat Malone, and that's the

TRENT MUNRO

way he'd like it to stay. 'If you blow in, blow out, blow-ins,' he laughed.

This was also the year Trent landed the Australian Junior Series title. In his last year as a junior, Knackers marched through the series with a potato sack full of trophies to take home. 'I'd paddle out every time and just know I was going to win,' he said. 'I think I won at least four in Oz, then I won in France too and got a wildcard into the WCT event at Lacanau.'

For Trent, this was the first taste of where he wanted to be, and he exploded out of his hometown stable like a bucking cow. 'I surfed against Sunny [Garcia] in that French event [the Rip Curl Pro] and I think that was a real turning point in my career; just surfing that first event and seeing how it is, really made me want to get there. All the best surfers are hanging out, going mad. I wanted to be one of 'em.'

But the country kid had his eyes opened during his first full year on the WQS. 'The first year I travelled away, I was so young. I was just going, "Wow. Look at all these parties, look at all these chicks." I pretty much wanted to lose my heat a lot of the time, because if you're the last one in the contest, you're devastated because all the boys are going out and going mad.'

He paused, realising he was on his old tangent and sipped his beer. 'What a faaarken idiot! Ha!' It's unreal how he laughs at everything. I guess coming from the country, everything is new to him. 'I reckon I qualified at the right time, though. There's no way I could have done it when I was only 18. I totally understand why Taj didn't want to do it [Burrow knocked back a spot on the WCT when he was 19, believing he needed more experience]. It's a big thing. Not just for us country boys, but just being that young.'

After winning one of the final events in Florianopolis, Brazil, in his third year, Trent qualified for the WCT. He was on a roll. After signing with O'Neill International, he was riding high, ready for a shot at the WCT for the start of season 2001. But things didn't going to plan.

The year he qualified he only rode two boards in contests, but just before the start of his first WCT season he ran into contract problems with his shaper, Greg Webber. 'I was coming into the start of the tour going, "Fuck, my boards are going great, everything is going to be spot-on", then I was thrown in the deep end again, just before the events, without any boards.' Then he tweaked his knee, putting him out of the water for five weeks prior to the season's kickoff.

This proved to be a true test of character. He had three straight lasts — the first against Guilherme — and found himself backed against the wall. In hindsight this baptism of fire was probably the best thing that could have happened to him, because it forced him to come out swinging. 'Hey! I worked hard, don't you worry. I worked so faaarken hard on my boards. As soon as Webber smoked me, I said, "Faaark this, I'm not gunna let that get me down. I am going to be on!"' I was waiting for the 'Ha!', but he was serious.

'When Trent arrived in Rio in early May, he had that look,' said Sarge. 'He looked at me and said, "You know what, Sarge, I ain't gettin' another 33rd." He would come in from a heat, absolutely annihilate someone, and have this look in his eyes, like, "Who's next?". He was backed up in a corner.'

'I beat Parko, Taj, Andy and Hog [Nathan Hedge] along the way,' said Trent, 'and just thought, "Faaark! This is just like the pro junior." Ha!'

Trent went on to beat Occy in the final, only the fourth event of his WCT career and the earliest win after a WCT debut in ASP history. With a victory under his belt, he kept the formula going, arriving early in J-Bay, the next event on tour, to get to know the wave better and keep the roll going.

TRENT MUNRO

He was full of confidence and came up against someone equally self-assured, Joel Parkinson. According to his peers it was the best heat of the year. 'Easy,' nodded Sarge, bringing a new round of amber to the table and rejoining the conversation.

'Ha! I was looking for him for days when I found out I was surfing against him,' said Trent. 'Then when I finally saw him, I looked at him hard and said, "Fuck, are you ready!"'

'We went at it, mate, like faaarking craaazy! He actually fell off first wave.' He paused. 'If someone falls off on their first wave, I just go on this automatic high where I'm going, look-the-faaark-out. Then before I knew it, he's just popped these three faaarking scores out of his arse. Faaark I was angry. I wanted to destroy him. I was just sitting there with steam coming out of my head, going "Faaark, give me a wave, Huey [the surf god], ya faaarker! Let me at him!" I was so angry, but you can't control everything.' Trent looked down at my empty beer a few minutes later. 'Whatcha drinkin'?' He stood up and fetched his shout, chatting to one of the old boys at the bar for a while. He takes pride in his beer etiquette and is down to earth enough to talk to anyone. During his absence at the bar Sarge and I talked about the push the Coolangatta kids are getting and how Trent is actually as good as Parko, Fanning and Morrison and how nobody even knows it, because he's from the sticks. I put this to Trent as he put the beer on the table.

'Mate, those guys can't go surfing without someone shootin'' them. I'd like to think I could get that much exposure if someone was videoing or shooting me every day as well.'

I asked him if they are his biggest threats. 'I don't give a faaark who's who,' he said, 'I want to beat everybody. I reckon everyone in there [the WCT] deserves to be there, and it is the best surfing in the

TRENT MUNRO

world. I'm a part of it and I want to win and they're all just getting in my way.'

Two weeks short of a year after losing at Bells, Trent was back there with good mate Nathan 'Hog' Hedge, one of the surfers he'd eliminated in Rio. They were there to tune up in a pulsing eight- to 10-foot swell, and Trent was keen to erase the memory of the horror start to his WCT career.

'Last year I blew it,' he admitted. 'Just inexpeeer...' He thought for a second. 'Nah, I was just faaarking stupid! I want to really learn how to surf the breaks so I can rock up to events and go, "Hey, you know what? I know what I'm doing now."'

In the first few heats at Bells this year he looked unstoppable. He dominated the highest scores with surfing that had more drive than the Great Ocean Road. He was almost going too hard, going for turns he didn't even need to attempt. 'I'm pretty confident with Bells now,' he said. 'After going down there throughout the year, I've learnt more about the wave and how far you can push the lip. I wasn't going to pull back.'

The country kid was as crazy as a cut snake, spitting venom at three consecutive beaten opponents, until he met another farm animal in round four — his Bells sparring partner, Hog. 'Yeah, you know what? I wish I didn't go down to Bells with the bastard now. Ha! How's that? When I drew him, I just couldn't believe it.'

The two went at it like pit bulls, but in the end it was Hog who brought home the bacon, and Trent was gutted. He climbed the stairs at Bells Beach and stormed into the competitors' tent, where he gave Hog a look that could have cut stone from the Bells cliffs. He pointed at him and yelled at the top of his lungs, 'One-all, Hog!' It was intense.

TRENT MUNRO

There's a different edge to Trent these days. He looks a little more serious. The initial fun and excitement of the tour is over for him. Now it's all about business. The sun was going down and the three of us left the bowlo. At most places around the country Trent's peers would just be starting to think about going out, strapping into their designer Tsubi jeans and gelling their teased hair. Soon Trent would be in his ugh boots, pumping up for Tahiti, where he'd bomb down 10-footers to nail a third-place finish.

'Those guys can have it, mate. I'm happy with who I am and I'm gunna do it my way. Ha! Deal with it.' A lot had happened since that cold day at Bells last season.

TRENT MUNRO

Luke

HITCHINGS

Somehow I just knew he was going to do it. As he came off the bottom there was a look of determination I had seen before. A look so focused you become a part of it, though that's as close as anyone ever gets. There was only one place he was going now. The draining reef below was further away in his mind than his surfboard as he powered up the 12-foot face, bottom turning vertically toward a lip that could have killed him. He defied it, like a small fly evading a giant swat. This was intense. As I paddled up the face, looking

SARGE

down, I followed his eyes; eyes that seemed to roll back in his head like a shark ready to attack. Aaron Graham (his best mate and a former pro surfer) and I looked in disbelief as he struck, smashing vertically into the thick pitching lip on his backhand. His body coiled into a position that reached out and slapped you in the face, screaming, 'This is commitment!'.

Luke Hitchings had just busted his 7'2" through the roof of a 12-foot pitching lip on the remote island of Asu off Sumatra. Fins out and coming down through the barrel. He made it and I'll never see anything like it again.

'Are you for real?' Our eyes must have been the size of basketballs. 'What were you thinking — that was a 12-foot barrel. It was already going over your head halfway through the bottom turn.'

'It was just a re-entry,' Luke humbly replied, his head red and on the brink of spontaneously combusting. This is Luke Hitchings. A humble technician with a bit of the animal in him. A raging bull that sees red in the most challenging situations.

'He was always into sports,' says Luke's dad. 'He surfed from when he was young, but he was also into rugby,' he laughs, 'until he was starting to get his head ripped off too much and couldn't surf because he was always sore. He's into golf and tennis at the moment.'

From a young age Luke developed a quiet ability to 'have a go'. 'When Luke played rugby,' says former schoolmate Gavin Bishop, who now plays fly half for Randwick, 'he wouldn't think twice about tackling anyone, and back then he was half the size of everyone else. The thought of pulling back wouldn't cross his mind. Even if he got hurt. He'd get this look in his eye and just keep going.'

Though Luke admits his fading from footy was a consequence of the unsettling realisation that he was increasingly looking up at everyone he was tackling (Luke didn't enjoy the growth spurt of his peers), his short, stocky build was starting to be an advantage in his true love, surfing, and a career began to poke him in the back pocket.

'It wasn't until my first year at uni [Luke studied building at the University of Technology, Sydney] that I realised I could make a career out of it,' says Luke. 'I had a good year on the Australian circuit and just through that I got the opportunity to do it for a living. So I packed up my uni studies and off I went.'

Finally Luke was off the fence, but it wasn't until the World Titles in Brazil later that year that people really began to take notice. It was in the middle of an era when the Americans were dominating and Luke was the last man standing for the Australian team in the prized junior division. He had just scored an interference in his semi-final against Andy Irons, which meant only his best two waves would count in his final tally rather than the usual three. A loss here would put the Aussie team back to third, with daylight a clear second. That's when Luke got that look again. He dug deep, found a fitness that simply wasn't there and powered into a wave with a minute to go. 'I knew I wasn't out of it,' says Luke. 'It's all about determination. When you get into a situation like that, you just go.'

Enter the animal. Hitchings pulled into what seemed like a six-foot closeout from way behind. Enough time had elapsed for coach Rabbit Bartholomew to nervously skull two beers, grow 14 grey hairs and bite his nails back to his elbows. Everyone was freaking. Luke came out, probably on the verge of the 9-point ride needed. He then smashed the lip with less respect than a bare-knuckled boxer. 9.83. Hitcho had done it; he was in the final. His response: 'I couldn't stuff that wave up. It was such a good wave.'

LUKE HITCHINGS

It was here that Hitchings earned the nickname 'He-Man'. 'It's like he has this superpower,' says good mate Oscar Wright, who was also in the team for the event. 'He transforms into this power lord and does the biggest turns. I don't know how he does it.' Hitcho went on to place second behind Kalani Robb, with Corey Lopez third and Neco Padaratz fourth. All of these surfers are now in the top 46 of the world.

We are down the road from the *Tracks* office in the middle of Chinatown in Sydney. 'I'm a rookie here,' admits Luke. 'You better order me what you're having.' Halfway through a question I notice him pouring green tea all over his meal instead of the cup of sweet and sour provided. He never did fuss much about food. 'Ah, no worries, it all comes out in the wash.'

Half an hour later we're in George Street where *Tracks* photographer Andrew Buckley is taking some portraits. Luke's brother Vaughan rings, then his dad. It's something you get used to in the closeknit Hitchings family.

'My dad has probably been the biggest influence on my surfing,' says Luke. 'He'd always make me go out when it was big, even if I didn't want to. I'd come in all the time and he'd say, "What are you doing? You're surfing like a girl out there. You're meant to surf a big wave just like any other wave." So that's just how I sort of approached it when I was younger. And I guess it's the way my surfing's probably gone. Yeah, it doesn't feel any different really. Just go out there and try and hit the lip.'

But there's a lot more to it than that. While the animal within him still lurks restlessly, he's also developed a technique over the years that has coaches all over the world foraging beneath the cracks of the lounge for the remote control.

'My favourite surfer has always been Tom Curren,' says Luke. 'Occy as well. I still watch Curren now. He seems to be in such good rhythm

LUKE HITCHINGS

with the wave and just does everything right. He never makes mistakes and that's the way I want my surfing to be. I also want to have a bit of that Occy thing where you're just busting down doors and you just don't know what's going to happen. I sort of try to have the mixture of both. Smooth with a bit of the animal.'

It's an influence that seems a generation out of place for Hitchings. 'It's hard to surf exactly the way you want when you're doing the tour,' Luke admits. 'Sometimes you just want to go along and do one massive turn. But you sort of have to link them. But at the end of the day conforming can make you a better surfer, so long as you don't lose sight of what you're really about.'

It's five o'clock in the morning in Bali, Indonesia. After a massive night on the streets of Kuta, Hitchings has come to rest in a peculiar position. Just one hour earlier I had busted him asleep on the dance floor at the Sari Club, resting comfortably in an upright position against a wooden pylon that was about as straight as his posture. He wakes up suddenly from a snore that makes Bon Jovi, which is playing in the background, sound like a death-metal band. 'Oops, sorry boys.' He's back. 'My shout is it?' Off he goes to the bar. About three hours later when I wake up for the early he is asleep on a cane chair outside the room, clothed only in a pair of boardshorts and a thick layer of mosquitos. 'Ah fuck 'em. I'll be alright. They won't bite me, I've drunk too much piss. Let's go.'

It's moments like these that you get a true insight into his character. Day to day, hour to hour, Luke Hitchings answers the call of duty. Action! He starts where most people's limits begin. 'He is incredible,' says Taj Burrow. 'He's so good to watch because he is so powerful and stylish and he smashes lips most people wouldn't touch'. However, he can be quite shy and reserved around people at times.

LUKE HITCHINGS

While this is sometimes mistaken for being stuck up, the simple fact is, Luke basically doesn't like talking about himself.

Determination has always been the substitute for fitness for Hitcho — and such a good one that it has surfers in the top 46 questioning their routines of blood, sweat and tears. 'I thought Luke was so fit,' says Oscar Wright '. . . before I actually got to know him, that is.' Though Luke attacks his sporting endeavours with the ferocity of a lion, he also rests like one. He intellectualises his winning formula as subtly as his turns. 'Fitness doesn't mean that much. It's all in your head. It's all about determination.' Determination and smart play will always succeed for Luke. A technical style complemented by a simple philosophy.

Durban, 1999. Semi-final one and the waves are pumping. Hitchings takes off on the best-looking wave of the day. The long righthander presents itself from the pier like a free ride to the final. Hitchings sets himself. Waits the familiar fraction of a second for his first turn — like he's slowly pulling back a rubber band. The 10 000-strong crowd goes silent. I hear a paper cup drop at the back of the competitors' area. Everyone is drawn in. First turn. Through the roof vertically, spinning the tail. Luke Steadman and Tommy Whitaker go, 'Orrr!' His concentration can't be broken now. Second turn, even bigger. About 15 people go, 'Orrr!' He's off. Third turn, a massive hook tail slide. 'Orr!' The whole competitors' area has been drawn in, producing grunted 'Orrs!' in sync with the animal unleashed as Luke attempts turns he has no right to even think about, especially with a competition singlet on. The raw emotion from Luke and the crowd is intense: 'Orrr!' He is only halfway through the wave and another perfectly timed forehand gash stuns the crowd. He's growing in confidence with every turn. I look around. What started in the competitors'

area has scattered like rabbits into the crowd. The boardwalk is congested
with onlookers, eager to investigate the source of the commotion. The
crowd gasps again, in sync with a turn that looks way too late, but
there's no stopping him now. He's way too balanced, way too charged.
By the time he's finished the wave — a 10 — the whole crowd is
screaming in appreciation at the fierceness of every turn. Then there
is silence as they focus with him on the next bottom turn. They're
watching the best surfing they've seen since Occy down the road at
J-Bay 15 years earlier and they don't even know this guy's name.
It's a bizarre moment that encapsulates Luke's quiet charisma
and raises more questions about manufactured marketability.

As per usual, Luke played it down: 'I was so lucky I got
that wave.' Luke went on to win that event and anyone lucky
enough to have seen it would not have put his victory down
to luck. As he travels around the world, he touches people
like this, turning heads and dropping jaws everywhere he
goes. Everyone who knows him and his surfing proclaims he
is one of the best surfers in the world, a massive call
unfortunately spoken in whispers. But Luke's humble
persona masks the realisation of the masses. He does not
have an image to cultivate or maintain and this is the biggest
mistake of the new sporting age. 'No image is my image,' said
Simon Anderson (inventor of the thruster) back in the '80s. But
these days it doesn't seem to work.

Luke hides an intrinsic desire and confidence to rise to the
occasion. To raise the bar. He has been taught by his dad to go
big, to 'treat every wave as if it was a two-foot shorey'. He has been
taught love, generosity and humbleness by his mum, Leonie. And he
has been taught a non-image-based, down-to-earth mateship by his
brother and friends at Bronte, where there are more sports stars than
cafés.

LUKE HITCHINGS

As he continues in his fifth year on the WCT, Hitchings is growing in confidence. Deep down he knows what he is capable of and he wants a top-10 finish. But don't ask him how he'll do it. Ask one of his peers, or better still, watch him. Luke is not outspoken and he is not a pretty boy trying to create an image for himself. He is a no-bullshit surfer and a no-bullshit person who has a rare mix of style and animalistic aggression in his surfing. The bull and the matador in one.

LUKE HITCHINGS

Rob
ROWLAND-SMITH

As soon as you walk into Rob Rowland-Smith's house at Newport on the northern beaches of Sydney, there's evidence of a proud man married to fitness. Detouring through the side gate, a sign welcomed me to 'Muscle Beach'. On the same sign, there is a drawing of a pair of cartoon biceps with the caption, 'You don't get these picking cherries.' Rob laughed, 'What do you reckon, Matty? Pretty good, eh?' Even his voice sounds like he has been gargling nails. His semi-loose shirt revealed the body of a silverback gorilla.

This man is hard, despite his age, which I guessed at mid–40s. His face is equally strong; it too has seemingly been cut from stone.

Muscle Beach is a big sandpit, complete with backyard gym, boxing apparatus, chin-up bars, dip bars, hand weights and sit-up benches. It is Rob's world and he definitely doesn't pick berries here; he'd crush them by looking at them. Even the chin-up bar is scared of him.

It may not be a normal backyard, but the Sand Hill Warrior, as he is known, is not a normal man. He has trained some of the best athletes in the world. His age is unknown to him; he basically doesn't care. Each year he vows to get fitter, stronger and faster than the last. Rob Rowland-Smith lives with pain, it has become his friend, and through this, he has discovered the essence of life.

'I have a few philosophies,' he said. 'One — pain is weakness leaving the body. You have to make pain your friend, learn how to deal with it. If you learn to go through the pain barrier, you know when you come out the other end that you're going to be physically and mentally fitter and tougher than before.'

The Warrior goes through three or four workouts a day. He carries injuries but he never gives up. 'When things get tough I say, "Bring it on, how much tougher can I be, how much more can I take?" Pain is a challenge and I meet it head-on, I don't sidestep it. The people that I train, I say to them, "Accept the fact that it's going to hurt. You are going to get out of your comfort zone. But once you learn to get out of the comfort zone, once you know how to step up to the plate and into uncharted territory, that's when you grow as an individual."'

This is where Rob has discovered the essence of life — and that it can also relate to emotional pain. 'We all deal with it,' he said. 'Accept the fact that it's going to hit you and accept the fact that it's going to hurt. You have to deal with it. The more pain I feel, the more shit I'm getting out of my system. I'm getting physically and mentally tougher, and that is what gives you the edge for everything in life.'

Rob looked as proud of Muscle Beach as he did the muscles on his own body. 'What do you reckon Matty?' he kept asking me. I'd been to his place a few times now and each time he greeted me like a best mate, such is his energy and friendliness. 'Come here, Matty,' he said. 'I've got to show you something.'

Walking through to his house I was struck by a living room of memorabilia. It was like a museum of fitness, or of the Sand Hill Warrior. There are framed posters and magazine cover shots of people he has trained, scribbled with thank-you messages and personal words of inspiration. Guys like league great Peter Sterling, and surfing world champions Kelly Slater, Gary Elkerton and Tommy Carroll, who he admits to having very competitive sessions with. 'All these people have touched my life,' he said. 'These people that you see in these photos, they all mean a lot to me because with training, when you work out with someone, there are no egos, there are no agendas. We are all equal and you really get into the soul of someone, because you are taking them into your world and it's going to mould them physically and emotionally.'

He then pointed out to me a framed photo of a massive sand dune that looked like the Sahara digesting itself. He put some glasses on. It's his only sign of age and it startled me. 'Yep,' said the Sand Hill Warrior, 'that's the dune in Pilat, which is in the Archacon Basin just north of Lacanau in France. And there's a story there.' There's a story in everything with Rob Rowland-Smith.

'I was training in Morocco with Quiksilver's team manager for Europe and we were running sand dunes in Morocco. He said, "Rob,

ROB ROWLAND-SMITH

when we go back to France, I'll take you to perhaps the biggest sand dune in the world." I couldn't wait — not only is it really high, but it's almost 90 degrees. I got there and I said, "Righto, I'm going to run this, but I'm going to do it in uniform", so I stripped down to my speedos and took it on. I ran for three hours and by the time I got to the top, my heart rate was 200 beats per minute. It was the toughest thing I've ever done. I loved it, because like anything, it's a challenge. That's why it sits here at Muscle Beach, because it's a challenge and I'll go anywhere around the world for a challenge. I love that sort of stuff. Hopefully I can go back there and kick its arse again.'

As I looked around his living room, he brought my attention to a hand-painted clay bowl that had a picture of a mosque in it. He laughed. 'There's a story in that one, Matty. I was in Morocco and had to stay a night in Casablanca. I got up the next morning to check it out and go for a run. Everything there is white so it's easy to get disorientated or lost.'

Rob trains every single day, four times a day — minimum. If he's on a plane you'll see him doing push-ups in the aisle or dips from the seats, often in Speedos. To him there are no excuses, but often it can get him into trouble.

'I ran down along the water's edge and out of the morning mist and I saw this beautiful mosque. So I ran up the stairs like Rocky does. I did a few laps and then I started to do some push-ups. I heard a few voices but I didn't do anything, I just kept on doing my push-ups. Then I felt the cold hard steel of an AK-47 pushed into my ribs from these soldiers and they're telling me to get up and I'm going, "Hang on guys, I've got one more set to go," he laughed.

'They arrested me and took me to this little station about 50 metres away from the mosque. Now, I didn't know it was Friday, a holy day, and here I am on the outside of the mosque doing push-ups in my Speedos. So I'm in this guardhouse and the soldiers are arguing with their commandant and I'm thinking, "Hang on, I'm in trouble here". So while they were arguing, I just bolted straight out the door. They chased me and were yelling at me in Arabic and I just kept running. The next thing I hear these gunshots going bang, bang, bang, over my head. I just kept running and running — and that was one defining moment in my career, where I thought, "Thank fucking Christ, I'm fit, so I can outrun these soldiers. Thank fuck I'm the Sand Hill Warrior"'. Two weeks later, Rob found the hand-painted bowl of that very mosque he'd been arrested in. 'It takes pride of place here,' he said.

From his living room to his backyard, he lives and breathes sand and fitness. Of course, he was a disciple of fitness before he became a preacher. He started off when he was young, and like now, he always trained in uniform. Whether it's running through the Domain in Sydney, or sand dunes at Palm Beach, the Sand Hill Warrior always wears Speedos.

'Ever since I was a kid, I've never worn underwear. For some reason, I've always worn Speedos. I used to wear them to school. I'd wear them under jeans, I'd wear them out socially, I'd wear them everywhere.'

'Have you got some on now?' I asked.

He reached into his tracksuit pants. 'Hey Matty, what do you think they are mate? A ham sandwich?' he laughed.

'My mum reckons I was born in them, she reckons I never wore nappies. She says all I had were these tiny little pairs of Speedos.'

Growing up, Rob Rowland-Smith was always into sports. 'There was a stage when I was younger when I was into everything — running, rowing, footy. To cross-train wasn't really heard of back then.

To get fit for footy, you played footy; to get fit for rowing, you rowed. I sort of worked out that, to get the edge, I had to do something different to make me mentally and physically stronger than the opposition. I worked that out when I was about 15.'

For Rob, like anyone, it started out as a simple goal. He wanted to make the rowing team at school. 'I wasn't that big compared to the other guys,' he said. 'So how was I going to get the edge? I'd do some resistance training, some extra miles on the beach, which wasn't heard of. Three things happened. One, I made the crew; two, I started to get really good at what I did, and three, I started to win races, and I thought, "Hang on a sec, I'm doing something that's pretty right here".'

Rob had almost invented cross-training, and it would change his life. 'I started to feel really good about what I was doing and why I was doing it. I developed confidence and an outlook on life like, I can deal with this problem, I can deal with emotional problems, I can deal with physical problems, all of a sudden I can stand up in front of a crowd of people and talk. By being physically and emotionally fitter, and pushing through comfort barriers, I developed the confidence that says, no matter what, I can do this.'

The more Rob trained, the more disciplined he became, and the more disciplined he became, the more successful as a person he became. He would never take the soft option. He was doing the hard yards to get the results. 'Nothing in life comes easy,' he said. 'If you want to be successful in whatever it is you want to do, you've got to work hard at it, no short cuts.'

This attitude soon became a lifestyle. He went to uni, got a degree in sports science and in teaching. He was playing footy and was doing very well. 'The people were seeing my results and going, "Shit, can we come and train with ya? Can we come and lift weights with ya?"'

Rob went to the Western Suburbs rugby league team, trained them, and then went to Parramatta for 15 seasons. It wasn't long before he met Tommy Carroll (twice world surfing champion) and got into surfing and training with the best surfers in the world like Kelly Slater. It became a full-time career for him.

To get an insight into the Sand Hill Warrior's life, let's take a look at his average daily routine. He awakes at 5.30 a.m. and drives to Palm Beach where he runs sand dunes, paddles boards, and does multiple sets of push-ups, sit-ups and dips. He also swims, with some boxing and other cross-training. That's an hour and a half. He then drives to the city to train a group of women. Then he goes into the Domain for what he calls 'Pain in the Domain' — 20-plus businessmen on their lunchbreak. He trains with them for a full hour, in his Speedos, and it's hardcore. Running, push-ups, dips, sit-ups — a full cross-training workout.

He then gets back in the car and heads to Narrabeen for a paddling session. Then it's off to Quiky headquarters at Newport for staff training. Then he trains a disabled kid before a couple of weight sessions with some of the surfers. Then he trains the Newport Breakers rugby team. Oh yeah, and Tommy Carroll was coming over that night for a session at Muscle Beach. The scary thing is, Rob trains with all of them.

'I have to lead by example. I'm a warrior and I lead a warrior's existence. To make sure I've got the edge on these guys I often train by myself too.' He does this mostly by running dunes.

'I have a philosophy that the best gym in the world is on the beach. You've got everything. You've got the beach to run, the surf to swim. Training to me is working out there in nature and that's how all this came about — I've run sand dunes every day of my life. I'm very basic and no frills, but I'm hardcore. Like this morning it was

ROB ROWLAND-SMITH

10 degrees, but we were still up and at it. You've got to have that warrior outlook, where you go back to basics. You deal with it when it's hot and you deal with it when it's cold, and that toughens you up mentally.'

It's the Sand Hill Warrior's love of life that keeps him getting up every morning. 'You're here once,' he said. 'But you're dead a long time. I see so many people stressing over material things. Death doesn't come with a luggage rack; you can't take it all to the big sand hill in the sky. But right now, your body is your luggage. I try to extract as much as I can out of the day. There comes a time when you've got to go inside yourself, to push through pain barriers, and by doing that not only are you better equipped to take anything on, but you get to know yourself.'

To Rob, fitness is not just about being strong, flexible, agile, powerful, and cardiovascularly invincible. It's about being able to enjoy relationships, making decisions with a clear head, and feeling good about yourself. 'We knock the tall poppy too much in this country and put people down,' he said. 'I want to pick those people up and say, "Come on mate, get up, we can do this." We are too critical on ourselves. Each one of us has gifts and I say to all the athletes and people, be the best you can be, don't let the music stop inside. It doesn't matter what you do, whether you're a boxer or builder, we are all equal as human beings. If everyone could be the best they could be, and therefore happy within themselves, jeez, we'd have a happy society.'

When Rob was young, he had a teacher who knew he was a little different. He saw the warrior. Before a rowing race, he'd say to Rob, 'You've done the kilometres, you've done all the hard work. For this 2000 metres, I won't be with you, but I'll be inside your head.' Rob

ROB ROWLAND-SMITH

looked at that guy who had done so much for him and out came the warrior. He thought, 'I'd fucking die for you.'

Rob is now that coach, that trainer. He can't run the race for you, or do the laps for you, but he'll be in your head. 'I want people to read this and go, "Hey, if the Sand Hill Warrior is that high on life, how do I get there?" If someone could read about what I do and how I do it and why I do it, then they can go, "Bang, I can do this too." It is in you all. You can fulfil that potential, you can hear the music, and you've got to have a personal goal that says, "I want to be the best I can be." When you get to the big sand hill in the sky, I want to meet you and I want to hear you say, "G'day Warrior, what time are we training today?"

'If somehow I can touch someone with what I do, then I've fulfilled my job as a human being. If you can walk away from here feeling better from knowing me and I walk away feeling better from knowing you, we'll both walk away a better person. That's what it's all about. If you can walk away from this, or at the end of a training week, and feel better than when you started, then that's all I want to know.'

The Sand Hill Warrior doesn't go to work and he will never retire. 'I don't believe in that word,' he said. 'I want to get fitter, faster and stronger than the year before. Age has no limits. I will keep pushing myself and discover more about myself and more about life. Pain will be my friend and weaknesses will continually leave my body. It's not a chore, it's a way of life.'

ROB ROWLAND-SMITH

CJ

've never felt like I was as good as these guys,' said CJ Hobgood, a small mushroom on his fork as he pointed around the room like a kid playing with his food. CJ, the new world surfing champion, had been crowned during a win-less year in which — due to September 11 — only four events were counted, and his victory had come on the back of perhaps the most worthy string of world champs in history: Slater, Occy and Sunny Garcia. Ironically they were all here now, eating breakfast after the world champion's dinner at Newcastle, watching me interview CJ, remembering how in previous years it would have been them in his seat.

I looked around the room again. Sunny was sitting with his wife and a plate of eggs. Soon he had a heat in the Newcastle City Pro, a four-star event in the WQS tour. Shaun Thomson was sitting with Rabbit Bartholomew, a pile of bacon and the morning paper on the table in front of him. Derek Ho sipped at his second cup of coffee and Damien Hardman took his toast slightly burnt.

'Not just these guys around me,' CJ continued, 'but even on tour. I've always felt like I have to get better. I'm really humbled by the company I'm in, especially right now.' It was a surprising admission from a guy so seemingly confident in his calculations. 'For me, this is just my first chapter. I want more and I think I'm capable of more.'

At 22, CJ may be exactly what surfing needs, a young world champion. And despite his protests, he carries the air of someone who fits the bill of a champ: hugely driven, intimidatingly competitive, intensely focused. You don't notice it in his facial expressions, but it's there, waiting.

It's not evident either in the way he talks. CJ's Floridian accent is slow and drawn out, a long way from the Californian accents that bombard our TV and film screens. Fluent, relaxed, entertaining and easy to understand: it's the way he surfs too. Nothing's forced. He finds pockets like a thief and surfs from one foot to 20 with effortless flow. It's a technique so precise that it borders on loose-limbed robotics, but it's jump-started with a hard drive of speed and creativity.

Like most Americans, his surfing seems influenced by three-time world champion Tom Curren. But he has added his own edge to Curren's smooth attack that he can call his own. 'I'm not the kind of person who just jumps all over the wave,' he said. 'I just don't have that kind of energy. I want to be smooth but sometimes that can work to my disadvantage.' He cut a bit of bacon and introduced it to the scrambled eggs. 'Last year, Shane Beschen was telling me I've got to learn to be not as smooth, because when I make a mistake and bog a slight rail or something, you really notice it. Especially in small waves.'

Before the interview I'd been down at the beach, watching CJ's first heat in the Mark Richards Newcastle City Pro. He was introducing himself as the new world surfing champion in a place that knew its surfing history like family. The surf was tiny, made even worse by an approaching southerly wind. CJ took off on a solid one-foot set and went deep into a bottom turn as if it were pumping, extending into a full rail cutback deep in the pocket. So much so that you'd expect him to fall off the back of the wave. But he completed the turn right in the sweet spot of both the wave and his board for maximum speed and control — the complete technician. If there was any aggro in his surfing it was clouded by a smooth style. He was flying across the wave with the spared energy of a glider. It was as though his board wasn't even touching the water. When he made the last section he launched into an air reverse, landing casually in a crouching position (that typifies his control), almost playing with it. When he finished his first heat, the people on the beach were impressed, or maybe just satisfied that he was worthy of his title.

I waited in the competitors' area for him to return. It took at least three quarters of the next heat for him to sign autographs and speak to various media people. I paced back and forth, waiting for my turn. The previous year he would have walked through unobstructed, despite being most improved surfer of the year and winning his first WCT event in France. But now he is a world champion and they are not treated lightly, especially in Australia. We agreed to meet in his hotel room 15 minutes later, so he could shower. Then we'd have breakfast.

'That was a good comeback in that heat, eh?' I said, as I entered the room which overlooked the surf from seven floors up. There were about 15 surfboards lying around the room with towels, wetsuits and contest draws scattered about the place. A hooter sounded in the background as yet another heat got underway in the event. I walked to the balcony to see whose heat it was as I waited for CJ's response.

'Yeah, I didn't get to see much of it, but he got through, huh?'

Fuck, right family, wrong brother. 'Hi Damien. How are you?' I laughed. Apart from a world title, CJ also has an identical twin, Damien, an incredible surfer in his own right who was ranked number 10 in the world last year. At times, their surfing seems as hard to separate as their facial features. I hadn't seen them that much lately and wasn't on the roll of familiarity you need with identical twins. Haircuts, scratches, facial hair, food scraps. You really do need to be around them day to day to know who's who. As far as identical twins go, these guys are like walking clones. I guess that would make them very forgiving. I hoped so anyway; it was too late now to apologise.

I remembered the busted nose someone had told me about: 'CJ's nose is a little crooked, that's the only way to split 'em.' I made a mental note — busted nose, CJ.

On the balcony, Damien was on the phone to his shaper back at home (Rusty Preisendorfer), ordering boards for an upcoming WQS event at Trestles in California. When you're snapping boards and travelling as much as these guys, you've got to plan ahead. They get boards thrown at them everywhere they go. Most aspiring shapers give up their time and money willingly to get world champion feedback. CJ and Damien are both just doing what it takes to be the best.

'I got you a 5'11" and two 6'0"s. Do you want a 6'1" as well?' Damien looked to his brother, who'd just walked out of the shower.

'If he'll make it, yeah, for sure.' CJ looked unbothered by the phone call as he towelled off. The youthful excitement and anticipation of getting a new board was no longer apparent. It was all work now and as for accuracy, he knew his brother and long-term shaper would take care of it.

The trust between CJ and Damien is amazing. They don't fight, which for Australians can be kind of annoying. They know each other inside out. Their surfing is almost a mirror image, too, and you'd expect them to benefit from each other's equipment, but in fact they rarely share it. 'We actually don't ride the same boards,' said Damien, as I picked up a few of their tools. 'They're a little different.' I compared two of their shortboards and the minute difference I perceived I put down to an intimate knowledge of their own equipment and a struggle for individuality. All that aside, they looked fast and light. The rails were smooth and the bottom curves were perfectly accurate. It was obvious the shapers spent a lot of time on them. One of them, the wet one, I noticed had a flex tail. There was no stringer and the thin tail allowed a little bit of bend.

We jumped in the elevator and pressed 'Ground Floor, Breakfast Room' as CJ elaborated. 'I've been riding them a bit lately. In small waves they give you that bit of extra whip. It's totally insane that board.' CJ was wearing a black Rusty brand shirt, Damien an Oakley long-sleeve shirt. I looked at his nose and made a mental note. Then I looked at Damien's for comparison. Slight bump in the bridge of CJ's, hair a little shorter, perhaps thinning. Different coloured shirts. OK, I was ready.

We sat in the room full of former world champions. Occy, Curren, Bartholomew, Townend, Hardman, Richards, Potter; they were all here, our heroes walking around like moving statues. To say CJ was out of place would be premature. All legends ripen with age. 'I believe I'm only in my first chapter,' CJ said of his story. 'I'm so stoked to be where I am right now, but I believe I'm capable of a lot more.'

If his hometown peers are anything to go by, he will. Kelly Slater, Lisa Andersen and Margo Oberg have all gone on to win more than three titles each. They have dominated the lines between the lines in record books. How the hell does Florida, where waves break like falling feathers, produce so many champions? The small wave expertise I could understand. I'd just witnessed it. But how do these people collect world titles like baseball cards?

CJ answered. 'I think it is 17 world titles now for Florida, right Damo?'

His twin nodded. 'Something like that.'

From what I'd heard, Florida's definition of a swell is when it's breaking. 'These guys are so gnarly,' says *Surfer* magazine's Matt George. 'They will travel eight hours in one day just for one session. You see this junk out here,' he pointed to a miserable-looking Newcastle Beach, 'this is a swell for them. They'd be surfing all day if this was at home.'

When I first sat down and started talking to the twins that day, they asked me where I was from and what the waves are like there and where is good at this time of year. It wasn't just a business trip for these boys, it was a surf trip. No wonder these guys travel so much, I thought. No wonder when he's away, which seems to be a lot of the time, he surfs 24 hours a day.

I think that's the difference between these new guys and the rest. Parko, Mick, CJ, Andy Irons, they all surf three or four times a day, practicing for hours on end. They have a pure love for surfing and their excitement shows on every wave. To add to that, CJ was brought up in a town where a six-hour drive is a walk in the park for a surf. To understand his motivation to find waves, first we need to understand where he is from.

CJ lives in Satellite Beach in Florida. 'It's where the NASA launch pad is, so there are so many mad scientists running around. Then there's a whole bunch of surfers. But where I live it doesn't even break for a few months a year, so you learn to start travelling for your waves,' he said

He looked at Damien and a hint of a laugh initiated his next sentence. 'Oh yeah, then when it starts breaking at home, sometimes it's because of hurricanes. Just when we think we are going to get waves, we have to evacuate. It's pretty crazy when you see people driving over the bridge, evacuating the town and there are surfers trying to go the opposite way to surf it.'

It's easy to forget CJ is the world champion when you are around him. He is, in essence, just a really keen surfer. That was what had him heading over that bridge on a daily basis looking for waves.

'I started travelling when I was really young. We didn't get waves every day, so it was just a natural thing for me to do. I grew up having to travel for my waves — even now, it's the way I live. I used to go to the Caribbean for three months every year when it was flat at home. Then when I started doing contests, I was travelling over to the west coast a lot more. I went to Tavarua [Fiji] when I was about 16, too, with my sponsor, and from there just started going to Hawaii every year and hanging out there.'

CJ quickly became respected as a charger, another bizarre Floridian trait. He concentrated on Pipe and focused on being on the best waves that came through. It wasn't like he had waves to go home to, so he made the most of it. 'I started going on lots of trips and started competing more. Before I knew it I was on the road a lot.'

Results were CJ's ticket out of there, the fire that lit the way. I was starting to paint a pretty miserable picture of his home state and he put forward his first and last hint of defence. 'It isn't that bad.' He searched for something better, like a wave, a secret they've withheld from us. He looked to his twin who was face down in scrambled eggs. 'Yeah, um ... maybe it's not so good.' They laughed. 'But surfing and travelling is what I do. The better I did, the more I got to travel — and that's what I love doing. Surfing good waves with the best surfers in the world.'

With the wind in his sails gathering momentum, CJ sailed the world, and he went wherever the winds took him. Even as far as Australia. CJ was one of those surfers who did the hard yards. He came out to Australia to contest the Pro Junior, every year. He had studied his elders who kickstarted their careers at this very event and mapped his path.

At that stage his surfing was a little slower, perhaps not as tight. But he was so smooth and his technique was so spot-on that when he became tighter and faster, he was on his way to becoming a world champion.

He pointed around the room. 'I take advantage of it — all these guys here. If I'm to be the best, I've got to be around them. Sometimes I miss home, but I think of the waves there — and the waves here. Like, I didn't need to be out here doing these WQS events, but I love the waves out here in Australia. As soon as Bells finished last week, I bolted across to Margaret River. I wouldn't be getting those waves at home, and I also wouldn't be getting the talent around me right now. Trying to continually improve is what drives me and I don't have a better opportunity than right now, with these people.'

When it comes to innovation, CJ has his finger firmly planted on the pulse. He has been doing moves such as rodeos, following in the footsteps of Kelly Slater, but also another move that has almost become his own, a backhand 360 air. 'I first started making them when I was going for rodeos,' he said, playing with his food like it was a wave. 'I was trying to a do a one-handed rodeo one day and it sort of turned into this 360-air thing. Sometimes it just turns out that way.'

It was these new moves that took CJ to a world title last year, but despite his talent, he has his critics. That year, CJ became the only man to claim a world title without winning a single event. It was the shortest year in pro surfing history. We will all remember 2001 as the year when our world changed. And America's world changed the most.

The reverberations of September 11 were felt throughout the world, and surfing was no exception. The European leg of the tour was about to take place, but the Americans were reluctant to travel at such a turbulent time. Only days after September 11, the ASP forced CJ and Co. to make a decision. 'No, we can't come yet,' said the Americans. After the three event sponsors got involved in the discussions, the European leg was cancelled. The surfing tree had been cut down mid-season: four events lost, with just the Rip Curl World Cup at Sunset Beach left unscathed. It was deeply controversial; no other sport had cancelled events, let alone whole legs.

I talked to CJ soon after the cancellation and he had this to say: 'Pat [O'Connell], Taylor [Knox] and all the Americans were speaking to each other at great length about whether we were ready to go. I told Pat that whatever they decided, I would go along with it. I didn't want to rock the boat. It was a heavy time for us and we had to make a decision overnight. Just when we were ready to go, President

Bush came out and said there was evidence of further terrorist attacks, and that it was not a safe time for Americans to be travelling, so we decided it wasn't in our best interests to go right then and there. But we didn't know the whole tour would be cancelled.'

What this did for CJ was fuel speculation over the worth of his 2001 world title. 'It's a blow-off,' said Knox before the climax. 'This year's world title shouldn't mean anything.' It was an opinion shared by many, unless someone like Occy won, of course.

CJ agreed. 'If I win the world title this year, I'll have to win it again to substantiate it,' he told me at the time. 'If someone like Occy or Sunny wins it, they've already won once, so it will be justifiable. If I win, I'll have to win again — and I'm ready to do that.'

Only one month after the cancellations, CJ packed his bags and went to compete in the Reef Biarritz event in France, ironically around the same time the cancelled WCT events would have been held. This offended some in the surfing world who had been in Europe ready to go when the Americans decided not to come.

'I did want to go to Europe,' responded CJ. 'I wanted to win events. But I didn't want to put my own personal mission in front of what was a really heavy time for everyone here in America. I told them I didn't want to rock the boat — and it was called off. Then I had an opportunity to go and compete in another event. I'm a professional surfer, that's what I do. But I'm also a surfer who needs to travel. It feels weird for me to be at home for too long. I had to go on another surf trip.'

That is the difference between CJ and the rest; he doesn't just go away for a job, he goes away to surf. CJ won the event in France and went to Hawaii full of confidence. But what could have been one of the most dramatic of finishes ever on the WCT turned out to be an anticlimax. In the end, CJ didn't have to fight for his world title, as one by one his opponents lucked out in the Sunset Beach death pit — and for the first time in a few years, we had a young world champion.

CJ represents a new age of professionalism and has injected some much-needed youth into the sport. It's a timely breath of fresh air into gasping lungs. So how has life changed for CJ now that he carries a world title on his shoulders? A bit of scrambled egg fired out on to his plate with my question and I hoped he didn't notice.

'It hasn't changed that much. It gives me more opportunity to help and motivate the kids — and I love that. I remember being a grommet myself and being so motivated by my heroes. That's the pure aspect of being a surfer and wanting to get better, and that's what I'm all about. If I can create something like that and help push the kids and keep them surfing, then that's been the biggest advantage to me.'

CJ has been doing the tour for three years. In his first year, he was named best rookie of the year. In his second year, he went straight to the top 10 and was named ASP's most improved. He won the world title in his third year. Still think he's not a worthy champ? He jumped out of his chair and raced out for his third surf at 11 a.m. The other world champs were still on their second cup of coffee.

The

CAMEL

I was deep in the jungle near Java's famous lefthander, Grajagan, where the Camel resides. The Camel is like a mythological figure here, an expat Aussie who spends the entire dry season of each year — six to eight months — in G-Land. I'd heard how he arrives for the last day of the rainy season and stays until the absolute onslaught of the next when the swells are no longer good and the wind's no longer trading offshore.

I sat on a bamboo chair, damp, in between surfs and looked for something to pass the time. I asked myself

the obvious as I stared into a portrait I'd found of him in a magazine. What kind of surfer gets the nickname the Camel? Sure, the Camel's nose was striking, if not abnormally protruding. His hooves had no doubt been toughened by constant walks over rocks and reef, and it was obvious he could withstand long periods before acquiring a thirst for Western-style hydration. That could work, but 'the Camel'? One thing seemed certain. The Camel did appear to be an animal, and he's doing something every surfer and adventurer dreams about but probably lacks the courage to do themselves.

I had to come to G-Land in search of something deeper myself. In doing so I had come alone. By breaking a personal boundary I figured I'd open up some new ones within my own surfing experience. I was thinking a lot about adventures when I arrived in G-Land. I was lying in bed on my first night when a filthy big mosquito started buzzing around my mozzie net. Every adventure presents a challenge, I guess. Whether you're a stinking little disease-harbouring mozzie, trying to penetrate the fine grade of a mosquito net for a rationing of blood, or a surfer breaking cultural and comfortable boundaries to sample abundant barrels, the adventure is what's remembered.

The Camel has inspired many through his adventures, like the way we stand in awe of someone climbing Everest but just never get around to doing it ourselves. His stints in G-Land inspire many surfers to drop tools and do the same thing, but they never seem to go the distance. It's moist, uncomfortable. Most surfers usually turn back after the second flat spell towards McDonald's, The Sari Club and the security of what they already know.

The Camel's been coming to G-Land for over five years, working in one of the camps as a guide with his knowledge of the people, the place, the surf and its language. The Camel is originally from Western Australia and perhaps this is where he gets the nickname from — sojourns up north where the desert meets the sea around Carnarvon and perfect waves are your only saviour. People have literally gone mad up there. I reckon the Camel must have spent a lot of time up north before he discovered G-Land. Being in solitary places like this really tests you: just the waves and you. It's an existence where you really learn a lot about yourself, like walking into a room of dusty mirrors.

I couldn't wait to catch up with the Camel. His existence here was guaranteed, like the rusty old ping pong table that's been there since the camp first opened. I'd read about him, but hadn't actually met him. Talk around the camp always seemed to contain his name, yet he remained an enigma to me, and I think to everyone else too, as the stories seemed to change a lot during attempts at conversation at dinner, where most people were strangers looking for common ground. I'd seen him once or twice since I'd been in G-Land, but always from a distance. He always seemed to surf at peculiar times and I don't think it was because of his work commitments. The Camel found a way to be in the perfect wave every day. He would paddle out, up and down the point, always away from the pack. His ritual was consistent if nothing else. He'd enter the line-up on a weird-looking board, nail a wave from start to finish, then retreat back to the jungle with the evasiveness of a mosquito and the mystery of a Javanese tiger.

I had two reasons for wanting to meet the Camel. One, I wanted to paddle out at the perfect time as well. And two, I wanted to claim I had actually met this mysterious character. I'd heard he'd put a ban on all interviews because of an unfavourable interview with him previously. So I passed as my normal self — a surfer — and began to

THE CAMEL

draw different lines in the surf. It was bizarre, though an interesting experiment. You've really got to find other things to do in the jungle, otherwise you'll go ... crazy? I'd paddle right up past Kongs (part of the break) up the point where I'd seen him surf a lot, busting away from the pack. It was sort of like a mating ritual that lasted a couple of days but presented no reward as I had not yet crossed his path. I would also wander aimlessly around the jungle camp, posing as the soulful individual with an acquired taste for adventure, but the Camel was like a ghost.

Every now and then I would see a lone figure right up the point take off while I was checking the surf. The Camel rides strange boards, but he seemed to know how they fitted in the wave — he did shape them himself and he'd without doubt ridden more waves here at G-Land than anyone before him. At the first sight of him I would run and grab my surfboard and paddle out, but he'd be gone every time. And there are so many places to hide in the jungle at Grajagan. I'd be left in the line-up by myself, just minutes after his exit, and I'd always seem to catch a good wave. My bizarre experiment was working — for my surfing, if nothing else.

I left the flock that week for an inter-camp mission, meeting different people from different places, running up a tab in every camp. Just wandering, never still. It was a cool social experiment that was definitely keeping me entertained in its peculiarity. I'd surf different parts of the point and ride my bigger boards at different times. It was very refreshing. But a thirst developed. Like any new thing that feels good, you want more.

'Did you guys see that?' A young, blond-headed kid ran into the camp looking as though he'd seen the first tiger since '92. 'Someone just got the longest barrel. It must have been eight seconds.'

The Camel! I ran for my board. It was quite big that day, probably about eight-foot plus, but not a clean swell. People were having trouble getting out the back. Like J-Bay in South Africa, there is no channel to paddle out which means you have to paddle straight through the waves. It requires a lot of skill, patience and strength. There were two other Hawaiian guys out there I had already met. They were towing in and it was starting to break on the bomby consistently. It was pretty big.

I struggled to get through the white water. It felt like I was swimming against a waterfall. As I edged closer I saw the Camel right up past Kongs on the outside where the brunt of the swell hits the point. It was a few feet bigger there and I felt like a caged dog watching other dogs play. Twenty minutes work and I was still paddling. I barked profanities, cursing just about everyone I knew until I finally made it out the back, exhausted, with determination leaking a death stare into my eyes. The Camel had just caught one past me and I hoped it wouldn't be his last, though I knew it would. I was now alone in the line-up. This left me with a choice — go down to Speedies where the other two were surfing or have a go right out the back on the outside where the Camel had been. I stuck to my guns and took a dramatic left turn up the point. Being stuck out the back by yourself on a big day is an incredible feeling, merging fear and excitement. Something every surfer can relate to, no matter what level you're at.

I had the spot lined up from the beach with a couple of palm trees and I sat and waited, the ocean chasing me from all angles. Half an hour had passed and I still hadn't caught a wave. I was riding my 7'2" and it felt like a toothpick. It was pretty big now, 10-foot sets were coming through and I was beginning to feel out of place. Even more so when I could see the two Hawaiians way off in the distance plucking off a couple in front of Speedies, riding them all the way through from the bomby behind jet-skis. Stay strong, I told myself, and stay put; it will come. Just knowing you may have only one chance is the spark to my adrenalin when it comes to riding big waves. You've got to take that chance because regret always hurts more than anything a wave can do. Too many times stuck in the rip at Haleiwa taught me that. Miss a wave there and you're gone for at least half an hour.

Then it happened. The ocean rose into a Himalayan contortion as water began to drain from the reef into parabolic gorges. I scratched for position though I didn't have to move an inch. I paddled into the wave with all my senses. Weightless, I waited for my rail and fins to grip so I could pull the reins and establish direction. I made it around the first section and saw the most perfect wave I had ever seen. What's more, I couldn't see the end of it! I could see Mount Krakatoa in my line of sight. People said it was ready to go off. I knew it wouldn't in the next minute. When I finished the wave, I just wanted to shout out to the world with joy. Instinctively, and slightly egotistically, I looked to the beach to see who was watching and was immediately cleaned up by a massive wave of instant karma. The wave washed me over the reef in one hideous swoop. In my disorientation, I could vaguely make out a figure in the jungle: the Camel. He was like a chameleon. He was watching me. I'd never seen him watch anyone before — he always seemed to watch the wave. I guess I must have been in his spot.

I walked out to the wooden table overlooking the break that evening and enjoyed a beer by myself as the sun enveloped a memorable day. All of a sudden the Camel came out of the jungle and sat next to me, watching the waves, appreciating the stillness, drinking a beer. For an hour we sat there, watching in silence. I realised nothing needed to be said. My reasons for wanting to meet him had been resolved. Then we both left. He walked back to the camp ready for another day in his little patch of heaven. I packed my stuff, ready to leave the next day. I still hadn't found mine yet.

THE CAMEL

Koby

ABBERTON

'Is Koby there, please?' I asked.

'Who is it?' came the muffled reply. It sounded like one of his brothers.

'Griggsy . . .'

'Who?' OK, it wasn't one of his brothers. I was starting to get confused.

'Matt Griggs, from *Tracks* . . . ah, I did the tour with him for a few years . . . ah . . . ah, you know, Griggsy.'

'Who? . . . who? . . . who?'

By the time I'd described myself better than even my mum could, I realised I'd been taken for a ride. 'How are ya Koby, ya bastard?'

REILLY

'Yeah, Griggsy!' Koby screamed. I could picture his face during the whole charade and we both broke up in fits of laughter.

At just under six feet tall and 82 kilograms, Koby Abberton is starting to look more like a heavyweight boxer than a surfer. His lunacy in big waves and courage to stick up for himself, in any situation, has created both enemies and a deep-seated respect in surfing circles. It's a two-sided coin that he is only too willing to toss. Koby doesn't fuck around, and the fact that he has eaten up life without the benefit of a silver spoon just adds fuel to his growing legion of admirers.

But Koby's muscled and tattooed exterior belies a cheeky and contagious nature. Wide-eyed and keen to prod anyone for a game, he jokes around more than his intimidating persona would suggest.

Koby grew up in Maroubra in a family with one of the most respected names in town: Abberton. He got away with lots, but copped a lot too. As a result, he learnt to push the envelopes of cheekiness and toughness. 'Maroubra made me what I am,' he said of the tough beachside suburb also known as 'The Bra'. 'If I didn't grow up here, I'd just be a soft little puppet like the rest of the sheep out there.'

Koby was never handed anything on a silver platter. He was never handed anything, full stop. He moved out of home with his 18-year-old brother Sunny when he was just 12, running away from a family life most of us take for granted. He moved to a little flat near the beach at Maroubra, where he lived on child support. It was the start of another life in his and Sunny's new family called the 'Bra Boys', a group of like-minded individuals who had all felt the pain of a broken home. They came together to produce a stronger unit than any family they'd known.

Koby has no vendettas, or energy-draining issues from his past. What he does have is a nine-year-old little brother named Dakoda who he wants to protect, and a new family he wants to spend his time with. 'It's just life, you know, it's reality. I didn't agree with a lot of things my mum and dad did. I had the courage, I guess, and right of mind to not put up with it. Personally, I don't give a fuck what you write but Dakoda doesn't need to know about that kind of reality yet.'

I asked Koby if he thinks his childhood experiences created the attitude he now has. 'Your mum's the closest thing you're going to have in your whole life and once that goes out the door you don't believe in much, and a lot of things go with it. Lucky for me I had my brothers and a lot of mates in similar circumstances. It could have been worse, you know, at least I had my brothers and stuff. It's just another little hiccup in life and you've just got to ollie over it.'

What Koby ollied into was an unconventional family life that stretched far beyond the boundaries of blood. It was a brotherhood unlike any other and the Abbertons were the nucleus of it. The Bra Boys take care of business; a family business that looks after its own better than a parent could know how in the hard streets of Maroubra.

'We teach the grommets to take care of themselves. Get them healthy and keep them off the streets. I have a gym in my backyard and we send out the message that all the local kids are always welcome. If they want to train with me, or need to talk about something, we are always here for them. It's pretty hard growing up around here, there are so many drugs and stuff. There aren't many of my friends who don't take drugs on the weekend or smoke pot at night. It's just reality, but we are trying to keep the kids off drugs and teach them how to fight.'

KOBY ABBERTON

In Maroubra gangs roam the streets and bordering suburbs, and sticking up for yourself is a matter of defending your territory. For the Bra Boys, it's almost instinct. 'Mate, those fuckin' idiots [the gangs] come and cause so much trouble. Everyone who says otherwise doesn't see what we do; they are not exposed to it. It's a different culture here. They've got weapons, mate. They come out here looking for trouble, bringing their own cultures too. Of course we are gunna stick up for ourselves.'

For Koby, being able to stick up for yourself is a prerequisite of life. Of his, anyway. 'I reckon if you can stand there in a situation and know that you can come off better than the other person, it's a big confidence-booster. As soon as you know you can knock someone out with one punch you just have this air about you. You walk around with your head up high and have the confidence to do what you like without having to worry if someone is going to do something back.'

The gym in Koby's backyard has seen a lot of sweat, blood … and tears. A sanctuary of both pain and hope, it's nestled just a couple of blocks back from unit-riddled Maroubra Beach. It's like walking into a gangsta rap film clip. Hip hop music bounces off a weathered duplex house and off the huge shoulders of the Bra Boys, who have obviously spent the better part of most days in Koby's gym in between surfs. Like Koby, the Bra Boys look and are potentially very dangerous, but deep down they are actually a fun-loving family of brothers who love to surf and live life to the full. They give so much time and energy to everyone they meet, but unlike Joe Average, they have the pride to stick up for themselves if someone's 'a fuckwit', and the ability to back it up. They are brought up different in this part of Sydney.

'The way my pride and self esteem is, I'd rather get bashed 10 times over than feel like a dog in my heart,' said Koby. 'Whether it's surfing, fighting or anything. I think it's best to say how you feel, rather than listen to what someone else feels. It's no good to just sit back and suffer your whole life, when you can just do everything you want without having to worry about what people think. I couldn't give a fuck what people think.'

Koby is not an angry man and prefers to have fun rather than look for fights. But if someone threatens him he deals with it quickly and efficiently: he is the first to throw a punch. Word on the streets of Maroubra is that he is one of the best boxers down there at training every week in the sparring sessions. 'I think if I was introduced to boxing a little earlier I might have pursued it. I still might. There's nothing like it; it tests everything.'

Koby's power and ability to fight is unquestionable, and he enjoys the thrill of boxing as much as anyone. Now that he is not competing full-time any more, despite coming close to qualifying for the WQS a couple of years in a row, he is hitting the bag a lot more.

'It [a boxing career] has been in my mind for ages. But it's still hard — I'll train really hard for a month or something. But then when I'm really fit and ready, I'll have to do another trip. It's a choice. I just want to surf right now, but I'll keep fitting it in, and maybe later on. It's definitely something I want to do.'

I hadn't been in the Bra for about a year and hanging there for the day made me realise just how much Koby is looked up to. There were mini-Abbertons running around everywhere. They were all wearing his MCD clothes and riding his Warner surfboards, greeting each other with the Bra Boys handshake and look in the eye that signified their respect. The handshake is tagged in ink on all Bra Boys and it symbolises their close bond and brotherhood.

KOBY ABBERTON

The influence Koby exerts also extends beyond surfing. 'I got this letter the other day from some kid in Brisbane,' he laughed. 'He said he wanted to be a Bra Boy. He wanted to get the tattoo and beat up homies. I don't know how he got my address — he must have looked it up or something — but I've had a few letters like that lately. It's weird.'

Koby and I went surfing that morning. A few of his mates were around and were keen for a surf with us. As per usual, they were riding his surfboards and wearing his wetsuits and boardshorts. 'That's pretty cool, hey Kobs,' I said, 'how you buff all your mates out.'

'To tell you the truth, they just take it, or usually my brother Jai hands them out. Mate,' his eyes were starting to light up again with that familiar grin before completing the rest of the sentence between gusts of laughter, 'I come home from overseas and I've got nothing left. My brother's gone through my wardrobe, clothes are gone and my boards have been snapped. Sometimes I'll be hanging in my room and I'll hear one of my boards being picked up. I'll look out the window and it's one of my mates running down for a surf. That's cool, though. I'm in a much more fortunate position than they are so I've got no problem with it. Clothes are fucking expensive too, you know. Brett [from Warner] is starting to wonder how I snap so many boards, though. I just got back from Hawaii where I snapped eight of them. All you have to do there is fall off and you break a board, but when my mates are home clocking them up too it gets a bit heavy.'

Breaking boards is part and parcel of Koby's big wave rep. My first image of him as a big-wave surfer came when we were barely teenagers. I was surfing Voodoo, a gnarly left-hand reef break in Cronulla, with a couple of mates and it was pretty solid. I was holding back quite a bit, watching some of my local heroes, trying to pump up, when this pack of Maroubra guys paddled out. Among them, a 13-year-old Koby was battling to win over his elder brothers' respect by taking off deeper and going harder than just about everyone out there. Not an easy feat and it was 10-foot and gnarly.

'Seeing my brothers charge and hearing stories just made me want to go harder and be a part of them,' said Koby. 'Everything they did, I wanted to do better. We still haven't had the chance yet where it's big enough, but I tell Jai we'll get our time to see who charges the hardest. We're gunna go to Tahiti together. I want to be able to go "Yes, I finally charge harder than him", but he's fucking crazy. He doesn't care about dying. I'd so much rather get smashed up and dragged over the reef and almost die than have all my mates sitting in the channel going, "You faggot, why didn't you take off?" That's the way I look at it.'

Winning the Gotcha Pro in Tahiti in 1997 showed the world what Koby can do in big waves. It was like his initiation. He continually took off on the sets that surfers such as Johnny Boy Gomes were letting go, making him a big hit in Australia and the States.

But Koby does more than dance in the face of death. He surfs incredibly fast for a big guy, mixing up carving cutbacks with the odd punt, hanging in and around the pocket waiting for sections, not forcing it. He also has a great, low centre of gravity. He doesn't particularly study his own surfing ('I've hardly ever seen myself surf, let alone follow someone else'), but he definitely takes his hat off to Taylor Knox. 'He's bullshit. Just surfs so hard and sticks to his guns. There have been times where he could have got through heats just by surfing soft, but he'd never do that. He goes hard.'

KOBY ABBERTON

And so does Koby. But when it comes to competing at the WQS the otherwise decisive Bra Boy is in two minds. A second place to Bruce Irons this season at Pipe enticed him into another attempt at the WQS. Though he had come frustratingly close to qualifying in previous years, in the end he gave it away, deciding chasing thick waves would be more fun.

With nine cover shots in one year, his sponsors were obviously happy for him to continue free surfing, but then he made the quarters in Margaret River while over there charging the Box. 'Fuck, I don't know what to do,' he said. 'I wouldn't mind doing the WCT, but I ain't doing the WQS heap of shit. There's not one good wave. All I want to do is surf — and those guys have the best waves now.'

I asked him this year if he was going to Newcastle for the WQS up there. 'Not if there's waves. I'd rather go surfing.' The morning he was supposed to get picked up for the two-hour drive there, he woke up and thought to himself, 'Fuck this, I couldn't be bothered driving to Newy. I'm flying [there instead].'

He makes these crazy decisions all the time. A year and a half ago he spent a couple of days in Las Vegas and walked out around US$8000 lighter. His craziness goes beyond the surf. As I was finishing this story, he went up to Bali for a couple of weeks to go surfing with some mates. He probably paid for them.

Chasing big, perfect waves is the only thing that will keep Koby out of Maroubra. It's the place where he truly belongs. It's tattooed on his back. He has also recently had 'Abberton' tattooed on his shin, just next to the devil's head on his knee, and 'My Brother's Keeper' across his chest. He probably got them just for the hell of it. He couldn't give a shit. He's either chasing barrels around the world, punching the shit out of a boxing bag or holding up focus pads to the next generation of Maroubra kids, offering them either friendship, fitness, or a family. 'I'm training really hard at the moment. I bulk up really easy which is good for Hawaii, but wasn't so good for the tour. My brother [Sunny] kept telling me to hang in there and he's done it, you know, he's made the WCT. I know I'm a good enough surfer, but I just can't surf those shit waves any more. Fuck 'em. They can have it. I'm doing what I want.'

KOBY ABBERTON

RASTA

I t was 6.30 p.m. just south of Lima, Peru. What was left of the afternoon sun waltzed through the resident haze and dissolved with the sandy colours of the world's driest desert coast. The Andes were a hundred kilometres behind us. The slopes continued to the surface of the water and disappeared into the Pacific. Somewhere in between was David Rastovich. He was at home — with himself.

'If I could be any man, I'd be a peli-man,' he said with poetic flair as I prepared my dictaphone. His words flowed freely and naturally, like his

FRANK

surfing — like him. His eyes were fixed on the ocean while he waited for the interview to start.

A group of pelicans glided playfully above the Pacific Ocean. 'We have incredible similarities,' he continued with a smirk. 'Big nose. We don't chew our food properly. We live off fish and vegetables and float through life as effortlessly as possible.'

Rastovich, 22, is one of the best young surfers in Australia. But he is like no other. He grew up with the likes of Joel Parkinson, Mick Fanning and Dean Morrison on the Gold Coast, joining them in a meteoric rise in fame and ability, but unlike his peers, he chose to follow a different path. A former world junior champion, he turned his back on an era where corporate colossuses have gone after anything with a young heartbeat and an aerial — and in the process, he's developed a spirit that is as profound as the ocean itself. For him, it all started on a green field out the back of his home at Burleigh.

'My new life started just after I won the World Grommet Title in Bali. I came home and was on my dad's property just out the back of Burleigh at Tallebudgera Valley. My dad had just adopted Buddhism and was into his new life as a naturopath and Chinese herbalist. He was the herb man,' Rasta laughed at the irony of it all, given that everyone thinks he must be on drugs (even though he's not), adding quickly with a chuckle, 'but it was the good herbs.

'I was on his farm hanging with these cows and my dad told me they wouldn't let anyone feed them or hang with them. I wanted to get past that, so I put myself amongst them. These big beautiful brown cows encircled me and allowed me to pat them and let me be one of them. I started seeing them as T-bones. These cows had just let me in their world and I was so grateful, I thought to myself I just couldn't eat them any more. I had become their friend.'

When you ask famous surfers about pivotal points in their life, it usually coincides with competition results. All Rasta's memorable moments surround his development as a person, or his spirit. 'My sisters were already vegetarians, so the idea was nothing new to me, but from that moment on I thought to myself, if I could not eat meat and still be healthy, then I'll become a vegetarian. My mum forced me to eat meat a lot when I was young, like most people, because you are supposed to eat carcasses, apparently. I was young and just accepted that. But when I felt better not eating it, it made me question everything about life. It made me realise what is perceived in your head and what is actually real.'

The sun had pretty much faded now. It left no blue, just a trickling orange watercolour. What light remained fell on a peculiar emblem-like tattoo on his forearm.

'It's the family tattoo,' he declared, rubbing it enthusiastically.

There's a story behind everything in Rasta's life. 'Every male Rastovich has one of these going back, a lot of generations.' How many, I asked, inspecting its obvious antiquity.

'So many I couldn't put a number on it.' It's about the size of a pocket watch and, like the Rastovichs, it originates from Vis, a small island off Croatia. 'I was meant to get the tattoo when I was 14, but my mum wouldn't let me. So I got it when I was 17. It means "Men of men".

'My dad actually went back there recently to try and retrace our ancestry. He told the locals his name. The name was a big deal apparently and in an attempt to prove his name and heritage, the locals asked my old man to find the family house, saying, "If you are a Rastovich, you'll know." He'd never been there before, but he walked straight to it and said, "This is it." They were blown away.'

RASTA

Rasta is very proud of the positive energy that flows through his family. His appreciation for his family history runs parallel with his acknowledgment and appreciation of the history of his biggest passion — surfing.

A board bag sat in the corner of the room, its contents spilling out. I had been itching to ask him about his quiver since he first carried that oddity through Lima airport, only two days earlier. He turned his attention to his surfboards and they came alive.

Six boards accompany him to most places he goes. One is a 5'5" stub vector, massively concaved, stringerless, epoxy creation for 'pockety barrels,' or Burleigh Heads. You get the feeling he could easily get bored with Burleigh and he fills the void with challenging equipment to experience new parts of the wave he hasn't found yet. Like Curren, his technique is so free-flowing and in tune with the wave that he is able to ride almost anything. Personally, I thought the boards looked shithouse. They were not performance boards that we had grown up with and accepted, but I loved why he rode them.

'You can ride it much further back in the barrel,' he said. 'Because it's smaller, it fits deeper and you can weave on it. The only rocker is in the tail and the inch or two of concave just grips.'

He then held a 6'1" shortboard to the light, feeling the rails like his fingers were saltwater. 'The 6'4" is a personal favourite, but this — Orr! This board is just beautiful.' He pulled out a 6'9" single fin. Despite its recent glass job, its contemporary rail line and characteristics, it mirrored a different era Rasta is trying to high-line into. 'I have a theory,' he said. 'In atoms there's 99.999999 per cent free space and 0.000001 per cent matter, right? I have a theory that in that 99.999999 per cent space is the bottled energy and stoke of every surfer who has ridden it before. You can feel it. I want to be a complete surfer and I want to experience everything about the ocean. To do that, I need to understand my past.'

Of course there is the seven-footer, for the bigger stuff. A 7'6" too, but taking up most of the room was ... could it be? A geriatric goose board only worthy of keeping middle-aged men afloat, and which has no regard for wave etiquette. It was a Malibu. A 9'6", and beautifully hideous.

'I want to have the perfect quiver. It's always been a dream of mine to have a different board perfectly suited for all moods and appreciations of the wave face. I love travelling with them all too. When it's tiny or really flat, I take my Mal out and have a ball while everyone else is struggling to catch the waves, or, worse still, not even surfing.

'I want to surf in different parts of the wave and feel the different parts of energy from the wave face. Riding different boards makes you take different lines. Especially single fins. They teach you to use your rail properly. When you get back on a shortboard after riding a single fin, it feels amazing. The way the surfing world is now, people are led to believe if you are not doing aerials, or you're not ripping 10 turns to the beach, then you're not surfing good. I want to show the world that you don't have to follow that to appreciate surfing. That you can just stand there and feel the wave and get just as big a thrill.'

Towards the end of his junior career, having claimed the Under–16 World Grommet Title, Rasta was starting to lose his early competitiveness. But he kept the ball rolling, even though it was shaped like a square. Confident in their champ, Rasta's major sponsor, Billabong, sent him around the world, perhaps prematurely, to contest the WQS when he was 17.

RASTA

'That was a really good experience for me. I was doing well but the waves were so bad that I was beginning to party a lot, chasing girls, discovering how much fun that was, and just starting to lose my will to compete. I was going crazy. The whole WQS thing works very masochistically. If you bomb out first day before the weekend, you just hit party mode, and if you are in a place that doesn't have waves, which in the WQS is generally the case, it becomes very repetitive and monotonous. But I had a lot of fun and it was a great way to be introduced to the world.'

There were times on tour where Rasta would run around nightclubs like a teenage boy on heat. I remember one time in particular in Durban when we were there for the Gunston 500. There were young girls everywhere and Rasta must have swapped spit with 90 per cent of them. He was going mad, dancing and chasing everything that moved. But that couldn't last forever.

He speaks of contests with little enthusiasm now, but there are definitely highlights. The most memorable win was up against good mate Joel Parkinson at his home break of Burleigh Heads in the Billabong Junior Series in 1999. 'Joel was in the lead with a minute to go. We had both just finished waves and got stuck in this massive paddle race up the point. We were side by side for about a hundred metres when Joel just went, 'Fuck, are you tired yet?' I was lactating seriously, but I said to him, 'Nah, not at all, are you?' The crowd was going crazy. Rabbit was on the mike calling it like Johnny Tapp. I could see in Joel's eyes that he was running out of energy, so I just gunned it. I got about 10 metres ahead of him and with 20 seconds to go this wave popped up and I got the score. It just came to me and felt so special.'

This typifies the relationship Rasta has with Burleigh Heads, a place where he has raised the bar already set high by some of the world's best.

He is the best surfer there, like Joel is the best at Snapper and Dean Morrison is the best at Kirra. 'I hadn't won a junior at that stage and it was my last year, and Joel being the competitive freak that he is was just winning everything at the time, so that was pretty cool. It was just nice to win at home. We actually travelled together a lot that year through Europe and it was hilarious. He won J-Bay and then I got a fifth at Mundaka. We were going crazy.'

'That was one of the funniest years of my life,' says Parko. 'We were pushing each other in every way. Out in the surf, partying. We were going pretty crazy just trying to outdo each other. Sometimes it's good that he lives at Burleigh because we are so full-on whenever we are together.'

Rasta talks of Burleigh Heads reflectively now, having only recently decided to move. 'I think moving is going to make me like Burleigh even more. I feel really boxed in there now. I have music jams at my house at least once a week where people come over and we just get together and play music and I've been getting complaints about the noise. I basically just don't want to have neighbours. I don't like the traffic lights, the noises, the crowds, the concrete, the stormwater runoff that is now at Burleigh. The way we travel as surfers, we go to such beautiful places within nature, and to have a home that's out of nature to me just seems stupid. So I'm going down the coast a little to get back in touch with nature and feel the dirt between my feet, see the trees, the animals, the stars, have clean water and smell clean air. But I'll be back when the waves are pumping.'

Rasta does an hour of yoga and an hour of meditation every day. It is after these moments that he gathers clarity. He actually completed a lap of both at his own request before I pushed the record button. It's how he clears his head and gets focused. We talked more

RASTA

about the cows. About how he hasn't touched alcohol or drugs in over a year and has never felt so clean. I asked him more about his evolution as a person and a surfer and how it led to where he is now. It all seems to have started for Rasta as an 18-year-old. While most people discover alcohol and drugs at that age Rasta was discovering vegetarianism and spirituality. He grew up early and matured even earlier. This ultimately brought him closer to the ocean and to his real self. We talked more about his growing up, before he met the cows.

'I was in surf lifesaving clubs when I was little and did really well at that. I was swimming and training against really competitive guys like Grant Hackett, so I was very competitive from when I was about seven till 18. But I think it really burnt me out. I got sick of wanting to beat people, a situation where someone has to be the winner and someone has to be the loser. That just didn't feel right to me any more.

'The things that I now consider important were against the grain of competition. It's no good for your soul. I was becoming bored and through that boredom I lost the desire to win. Contests just weren't important to me any more. My body couldn't handle it and my soul couldn't handle it. It just felt like the wrong place for my energies to be focused on.'

This is where Rasta's faith in life was first tested. 'I took a bit of a gamble last year with Billabong [his major sponsor] and just said, "I can't do this any more. This is not for me. I'm not competitive and can't pretend to be. I need time to do my yoga every day. I need time to do my meditation every day. Can I please do the free surfing thing?" Being myself was more important than something you're supposed to be. I guess I was marketable enough or had a strong enough personality for them to allow me to do it.'

RASTA

'Quite simply, not every surfer is a competitive animal in the 'first-past-post' sense,' says Billabong's Bruce Lee. 'Having said that I sincerely believe that Rasta has a lot of pride in being counted as one of the best surfers in the world, and he displays a level of confidence every time he hits the water which underlines this subdued egotistical trait.

'Having an ego, or more accurately in Rasta's case, a clear sense of understanding of his level of surfing ability, is a totally natural human characteristic, and rather than test himself against other surfers, Rasta prefers to test himself against the ocean. In this regard one can easily compare Rasta's ability to that of other surfers through assessing their feats at any particular surf break at which he has been previously observed and/or filmed. If Billabong discontinued our association with Rasta merely because he shuns competition it would not only have positioned us as a brand with a shallow outlook, it would also have cost us customers who identify with his pure love of wave riding.'

Rasta's organic marketability was now growing wild. Was it simply that he had something different? When you watch Rasta fade deep on an unpredictable bottom turn, hug the top of the wave face, then cut down hard and fast with Currenesque ease, sometimes you forget how bloody good a surfer he is. He is as good as Parko and Fanning. He is incredible. Sure his character is of interest, but his surfing is also like nobody else's. It is influenced by different surf craft and a different psyche altogether. It throws spray no one has seen before. It has this edge. It brings together several arts and combines them in a natural and effortless flow. Like the flow and grace of the single fin with the speed and creativity of today's innovation. But like that pelican he had talked about before, there is also a sense of humour to his surfing. When Rasta surfs, it is playful.

RASTA

The sun was shining on other parts of the earth now. The moon was half full and the stars were arriving one by one, but it was hard to tell through the haze of the desert. Rasta was naming them individually as they appeared. I hadn't asked a question in a while and Rasta was beginning to take charge of the interview. With him he had brought a message, an agenda, a plan. He switched the focus off himself — and I let him.

'I want to give the kids a choice in which direction they want to take their surfing. They don't have that choice at the moment.' This is Rasta's focus nowadays. He had been talking about it on the plane over, and it was an issue that gained momentum during our stay. 'The whole focus for companies right now is punky aerials and looking good. What happened to going to the bush with your mates, learning about the bush and the ocean? Just being an all-round waterman who can ride any board and appreciate the ocean in every way? At the moment, there's nobody showing them that there is a different way of bringing the ocean into your life.'

He searched for an example and found it in something everyone could relate to. 'Like Dorian, Slater and all that crew riding the bodyboards and body surfing in *September Sessions*. I thought that was unreal. Who gives a fuck what you're riding, as long as you're having a ball?' It was the first time he had sworn during the interview and it demonstrated his passion for the subject.

'If I can show that it's alright to experience the ocean in more ways, through videos, stories, interviews like this, that shows the kids two options — not just airs — that's something I'd really like to do. To me, nothing's bad, it's just a wave-like pattern, like everything in life. It gets to the bottom and comes back up. Right now it is at the bottom. The companies are only focused on the kids right now. Maybe soon the wave will creep back up and surfing's elders will be acknowledged and entertained for a change. A lot of surfers like to watch competition, but not many people do it. It would be nice to see every other form of surfing acknowledged so everyone has something to relate and aspire to.

'I think that's why I'm here ... to be a different role model for the next generation. Everyone looks at me and thinks I'm so different. I'm no different to thousands and thousands of people on this earth. But I am different to the surfers that are on this earth, so that's the reason I've attracted a bit of attention. It's not a different way of being a human, it's just a different way of being a surfer.

'But with all that, my goal is to be a respectful person, without an ego. That's important. I think that's why I couldn't compete. Competition doesn't do anything except satisfy the ego. It's good for nothing. But for a lot of people that's them — they're all ego. I'm not saying that's bad, it's just where they're at in their life.'

Rasta's influences come from yogis and gurus and he has applied their wisdom to his life as a surfer. On his bedside table was a book called *The Autobiography Of A Yogi*. There were several more in his backpack. Every day he would read something that would sink in and he enjoyed sharing it with me. He'd relate a passage to his own solitude. 'You can't learn anything when you are part of a cliquey crowd. Being a loner puts you outside the circle of influence. You become an observer and you can make judgments with more perspective because you are not trying to please other people or act like other people.' He would also write passages down, as well as other observations he'd make throughout the day. It helped them to sink in.

RASTA

I asked him whom he hangs out with. 'Nobody, just myself. That's all there is at the end of the day.'

During our trip he would often go missing; walking, surfing, meditating, mellowing at the end of the day. 'If you don't go within, you go without,' he said, reading a passage to me and referring to his meditation.

When we arrived at Machu Picchu (the lost city of the Incas) a week into our trip he almost had a sensory overload. It was considered the navel of the world by this ancient civilisation that developed to be the western hemisphere's biggest empire at the time of Columbus discovering the Americas. When I first offered him the trip with *Tracks* to Peru he almost burst. He knew all about the Incas, about Machu Picchu and the world's longest wave at Chicama. He admitted to getting goosebumps every time he thought about it. He also admitted being there before in his dreams.

'When you get déjà vu, it means your life is on track. Your dreams are as close to your real self as you can get, and when they cross paths it means you are on track. It's a comfortable feeling.'

His knowledge is quite incredible. He doesn't utilise his time just riding waves. He learns things, discovers things above and beyond his surfing sphere. He swallows charcoal tablets when he gets the squirts, he wears the 'om' symbol (a symbol of the universe) around his neck, and keeps different rocks and minerals beside him that offer everything from strength to guidance.

Like most of us, Rasta is finding his own path in life, with surfing his inspiration and major passion. He is as open and as free as they come. So much so that it's contagious. He attributes a lot of it to surfing.

RASTA

'Within us all is everything you need to know about yourself and life. We are taught or at least we learn in Western society a linear line of experience. Surfing is the perfect teacher because it is not always perfect. You live highs and lows. You can't always feel perfect every moment or every breath. Like a wave, you've got to accept the troughs, or the flat parts of the wave as much as the barrel, because they all have hidden treasures.

'Through surfing I have come to realise that all that operates in our existence has the qualities of a wave in the ocean. Every day of our lives flows up and down like the sea. For me, this was quite a realisation, as it allowed me to move up and down with the wave-like challenges of normal, everyday life. Previously, I had been thinking of life in linear terms, trying to exist in a straight line of security and consistency. By thinking that way, every time I was confronted with a wave — change — I would react either positively or negatively, because this wave was upsetting my straight and consistent way of living life. Now I know that the only consistent thing in life is change.'

I was tidying up a few words the next day when Rasta arose from his ritual dance with himself; one hour of yoga and one hour of meditation. It was his second lap of yoga for the day. He walked up to me and took a deep breath. A couple of pelicans and the smell of fresh fish attracted his attention. 'I can't wait for dinner, I can't wait for the surf tomorrow, I can't wait for Chicama, I can't wait to learn about the Incas. I can't wait for the next breath.'

RASTA

Kelly

SLATER

Robert Kelly Slater, the best surfer who has ever lived, declined this interview. Well, his manager did anyway. 'Sorry, but we are going to have to pass,' he said. 'Kelly is working on his own surfing book, and we are not at liberty to participate in anyone else's surfing book endeavour.'

It seems Kelly now comes at a price and it demonstrated how far removed from the rest of the surfing pack he has become. He is inaccessible, a superstar ... blah, blah, blah. His story is not new — and despite a three-year hiatus from competition, it is definitely not forgotten.

SARGE

In eight years on tour Kelly made the '90s his own, obtaining every surfing record available to him. In doing so, he changed the sport of surfing as we knew it, to one we are still trying to understand.

To compare Kelly to other surfers would do nothing but confirm how freakish he really is. To really research him, we must compare Kelly to other sporting champions. So how does the best surfer who has ever lived stack up against the best sportsmen of our time? Sometimes it takes one to know one.

Trevor Hendy, the greatest ironman ever, told me about 'the zone' one day, as we sat in his Gold Coast home overlooking the beach at Mermaid. 'I've been in races when I wasn't fit and had no right to win,' he admitted, eyeing some of the trophies that lined his living room like wallpaper. 'I just found something — this energy. You just know you're going to win. You know the wave will come. I can't hear or see anything, it's just all blocked out, and then when the race is over, you can barely remember what happened.'

Trevor, who was a six-time Australian Ironman champion and four-time world Ironman champion, related to me a story about Kelly, who also happens to be a close friend.

'Kelly once told me that, at times, he has felt so in time with the ocean, or so in the zone, that he could make a wave come to him,' Trevor said. 'He told me he has sat out the back of the break before, waiting for a wave, and with a minute remaining in a heat, willed a wave to him.'

Is this some kind of crazy witchcraft? Has Kelly lost his mind? Or has Kelly perhaps found his mind? The amount of times I've seen Kelly Slater win in the last minute seemed to bend this seemingly ridiculous statement back into reality. In a sport that relies so much on luck, Kelly has even bent the rules of Mother Nature to his will.

KELLY SLATER

In eight years on tour, he won six world titles, 33 events, became the youngest world champion ever, the second-highest money earner (Sunny Garcia is the highest), a rookie of the year, and secured the most victories in a season. He is a master of all crafts and all conditions, winning in small waves and in big waves, and he has influenced the industry like no one before.

In surfing nobody comes close to him. His supremacy however, can be compared to other sporting greats: Pele, Don Bradman, Tiger Woods, Michael Jordan and Carl Lewis. Looking at these guys, we are able to understand a little more about the zone and what it takes to be the best. Let's see how the champions stack up against a little ol' surfer from Cocoa Beach, Florida, who stole the imagination of a generation.

Exhibit A: Pele, born in 1940, the undisputed master of the world game, soccer, and the IOC athlete of the century, scored 1281 goals in 1363 games (an all-time record), meaning he scored 94 per cent of the time. In 19 years at his Brazilian club, Santos, he was 11 times the top goalscorer of the year. In 92 caps, he scored 92 goals for Brazil. He played in four FIFA World Cups, won three — and became the top Brazilian goalscorer of all time. Kelly, too, has been the highest point-scorer from day one. He doesn't just win heats, he annihilates them. He doesn't just win world titles either, with the exception of two years (against Rob Machado, in '95, and Mick Campbell, in '98), most world titles were won before his competitors were training for the last event.

Pele, who came from a poor family, had a dream of playing soccer. But growing up in the slums, he could not even afford a soccer ball. So he shoved pieces of newspaper in socks and played in the dirty streets before his talent paid its way. While Kelly also came from a reasonably poor family by American standards, it was the waves that put an uneven bounce in his dream. Coming from Florida, he didn't have as much opportunity to surf good waves, but he held onto that dream and kept surfing in those mushy little waves on any surfboard he could get until his dream slowly unfolded.

This drove his inner competitiveness harder towards success. 'It probably came from having an older brother and growing up like, "That's mine", "No, that's mine,"' Kelly told *Tracks* in 2001. 'I think a lot of my competitive intensity over the years came from more unconscious emotional places that I wasn't really aware of. I just became really intense about competition and I got super-psyched and I didn't really understand the reasons why.'

Exhibit B: Don Bradman, cricket's greatest ever batsman. At international level, 'The Don' had a career batting average of 99.94 (the next best is 61), far surpassing any cricketer that has ever lived. In 80 innings he hit 29 centuries and 13 half-centuries, with a highest Test score of 334 not out and an astonishing average in one series against England of 201.

Bradman, who was never coached, developed a self-administered style that he called a 'closed-face technique'. Apart from his technical high standard, Bradman was one of the fastest scorers of all time, scoring centuries like singles. 'Sometimes I did play reckless shots,' he admitted in an interview late in his life. 'And sometimes, I'd pay the price.' But 'The Don' rarely hit sixes, which displayed his control. He was so good in fact that he was inadvertently responsible for the controversial advent of 'Bodyline' — head-high bowling from frustrated English bowlers unable to hit his stumps, so they went for his head instead. He also used and experimented with different equipment, actually using a lighter bat, and had a complete understanding of its potential. So too Kelly, whose experimentation with narrower, ultra-rockered surfboards changed the face of shaping in the '90s.

'Kelly knows his sport inside out,' says his part-time trainer, Rob Rowland-Smith, 'from a deep understanding of his equipment to a complete commitment to training. The main thing I first noticed about Kelly was that he is deceptively strong. We've had some tough days in the dunes and he's not afraid of pain. He has a great attitude towards training. He knows what it takes to be the best athlete he can be and he works every component of fitness from flexibility, strength, power, speed and endurance to be the best. Kelly is the real deal, he approaches his sport on a much deeper level. Not only that, but he has this incredible ability to just switch on like I've never seen. He can deal with the media at an event or hang out with his mates and have a laugh, but when it's time to put on that singlet, it's all about business. That's what separates the world champions from the rest.'

Exhibit C: Tiger Woods, the current number one in golf, at only 26 years of age. Tiger has already scooped $30 246 327 (at the time of publication) from prizemoney alone — and thousands of dollars in endorsements are ticking over as we speak, like seconds on a clock. He was the youngest number one-ranked player ever at 21, youngest US Masters champion at 21, was the leading PGA Tour money-earner at 24, has the longest consecutive number one-ranking ever (two years), has 18 holes in one, is the longest hitter by far and has won over 44 tournaments (32 on the PGA Tour).

Tiger first learned to swing at two years old and went around nine holes with a score of 48 at the age of three. Like Tiger, who was on many TV shows as a kid, Kelly was also a child prodigy, one who survived the onslaught of media attention and fame to become the best he could personally be, not the best he was expected to be.

It's probably easier to compare Kelly and Tiger because they are a similar age and are still competing. Tiger was the number one-ranked player in the world at 21. Kelly was world champion at 20, the youngest ever. Tiger has won 40 or so tournaments, Kelly 33. Tiger has won the US Masters, the most prestigious golfing tournament, twice. Kelly has won the Pipeline Masters in Hawaii, the most prestigious surfing tournament, five times.

The biggest difference between the two does not relate to ability so much. The biggest difference is money. In the time it takes you to read this book, Tiger won more prizemoney than Kelly has in his whole career. In fact, Tiger won more money in the US Masters in 2002 (US$1 million) than Kelly's career earnings at the time of publication (US$827 055). In endorsements, Tiger is worth tens of millions a year. Kelly is speculated to earn a million a year from his main sponsor, Quiksilver.

Where they do coincide is their commitment to technique. In 2000, just when the best golfer in the world seemingly couldn't get any better, Tiger went and changed his swing. 'I looked at my technique and thought of ways to make it better,' he told *Time* magazine. In trying to hit the ball so far he was losing consistency, one of the most important things in golf. Tiger shortened his backswing and changed a few other technical aspects. It cost him a few titles that year, but he had more consistent top-five finishes than ever.

People like Tiger, like Slater, don't stop improving. They find ways to get better, even if it is, as in Tiger's case, just improving consistency. They don't look at what they can do perfectly, but at what they can't do perfectly and are not afraid to take risks to fix it. This is something Kelly did in his three-year break from competition from 1998 until 2002. He really worked on new turns and freeing up his technique.

Another thing these two guys have in common is their visualisation techniques. Before he hits a golf shot, Tiger sees the ball going straight down the fairway. When Kelly rocks up to an event, he sees himself holding the trophy before the first heat. He also sees himself doing those incredible turns in his head while on the beach stretching, so when he catches a wave, he already knows how to make the turn properly.

Exhibit D: Michael Jordan. In a 14-year career, Jordan averaged 32 points per game, an all-time record. He was five times NBA Most Valuable Player, won six NBA Championships with the Chicago Bulls, was selected for 13 All-Star teams, was twice Slam Dunk Champion, has scored 69 points in one game (the best ever), won Defensive Player of the Year and has the highest score in NBA history — 29 277 points. 'Air Jordan' had a simple philosophy: 'No matter how good you are, you can always get better.' Day after day he would adhere to this philosophy and spend extra time training to be the perfect player.

Relatively speaking, Kelly is as valuable to Quiksilver as Jordan has been to Nike. And he also changed surfing like Jordan changed basketball, bringing in new fans and inspiring countless people. The Chicago Bulls once estimated that Jordan was worth a decent percentage of their club's revenue (around 30 per cent) because of how many number 23 singlets he sold around the world alone.

'Kelly Slater has a tremendous impact on the Australian surf market,' says Quicksilver's Mark Rayner. 'He's the most influential surfer of our generation — including both his style in the water and what he wears on land. Just like Nike redefined sports marketing with Tiger Woods, Quiksilver Australia has never seen any one surfer influence the surf market like Kelly. He's the man that girls love and guys want to be like. It's impossible to measure exactly what his impact on sales for us is, but it's got to be a good chunk.'

Exhibit E: Carl Lewis, the king of athletics. In the 1988 Olympic Games Lewis clocked the fastest legal speed ever recorded by a human being at 43.3 km/h. In four Olympics he has won nine gold medals in 100 metres, 200 metres, relay and long jump — the most in Olympic history. Lewis met the former athletics great Jesse Owens (four gold medals in the 1936 Olympics) as an 11-year-old. His hero advised him to 'just have fun'.

Kelly had a similar relationship with Tom Curren (three-time world champion and his childhood hero), and the American public saw Kelly as Tom's heir, although Kelly never publicly accepted the mantle.

It is more than natural talent that makes these guys so good. It is their willingness to set goals and make sacrifices and train hard to achieve them. It is their confidence and determination not to stop training until they are holding a trophy. Like Jordan said, 'No matter how good you get, you can always get better.' No matter how good these guys get, it never seems to be enough.

'It's not the best surfer that wins the world title every year,' Slater said after one of his championship wins. 'It's the best competitor. This year, I was the best competitor.' With so many nurtured champions coming through these days thanks to growing professionalism and sports marketing, natural talent is more of a prerequisite than a right to win.

One thing Kelly has had that eclipses every one of these guys is the all-round game. Sure Jordan may have won one Defensive Player of the Year, but he was an offensive player. Pele was also primarily an attacking force, Carl Lewis competed in only three disciplines in athletics, while The Don barely bowled a ball in his career (his best bowling figures were 1–8).

Slater is a wizard of all conditions. He's won everywhere and is the best everywhere. No matter how big or how small the surf, he has been the best in the world for the last decade — and still is. Even now, as the sport breaks up into factions of big-wave surfers and aerial specialists, he still leads them all.

In his comeback in 2002, Slater had a bad start by his standards — a ninth and two 17ths at the time of publication. But results aside, he was, and still is, 10 per cent better than his opponents in ability. Want proof? In his first event at Kirra he held the highest wave scores and heat tallies from his best three rides. 'He may not have won the event,' said Luke Egan, 'but he set the standard for the rest of the year in the judges' minds.'

At Teahupoo, Kelly scored a perfect 10 on a borrowed board with no leg rope on, and a cake of wax in his mouth because he didn't have time to wax up or put on his leash after breaking his last board. In Fiji, Kelly also scored more perfect 10s than anyone, as well as the two highest heat scores from only three heats.

Do not doubt it any more. Do not be put off by a bad start or sold on the hype that Fanning and Parko and Andy Irons are better. They are not — not yet anyway.

'I was able to focus on my personal life and that sort of stuff and, I guess, figure myself out a little better,' he told Ross Garret in *Tracks* about his break. 'Being on tour isn't the best place to figure yourself out, but I feel now that I can separate the competition and the rest of my life.'

Kelly is well and truly back — and, like Jordan in basketball, he'll prove that he is still the best surfer in the history of professional

KELLY SLATER

surfing, even if it doesn't happen straight away. 'If it's just obviously clear to me that I can't win a world, then I wouldn't be there,' he said.

It's this scribe's prediction that it won't be too long before Kelly finds the zone and starts talking to the waves again. When that happens and he gets his rhythm back in heats, records will continue to flow, and everyone will remember who he is — the best surfer in the world.

KELLY SLATER

Pete Nolan with his brother during the chemo, 1994.

At home in Cronulla, 2002.

After the operation. Back in the water at Puerto Escondido, Mexico, 1997.

Of all the surfers who have gone to Shipsterns after David Guiney discovered it, **Kieren Perrow** has been the only one who has wanted to go back. He has had a ticket on standby ever since his 2001 trip.

Trent Munro knows how to surf Teahupoo now.

Luke Egan, Teahupoo, 2002. Always calm, always big.

Mick Fanning winding into a turn that wouldn't be possible without the speed that has made him famous.

The gnarly thing about **Taj Burrow** is not that he goes for turns like these on every wave, but that he actually *makes* them.

Wade Glasscock training for the 2002 WQS tour.

Magician **Joel Parkinson** about to land a six-foot aerial as if it were a floater.

The Camel keeping out of the sun at G-Land.

Ever-explosive Kiwi **Maz Quinn** surfing from dawn 'til dusk.

Peter Troy waiting to board the ship that would take him around Indonesia.

Troy, Bells, circa '66.

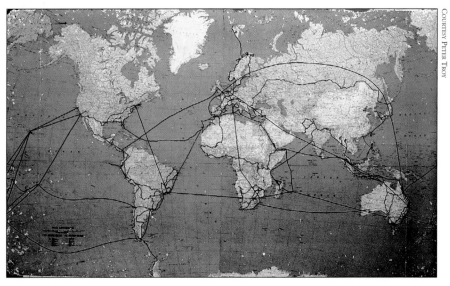

This map documenting Troy's hitch-hiking adventures hangs on a wall at his home, so that 'when I'm old, I won't forget where I've been'.

Pete
NOLAN

I first noticed a limp in Pete Nolan's stride when we were returning from the surf at Cronulla one day. We had only just met. 'What's up with ya knee, Pete?' I asked, admiring the high-tech brace that almost enveloped his whole leg.

'I've had surgery on my knee,' he answered.

'Oh yeah, did you tear your medial ligaments or something?' I said casually, frustrated by his slow walking pace.

'Um, no. I had cancer.'

I wondered how many times Pete had been asked what was wrong with

FRANK

his knee and I felt stupid having asked the question myself. I still do. Over the next year I became quite close to Pete, a true surfer who lives for the ocean. It's his one true passion. But like his leg, it was almost chopped from underneath him by cancer.

Had it not been for his passion for surfing, and life, Pete would not have been sitting in my house, telling me of his battle with cancer. A battle involving chemotherapy, a massive operation and, when it seemed it couldn't get any worse, the death of his father. But Pete's story is also of hope and inspiration, of one family's bonding, and one man's passion for surfing — a passion that kept him alive.

'It was 1994, I was 20, still at university studying for a business degree. I had just returned from Tasmania on a surfing trip and I knew something was wrong. I had this lump that was incredibly painful and I flew home straight away to see what it was. I just couldn't bear it,' he told me.

At the time, Pete related the pain — as did the doctors — to a sports injury, but after months of frustrating misdiagnoses, his greatest fears were realised.

'The GP brought me and my dad into the room to give me the results and ...' he sighed uncomfortably, 'I'll never forget it. Dad and I were sitting in front of him and he says, "Peter, you've got a tumour in your knee. Looks like it's an osteogenic sarcoma, which is a malignant tumour — a very nasty form of cancer. You'll probably lose your leg, but you should live."

'Just straight out, just like that! It was wrong. He should never have said it like that. What happened after that was a bit blurred, but I think I sort of said, "What? What do you mean?" He said, "We can't confirm it, but looking at the scans it looks like you have a very rare form of cancer. Apart from losing your leg, you should live."'

PETE NOLAN

Pete went home and the gravity of the situation sank in slowly. 'I was just looking at my leg, going, "I'm going to lose my leg." I was vomiting every day, just freaking. The doctor was coming over to give me shots of valium to calm me down. It was terrible.

'Then I went to the Wesley Hospital in Brisbane to see Dr Dickinson, my orthopaedic surgeon. We had to stop the car a couple of times on the way up because I was vomiting. The pain was absolutely unbearable, like a hundred needles just going bang, bang, bang! It keeps hitting you in the same spot.

Dicko said, "OK, I want you to know the first thing we are about is preservation, and that you shouldn't lose your leg." As soon as he said that, the relief was overpowering. It was like, well, that was all I wanted to hear. Surfing was the big thing in my life, and if I'd lost that, I don't know what I would've done. As a young kid, man, if someone tells you you're going to lose your leg, it's not something you can come to terms with. I felt like looking at my leg, touching it, and I felt like never cursing it again.

'It's full-on at that stage. I was doing all this counselling, being told what chemotherapy was, being told what cancer is. Cancer is such a terrifying word, to anyone. You just immediately think of death. For someone like me who had never been in a hospital before, it was just...' Pete's bottom lip began to quiver a little and I noticed he was fighting back tears, 'it was hell.'

Pete was really in amongst it now, with both cancer and chemo in his body. He was on a drug called cisplatin, which is highly toxic. 'I remember sitting there and being told what it is — a poison put into your body to kill the tumour cells. But the reason you get all these side effects is the drug affects every cell in your body. More rapidly producing cells such as hair follicles and saliva suffer the most.'

PETE NOLAN

His hands took to the air, simulating the war that was going on inside him, his face red with pain. 'I was told I was going to lose my hair in a couple of months. I was told I was going to have a total knee replacement, a big surgery to remove the cancer and all this type of thing.'

The knee replacement involved removing the knee joint, taking out the top half of the tibia (the shin bone), the top third of the fibula, and shaving the base of the femur. Then putting in a titanium hinge joint prosthesis. 'I had to do chemotherapy for about three months before the operation, to try and reduce the intensity of the tumour. In that time the prosthesis was being custom-made for my leg.

'The day of my first hit, Mum came up with some lunch for me from the hospital café. It was turkey. I don't know why but it was really nice. Then I had the chemotherapy and I remember a couple of hours later I didn't feel well at all. Then it started. I vomited. The worst you can ever vomit.

'This is disgusting,' he continued, putting his beer down and looking me in the eyes. 'It's very graphic and very real, but I'll never forget it. Think of British racing green. That was the colour of what was coming out of my body and it was just … evil. I vomited for 10 days. I didn't eat for 10 days and I went from 82 kilos to 62 kilos within two weeks. I was suffering.

'That was my first treatment of chemotherapy and I was scared and didn't know what to expect next. My tumour was classified as a high-grade tumour when they found it, which means it's had more time to grow.' It saddened me to think that there'd been cancer growing in Pete before he had stopped growing himself. The impact of the chemo was shrinking his body and he was fading away physically and mentally. 'I really wasn't tolerating it.'

He sipped a beer for a change of mood and brought to my attention a drum and bass track he liked. Another passion of Pete's is music. It's his release, especially when surfing and sports became a memory. We took a 20-minute intermission and talked about surfing.

'Then I turned 21.' He showed me the photos. It's one thing to hear about cancer and chemo, but it's another thing seeing it, especially at someone's 21st birthday party. He sat amongst his healthy friends who all had their arms around his frail body. He had no hair and he looked like he should look in 50 years. He smiled in the photo, but he didn't want to. 'It's hard to think you're not dying when you look like that,' he said.

'All these well-wishers were coming out of the woodwork and giving you advice and all these different ideas on natural remedies and books to read and all that kind of thing.' Pete told me how he'd received a framed Wallaby jumper signed by every player, as well as a signed poster of Luke Egan, his favourite surfer, that read, 'Dear Pete, get well soon'. It now sits framed on his wall.

'I was just psyching myself for the operation. I also kept asking my surgeon, "When can I surf? When can I surf?" I had to hang on to the idea that I could be surfing soon. In the end he said to me, "Look, you just need to relax because you're not going to be surfing for a while."'

As the operation neared, the scans were looking good and the cancer was responding to the chemotherapy. Another important step, as far as Pete was concerned, was to be shown the prosthesis by his surgeon. 'I was excited about seeing it, because I had heard so much about it and I was putting so much emphasis on the operation as a starting point in the whole thing.

'That was wacky, because it was this big contraption.' He fumbled for a photo of the prosthesis, handing it to me. It was the size of a

PETE NOLAN

baseball bat and looked like a piece of Robocop. I just couldn't imagine it in his body. 'You're talking about something that is a metre long. It's titanium, just this big piece of metal.'

'Dicko said to me before the operation, "My first priority is to save your life, and my second priority is to save your limb — and I'll do whatever it takes to save your life." So here I was being told that there was no guarantee that I was going to keep my leg. He said, "I'm confident it will go ahead well. I just need you to be aware of what the consequences are if things aren't looking good." I remember asking him if he'd ever gone in there really confident and it hadn't worked out. He said, "Yes it has".'

Pete went and changed a CD. He needed a break. We went out to the balcony and enjoyed the view over Cronulla Beach under a moonlit sky. The ocean was a midnight blue. He looked over it and told me how his dad used to stop by the beach at Nobby's, where he watched the waves. 'I couldn't surf, but just sitting there in the car watching it before I went up to Brisbane for the chemotherapy gave me a little fix. It wasn't even spoken of. Dad just knew to do it, because he realised how much I missed being around the beach. That was really good for me. It was calming and kept my focus and inspiration to get back in the water.' We closed the balcony door and sat back on the couch. We'd reached the point in Pete's story that he called 'Judgment Day'.

'I was just terrified,' he said, recalling the day of his operation. 'It was all out in front of me. After months of psyching up for something, I was outside the operating theatre waiting for an operation to save my leg and my life. I was thinking, what's going to happen if I wake up and I don't have a leg?'

Pete's mum and dad, his brothers John and Dave, and his then girlfriend, were all there. 'The doors of the theatre are like Customs at the airport where you're trying to say goodbye to someone, and I was in a pretty bad way. My security blanket at that stage was my family and I was just being wheeled through those doors, leaving everyone behind. Then I was in the operating theatre. Everyone is in gowns and it's go, go, go. Dicko came in and gave me a bit of a pat and said everything would be OK, that it would all be over soon enough. I was remembering my last surf in Tasmania and my last surf at my home beach at Nobby's and I couldn't stop crying because I thought they could have been my last.'

The operation took a marathon seven and a half hours. 'I remember waking up and I was really groggy. I pulled blankets off and I thought, "Oh!"' He sat up to attention. '"Do I have my leg?" I went to feel my leg, but I couldn't feel a thing.' He was feeling it now. Again.

'I heard some noise. Then a nurse came over and I just screamed, "Have I got my leg?" That's all I kept saying: "Have I got my leg?" She said, "Yes, it's all OK," and patted it. I said, "But I can't feel a thing." She said, "Don't worry, that's just the anaesthetic." I was still hysterical. I got wheeled out the door and Mum and Dad were the first people I saw. They both just had massive smiles on their faces. I knew straight away that everything must have been OK and this overwhelming sense of relief floated through my body; it was just amazing. I remember being giddy with excitement. I could see my leg and, though it had bandages all over it, it was there and I was so happy at that point. To me, that was a defining moment.'

It was to be one of many defining moments, good and bad. With chemotherapy, it is often said that the cure is worse than the disease.

'I had a couple of weeks with some basic physio,' Pete continued, 'just getting my leg bending, and then I went into this six-week course of a drug called methotrexate which is a very nasty toxic agent. The euphoria of having my leg back soon wore off when I started the chemotherapy because I was super sick the whole time.

'The chemotherapy was explained to me as taking me as close as they can to death, and then they let you get better enough for them to do it all over again. And that's how you live your life, for months on end, flirting with death. I lost every hair on my body, all over. I was so depressed, my self-esteem was gone. I suffered vomiting, my weight never went back on, I had a couple of epileptic fits and partial renal [kidney] failure. I couldn't swallow. Everything was bad. There were no positives — none that I could find, anyway. I wasn't coping at all.'

I could see the pain on his face. He hadn't touched his beer in a while. 'That was when I started getting into some dark times. Everyone was really worried about me because I was so depressed. Then I saw a psychologist and he had a great impact on me. He taught me coping skills including a technique that was called "my secret place". It was one of the biggest things about me getting better.

'I still use it to this day. No matter how sick you are and how down you are, you can go to this secret place and no one can touch you. For me, my secret place was being down on the beach at Miami Headland with my girlfriend and my dog, just surfing. I guess that's what I used to cling on to more than anything else — the thought of getting back in the water.'

The surf is there every day for most of us. For Pete, it was more than just there; it was his whole source of inspiration. He would sit there with his dad, weak from chemotherapy, hairless and barely strong enough to sit up straight, watching the surf. It's what helped him fight. But the fight was getting harder.

PETE NOLAN

'I worked my arse off for about six to eight weeks, I was so determined to get in the water. The goal was to get my knee extending to 30 degrees to horizontal. It was considered that if you get to 30 degrees, you could carry out day-to-day things, like walking. I finally achieved that. But I just kept working to get it to 15 degrees, because my doc told me if I got it to there, I could surf. Every day I would drag myself around on crutches, so weak. But I had to do it, I had to surf. The pain didn't matter. He didn't tell me, but nobody had achieved zero degrees in that operation before — and I made it. I'd made all these big gains and was starting to think about surfing.

'Then I got really nailed with the chemotherapy. I had these massive ulcerations in my mouth and was so sick. Everything that I had worked for, every gain that I had made in over eight weeks, I lost in one week of chemotherapy. I was just starting to think, "What's the point?"

'I was getting really depressed. I used to look at myself a lot [in the mirror], which for me, then, was not a good thing. I wouldn't recognise the person staring back at me because it was someone I'd never seen before, basically. I was skinny, white and pale-looking, without a hair on my body. I was thinking, "How am I ever going to get back to how I was?" This is after a solid six or eight months of the chemotherapy. All I was doing was going back for chemo, getting better and going back for more chemo, getting better and then getting hit again. It was relentless! Just when you start getting on top of things, you get smashed again. That was the point when, I won't say I'd given up, but I definitely didn't want to fight any more. I just didn't care. I was over trying to get better just to go back for more chemo. I thought, "If I go to sleep tonight and don't wake up, well, so be it, because I'm over it, I really am over it".

PETE NOLAN

'I was crying heaps. I remember sitting on my bed watching tears running down my cheeks thinking, "This is about as bad as life can ever be".'

In despair, he wrote a poem, pouring his emotions onto paper. Pete fumbled through his bag and passed it to me, then went to the balcony for some fresh air. 'That was the worst time of my life,' he admitted. The CD had stopped and I read it in silence.

You talk of self-preservtion. I'm at a point where I know nothing else. The poem was about 20 lines long and it was heart-wrenching. It finished with just a hint of optimism: *The light at the end of the tunnel seems far away. As time goes by, it gets no closer/Will it ever change? Will we ever bathe in life's full glory?/In a sea of light with no more tunnel to pass through. Perhaps it will all make sense!/It will all seem worthwhile. And self-preservation will be no more.*

He entered the room again five minutes later, saw the emotion on my face, and stuffed the piece of paper back in his bag without looking at it. 'At that stage I said to my family, "That's it, I'm over it. I couldn't care less any more." Then Dad came up and tried to talk to me but couldn't get through. He knew I was looking at my body in the mirror a lot, and he just came into my room one day and smashed my wardrobe to pieces. It tore him up that I was so sick and he couldn't help. I learned later that Dad went downstairs and cried too. He was saying to mum that he would take the needle for me if he could. All the pain, all the chemo, the leg, he would have copped it all.

'Then Dave, my brother, managed to get through to me. He said, "You're not going to die, you're never going to die. You've got so much life ahead of you, we have to get past this. We have to go surfing again." He just refused to accept the scenario that I was going to die. I had to keep fighting, you know. He was the only one who didn't have doubts and he connected with me better, I guess. He should have had doubts, though. Statistically, there was no certainty I would survive. But somehow he just got through to me. Sure it was bad and everyone wished it had never happened but there was just too much life to be had after it for me not to fight on. Whatever happened on that day, whatever he said to me had a massive impact and somehow I managed to pick myself up and keep going again.'

Pete, with his incredible determination, turned it around. 'It wasn't too much longer after that, that things started to get a little bit better with the chemo. I think I developed a bit of a tolerance. There was more of a space between each treatment; instead of a two-week break it might have been three weeks. I kept dragging myself to the physio almost every day, trying to get my knee-bend back to zero degrees. By the third week I was feeling pretty good and I was starting to play golf again with Dad — I tried to play one day a week which was pretty good. I was still on the chemo and I was still sick, but mentally I was getting a lot better. I could start to see that, yes, I was actually going to get back in the water and start surfing. That was my goal and a massive motivation for me.'

The beers were going down easier now. Pete, after a tortuous training program and still 20 kilograms under his normal weight, had finally got his knee extension back to zero degrees.

Now, he could surf.

'My first surf was massive. I went down one day to Miami [Headland] with Dave and it was tiny, one to two foot, howling NE, wind slop. I remember I was so excited, because I hadn't been in the water for 14 months. I was terrified, too, not knowing how my knee would hold out, whether I could stand up. My first duck-dive was

PETE NOLAN

amazing; anyone who's been out of the water for that long knows how good the first duck-dive feels. I remember the feeling of the water being all over me again and the board underneath me was just awesome. I got my first wave and went to get up but just stacked it straight away. I was laughing my head off. I think I probably got two or three more waves and then I stood up. I just went along this wave and I was just loving it. I was so stoked, just completely living for the moment. I was thinking about nothing else except how awesome I felt on the wave and in the water. All of those things that are quite indescribable. I realised how much you depend on surfing sometimes. It was the first time I'd been like that in a long time.'

Getting back in the water had been a huge milestone for Pete, and it seemed he was progressing well at last. Apart from the seizures, that is. 'The seizures were a side effect of the chemotherapy. I remember the first one — I was sitting at the dinner table when I just felt a few cramps. Then all of a sudden my eyes were rolling back in my head, I fell off my chair and just went into these gnarly convulsions. My mum and dad were freaking out apparently. They thought I was dying.

'I don't remember a thing from it, except that whenever I got a bit of a shake after that, I was petrified too. For the rest of my treatment I had to have someone with me all the time, no matter where I was. I wasn't allowed to go in the water in case I had a seizure, because it would increase the risk of drowning, so I was out of the water again.'

Things were on the improve though, with Pete enduring just one more seizure, and his chemotherapy finally coming to an end. But fate was about to deal him and his family another disastrous card. Two weeks after Pete's chemo was completed, his dad was involved in a car accident, suffering massive head injuries. He died about three months later.

PETE NOLAN

'The whole family had been so elated that I'd finished the chemotherapy and that hopefully I was going to get better,' Pete explained, 'and then everything fell apart. As a family they were pretty hard yards. They still are in many ways. Dad and I were really close and he was such a big part of my life, especially through all that. I remember he bought me my first single fin to learn how to surf. The thing is, too, he was a massive security blanket for me and then to have that taken away from me was horrendous. It took me a long, long time to deal with that.'

I noticed a tattoo on his arm, running across the inside of his bicep. It read in Latin: 'For you are with me.' It was from Psalm 23 in the Bible: 'Though I walk through the valley of the shadow of death, I will feel no evil, for you are with me, your rod, your staff, they comfort me.' I imagined Pete walking through that valley, his body riddled with chemo and cancer. I asked him about it.

'I'm not overly religious,' he said. 'But I have walked through that valley. Getting that tattoo was something I did with Dave because he was with me during it all — and so was Dad. So that's why it says "For you are with me", because I know my dad is with me still.'

Pete put on another CD and the conversation shifted. 'I didn't know what I was going to do with my life now. I went back to uni and finished that. I was well and truly back into my surfing at that stage, surfing heaps. That was my escape, my outlet. I was working and surfing, nothing else. I remember after Dad died I shut out a lot of my mates. It was just a really strange time. Then an opportunity came up for me to go travelling and I thought I've got nothing here and so much has gone on, so I booked a flight eight months down the track and just worked towards that — a big surf trip. That was awesome, a very big step.'

PETE NOLAN

I looked over my veranda as a plane flew across the ocean, and Pete continued: 'A lot of things came out of my travel experiences. As you do, you tend to get close to the people you're hanging out with when you travel. When I would tell my story people were just blown away. The response that I was getting from people really gave me a realisation of what I had achieved. I guess I hadn't thought about it much before, with having gone from being really sick and then Dad dying. Meeting all those people put things into perspective and helped me with the whole healing. I was getting more in touch with myself again and just building my self-esteem.'

Surfing had done wonders for Pete's spirit, but its impact on his knee joint was more problematic. Three and a half years after the operation, his prosthesis snapped and Pete found himself back in Australia. 'I was walking through a tube station in London and I just felt this buckle sensation. I stumbled but didn't fall and I felt a chill go through my whole body. I'm feeling it now, thinking of it. I bent down to feel my knee and the hinge joint just pushed back through my leg. I just felt it click and then dislodge.'

The titanium bone in his leg is supposed to last up to 11 years, but Pete is a surfer — and a damn good one at that. Hitting lips and floating over big sections is no good for even the best of knees. It was very bad for Pete.

'Basically, the joint will last for a certain length of time. It is hard to say how long because every patient is different with their level of activity. Generally speaking, an older patient could expect to have the joint for up to 10 years or more. For a young active guy who wants to surf as much as he can, that is definitely not the case.'

Pete has now had the operation *three* times, most recently in August 2001.

'Because I've been surfing for the past four years, it snapped again. When it did snap, I knew straight away that it was broken. The sensation was the same as when I first broke it in London.'

This is the most inspiring part of Pete's story. He keeps surfing. He knows it will snap. That's a fact. Every wave, every session brings him closer to the reality of surgery, a new titanium rod and a year's physio trying to get his new leg bending at zero degrees again. 'I remember when it happened. I was thinking, shit, here we go again — another operation.'

We are talking about cutting his knee-less leg open again, taking the broken titanium out and replacing it with another. The physio and recovery process is intense. Three to four sessions a week with the physio and a mountain of work at home before he can even walk, let alone surf. 'I was not as scared as when it happened in London a few years earlier, but I was scared nonetheless because I knew once again what was ahead of me — surgery, recovery, pain, physio, will I surf again, have I done any further damage? All in all I was not feeling good about things at all. Anyway, it's all behind me now. And I have another new knee joint.

'I've had conversations with my surgeon about whether I should or shouldn't be surfing. His opinion was that it was for me to make an educated decision because, if I kept surfing, yes, the knee will break and that's without question. It will fail. I will have to go through that same process. It will snap one day doing something trivial like walking across the street, I will need more extensive surgery and I will be out of the water for another eight months, without a guarantee that I will ever surf again. Whether it breaks in four or five or six years it's hard to know. It's been three years and then four and a half years. But if I didn't surf at all and it lasted eight or nine, personally I'd think of how much surfing I'd miss out on. So it

PETE NOLAN

would be no surfing for eight years just to get an extra few years out of the prosthesis. That's the effect surfing has on my knee, but it keeps my whole life worthwhile. The whole time, surfing was what I worked for. I wouldn't be here if it wasn't for surfing. I'd never change it.'

To see Pete surfing now is a joy. He's the man everyone calls into waves — and he's the man calling everyone else into waves. He enjoys it more than anything. Right now, he's ripping. He's had heaps of physio and time in the water and is blowing everyone away with his surfing.

'Surfing's made me who I am,' he admitted. 'It's brought me all these amazing experiences travelling and meeting great people. It's the experience. Like those days when you're surfing a perfect beach break with your mates and a dolphin pops up. It's those memories that keep me going through the bad days.

'Eight years down the track, I've gone through cancer, I've lost my dad and I've had three major operations on my leg. I'm probably more — no! I know for a fact that I am more — in touch with myself and more comfortable with myself, more at peace and more fulfilled, than I ever have been in my whole life. These last couple of months have been really good and I'm feeling really equipped now to deal with whatever else is put in front of me. I'm ready to go out and enjoy the rest of my life — in the ocean especially.'

PETE NOLAN

Wade

GLASSCOCK

H e's from Texas, originally. Then he moved to India for four and a half years, studying to be a guru. He has since lived in Hawaii and now Australia where he dedicates his energies studying to be a surfer. But despite his dedication, he has experienced limited success. He is a 40-year-old competitive surfer who has made few heats in a professional career spanning five years — and he has a message for all the judges around the world: 'Stop ripping me off!'

It's hard to reconcile this with the

SARGE

fact that he is widely regarded as one of the least accomplished surfers on the world circuit.

We were sitting on the sand at D-Bah, arguably the most competitive beach in the world. Glasscock had just returned from a free surf after once again losing his first heat in a WQS event that day, the Surf Cult Pro. He lit a cigarette and talked about his life on tour.

'I had a hard time this year because I started out by pissing off a few of the judges in Portugal,' he said. 'Ever since then, whenever those judges are there in Europe, which they usually are, they give me ones and twos.'

Glasscock has been following the tour for a few years now, turning up in all corners of the globe with his trusty 6'8" surfboard, by himself, ready to surf in high-level surfing competitions. But he has become frustrated by his results — or lack of.

'Last year I gave this judge the bird because he ripped me off in my heat. I totally dominated the heat — it was one of the best heats I've ever surfed in my whole bloody life. Every man and his dog thought I'd won the comp — everybody! But they were giving me point nines and point eights for every wave I got. Which is zero point eight and zero point nine. It's tricky going back there, but I have to, because that's the best leg.'

Wade leads a mysterious life of solitude, picking berries at his home on the NSW north coast to scrape together enough money to travel around the world and compete in the WQS. His life is like a jigsaw puzzle with missing pieces and he has baffled and confused all of us on tour.

There were rumours of him having progressed through a heat once in Portugal, but only because two other guys didn't turn up. But enough! I thought. Time to ask the man himself about those missing

WADE GLASSCOCK

pieces. But chatting with him I realised that, as far as ability goes, Wade doesn't see anything missing in his surfing.

'Often it's because I don't have any money,' he said. 'I have to catch buses and shit everywhere and I'll be camping on the beach or sleeping in my car before a comp.'

The tall, awkward-looking man pulled his wetsuit halfway down, allowing the fresh sea breeze to cool him. No money fell out and it's obvious he struggles financially. In fact, he has to pay entry fees of US$150 a pop and a further US$200 in ASP membership.

He watched the contest bank in front of us — professionals ripping across random peaks, advancing their careers and bank accounts with seemingly effortless flow — as I asked him the question we had all been asking for years: Who the hell is Wade Glasscock?

He spoke with assuredness and confidence of his introduction into surfing. 'I'm originally from San Antonio, Texas,' he said, with his unusual accent, a bizarre mixture of drawling Texan mixed with ocker Aussie. 'There are some waves there, but they are not that good. I then went to India and was initiated by this guru and hung out with all these other gurus. I just got into the scene. There were a lot of beautiful women that were practicing to be gurus, so it wasn't a bad place to hang around. I lived in the commune for about four and a half years. We were pretty clean. A few beers here and there, a couple of cigarettes, but not many drugs.

'When I was growing up I did quite a few [drugs], some pretty nasty ones. You know, LSD, mushrooms, whatever. But ganja [marijuana] is the only one I've ever liked. I didn't get into surfing until I was 25 when I moved to Australia and almost missed my calling, you know — my favourite thing to do in life.'

Wade is passionate about his surfing. He sees things that others miss. And through these self-styled visualisation techniques he has, apparently, been doing some pretty mean turns. 'I've been trying to do this 360 where you get a nice air and pull off the 360 and make the landing. I've been trying to polish that one off. But mainly I've been working on different airs and different carves inside the barrel. I can visualise 20 or 30 different moves on a wave. If I can find a point break, I can fit them all in, in one wave sometimes.'

With those manoeuvres in his head, Wade has been lapping the world in an attempt to make a living as a professional surfer. He travels to Europe every year. He has this strange habit of rocking up everywhere. 'This will be my third year on the WQS,' he said. 'I've been doing around nine or 10 comps a year. But I also did a few years on the ACC [Australian Championship Circuit] before that.'

'How did you go?' I asked, trying to remember.

'Good ... in some. I've had a lot of 33rds and 49ths here and there when things are going right but also a lot of 60ths and 80ths. It's been hard because I know I've been dominating the free surfing sessions.'

Despite the rumoured walk-through that had become legend, I was quite certain he'd never made a heat in my presence. I checked the current standings. At the time of publication Wade was sitting at 868 on the WQS ratings.

I asked Wade about goals; if he believed he could qualify for the top 46, to compete against surfers such as Kelly Slater, Mark Occhilupo and Joel Parkinson.

'Yes,' he answered. 'But I don't believe it can be done in a year. I've only been doing this thing full-time for two or three years. But I believe I can. I'd like to get in the 150 this year of the WQS. Then the 50 after that, and then the year after I expect to be in the WCT. I'm not

WADE GLASSCOCK

out of shape, it doesn't matter that I'm turning bloody 40 in a couple of months. I could go for another seven years.'

I looked over the surf comp again at D-Bah. Beau Emerton had just finished off a great wave to the beach. Behind him, Joel Parkinson went crazy. I looked back at Wade who was watching the ocean peacefully, drawing back on a cigarette that blew clouds between himself and his competitors.

'The standard is pretty high these days, Wade,' I said. 'What do you have that will make you stand out and hopefully qualify?'

He put out his cigarette. 'I think these days it's all about having an individual style that people like. Most of us on the tour these days do, so it's quite a battleground. Basically, I can do the sickest airs and floaters when I'm really surfing my best. They are probably my best features. Huge gouging turns also. People often comment when I do a nice turn, they'll say that was the sickest cutback they've ever seen. I'll be surprised most of the time you know, like "Oh really, that manoeuvre?" I thought that was just a weird nothing.

'When I'm really relaxed and in tune, which is probably one out of two or three comps, I'll just go sick, you know. I'll blow my own mind and people will come up to me and go, "Oh my God, I can't believe how good you were surfing. You blew my mind. You inspired me." To me, I'm very good at what we do, and that's surfing and competing to make money, and I'm only just learning the ropes in my third year. But I've got the potential to get right up there because I can do the things everybody else can do, and I can do some things no one else can do.'

Wade seemed so proud that he 'did the tour' and clearly loved being a part of the scene that was around us. I asked him to explain what he liked about the way of life he'd chosen.

WADE GLASSCOCK

'I do it for the lifestyle and the brothers you meet on tour,' he answered. 'There's a real spiritual vibe on the tour, where at least half of us would be just full-on soul surfers most of the time if we weren't doing this. That's part of it too, you know. I like to travel and I like to hang out with all the guys that shred — and there are hundreds of them these days.'

In actual fact, Wade doesn't hang with anyone. 'I just like to do my own thing,' he admitted. 'If I had a sponsor they'd have to be pretty easygoing. If they told me you have to do this comp, or you can't do that one, you can lose your individuality. There's a real balance there and I'm not interested in finding that balance unless the money's good. I'd rather do my own thing in my own way — and if I can win more money in the comps, then I'd be doing twice the amount of comps I'm doing now.'

Wade's is a story of inspiration, to follow your dreams. And he has some advice for aspiring surfers: 'I say, forget about the sponsors. Do it for yourself and let your results speak for themselves. When that happens the sponsors will come to you. It doesn't matter how old you are. If you surf 20 hours a week you're fit enough to do it. You've just got to pull out every move you can imagine. Try to visualise the most amazing manoeuvres to win your heat — and then pull them off. Anyone can do it as long as they've got a soul surfer's dedication to surfing.'

Wade left the Surf Cult Pro with another loss under his belt and drove back down to Evans Head to prepare for the European leg of the WQS. He is on a mission to make the WCT — and he has one more thing to say: 'For all those judges in Portugal, I've written to the ASP about you guys [not rating me] when I've shredded ... I'm going to get the 46 together and I'm gunna vote you out. If you don't lift your act I'm going to do whatever it takes to get you fired. Otherwise, I'm willing to forgive and forget.'

WADE GLASSCOCK

Mick

FANNING

I n the early hours of a winter morning in August 1998, residents of the Gold Coast awoke to the news of a tragic accident. It involved four youths in a vehicle that had lost control at Greenmount, Coolangatta. Two surfers riding in the rear of the car had died on impact. One surfer's name was Joel Green. The other, Sean Fanning.

Sean's two brothers, Ed and Mick, were at opposite ends of the earth when they found out. The youngest of the three brothers, Mick, was overseas competing. All of a sudden, the closeknit Fanning brothers, who'd lived and shared the dream of surfing since their childhood in the western suburbs of Sydney, were cruelly ripped apart.

The tough streets of Penrith, where Mick was born in June 1981, taught him how to kick an olly, spray a tag, but mainly to stick up for himself amongst similar kids with attitude. The Fannings also lived at Campbelltown, another tough suburb in western Sydney. 'We used to get right into skating,' says Mick. 'There wasn't much else to do out there.' It brought the family closer together. They had friends in different places, but they always had each other to go for a skate with, throw a footy in the backyard, or go down the road and throw stones at bottles.

It was when the Fannings moved closer to the beach, at Ballina, Coffs Harbour and finally the Gold Coast, that their lives took on some sort of shape. At this stage Mick was 12, the perfect age to get into surfing. He didn't know it then, but he would become one of the best in the world.

Mick moved to the Gold Coast at around the same time as Joel Parkinson made the move from the Sunshine Coast. Another hot young local, Dean Morrison, was also turning heads. They didn't know each other that well, but soon they would. It was almost as if destiny brought them together, because they shared and fuelled a healthy rivalry that would make most mortals sick. They lived and surfed at the most competitive beach in the world, Duranbah, and the three of them are now perhaps the most exciting surfers in the world.

'We all went to school together so we were hanging out a lot since we were at least 13,' says Mick. 'I was only young — I wasn't thinking I was going to be a pro surfer or anything yet — so I thought I'd just keep going with school, you know, try and keep getting through.' Mick, coming from the western suburbs of Sydney, knew nothing about the potential of a surfing career. He'd only just been introduced to the ocean, so every day was like a holiday. Funny thing is, it still is. But on the Gold Coast the possibility of a surfing career is as sought after as an uncrowded session at Kirra. Joel and Dean committed to the dream early, and of course this took away from their school life. 'It sort of pissed me off when they kept coming to school telling me that D-Bah was pumping or something. I was never allowed to stay at home, so it was just like, "Fuck off, idiot."'

Mick was starting to develop a style of surfing as individual as his character; reckless and quick, he darted across waves like a rabbit. Nobody could catch him. You didn't even have to blink to miss a turn. The scary thing was, he was barely a teenager.

'It doesn't feel that fast to me,' he says. 'It just feels normal. It's weird — sometimes I'll do a turn and think, "fuck that was slow", but when I see it on video it sort of does look fast.' Though he describes his surfing as 'out of control', one thing is clear. It is unique.

'I used to watch guys like Occ and Luke Egan a lot in all the Billabong movies, and Tom Curren. But you've still got to do it your own way. I don't know, I think I'm just like everybody else just out there doing it their own way. I guess it just turned out the way it did.'

Being the humble, shy person that he is, Mick did not have in his head how good he really was. He kept surfing with his brothers every day, pushing each other and having fun. Secretly, they shared a dream of one day surfing professionally and travelling the world together. But like their sessions, this was mostly kept in the family. Then, all of a sudden, Mick just hit this feeding frenzy. Like a shark rolling its eyes in the back of its head, he wasn't even watching, or

MICK FANNING

at least not taking notice; he was just feeding instinctively. He puts his success down to 'not caring so much'. His method aside, all of a sudden the world knew about Mick Fanning. And the universe wanted to know more.

'I think it was when Rip Curl came to the party when I first realised I could be a pro. They came to me and it was just like, "Oh shit". We are talking about a lot of money and a definite career in surfing. I thought, if it's gunna happen, then it's gunna start now.'

That was in '96, when Mick was just 16. He had signed a massive five-year contract with a company banking on him becoming a superstar. 'It was sort of weird,' says Mick. 'You always think of all these people getting heaps of money and then all of a sudden someone rings me up and says we want to give you this. It's like, what the fuck! Now I was one of them.'

Mick had signed a deal that made him the latest Aussie sensation and the new face of Rip Curl, one of the world's top three surfwear labels. But in Mick's eyes, most of the support was coming from his family. 'My mum and dad didn't have much money, but they went out of their way to give us everything we needed.'

Despite being one of the best surfers at D-Bah on any given day, Mick's brother Ed was starting to give up on his dream of a pro career. He couldn't quite reach the bar that Mick had just launched over, so he stepped aside to put all his energies into his brothers' careers. Mick and Sean were starting to do really well. Ed realised the talents of his younger brothers and was now all for them; the dream would still live on.

Like Mick, Sean was also starting to get noticed. He travelled with Mick around different parts of Australia and the world competing, and as a professional surfer he was really starting to kick in. But before Sean could pack his bags and join his brother on tour, the life they shared, or hoped to share, changed in the worst possible way. After a night out on the Gold Coast, Sean was driving home with Joel Green and two girls. The vehicle spun out of control, hitting an old pine tree at full impact on top of Greenmount Hill. Sean and his good mate died instantly.

Mick was barely seen for weeks as news filtered around the surfing world. 'I was just not doing anything,' reflects Mick. 'I couldn't understand it. I didn't surf for at least a week or two and I didn't surf that much once I did get back in either. I sort of just dropped everything. I couldn't motivate myself for so long because he was the one I did things with — he was the one who motivated me. Then he was gone.'

The two were much loved by the people of Coolangatta. It seemed that everybody felt the loss, and the whole town eventually adopted Mick as family. It brought everyone closer together. It was good friend Adrian Wiseman, in particular, who got Mick to carry on the dream.

'Ado was going to this contest down in Coffs Harbour and he said, "You've got to come. I'm not letting you stay at home any more." So I went in it and had some fun, and that was when I started to get back into it.'

If Mick needed any reassurance that he was destined to live out the dream he once shared with Sean, it came at a little place called Sandon Point, near Wollongong on the New South Wales south coast. It was the Konica Skins event where some of the best surfers in the world lined up for thousands of dollars in prizemoney, for head-to-head, best-wave surfing. As a skinny little 17-year-old, Mick tore through the pack like a Tasmanian devil. He was unstoppable with his fast on-rail surfing that evolved perfectly to the face of a point

MICK FANNING

break. By the end of the day he had beaten most of his heroes and walked away with $21 000. It wasn't a fluke — he beat everyone, one by one. It was a special day for Australian surfing, but even more special for Mick. On that day, Sean would have turned 21.

'That was pretty crazy. I just went into that thing going, "Oh fuck it ya know, I don't care. I don't care if I lose or not," ya know. I was still a bit down and a contest didn't really bother me too much. I was just this little kid coming up against Occy, Luke Egan and all the boys and I just kept getting through heats. I didn't know how much I was winning and then at the end of the day I had won 21 grand and it was Sean's 21st birthday that day. I do try and talk to him when I'm out in the surf, but when that happened I thought, "oh shit, that's a bit weird".'

He still talks to Sean a lot and according to Mick, 'It's almost like having another brother'.

'I try to speak to him all the time,' he says. 'Usually when I come home I try and go up to the tree where the ashes got buried and talk to him. I still feel really close to him.'

It's probably one of the hardest things Mick will ever go through. As a young man, he has handled it incredibly well. 'I guess I just think of the good times, you know, and just know that [Sean and Joel] are always there. Their spirit and their energy are always around.'

It seems to have spurred Mick on; like Sean really is there listening from the heavens where he probably shares a beach-view apartment with Huey, the surf god. Mick powered into the next part of his career, with Sean's and Ed's wind in his sails. With lightning speed, Mick continued his giant-killing run by winning the Hot Buttered/Ocean & Earth Pro Junior two years in a row, as well as the Mark Richards Newcastle City Pro (a WQS event) as an 18-year-old.

MICK FANNING

He went into the 2001 season full of confidence — and the world was watching him with anticipation. The first event was the Quiksilver Pro at his home break of Snapper Rocks. He didn't seem burdened by the heavy expectations on his shoulders; he became lighter and faster. He placed second, to Taj Burrow, and had a great start to the year, but it would get better.

Bells Beach, Easter 2001. Mick travelled down to Bells as a sponsored wildcard for the year's first WCT event and went one better. He won, beating the best surfers in the world. After it was over, he mentioned how weird it was having his name on the trophy list. How he was just a kid. His trophy was handed to him by Simon Anderson, the man who invented the thruster and won Bells on it in '84 to prove its worth. He is perhaps the most influential surfer ever. Simon spoke simply and powerfully: 'Look out world, here comes Mick Fanning.'

'I still don't feel worthy up against all those guys,' says Mick. 'I go in heats now and I think, "Oh no, how am I going to beat this guy?" But I just want to beat them all so bad. I guess you've just got to somehow believe in yourself and have a go, and never feel bad if you lose.'

Margaret River, March 2001. Mick was going from strength to strength. In the next event on the ASP tour, he stormed through all his early heats: he hadn't lost one in about 20. He was seen walking around the car park after his heats, or in the caravan park that night, thanking people who came up to him and told him how bloody good he was. He won that event too. Though his surfing was ready for the number one dais, Mick's personality wasn't ready for the attention. He was still the shy boy from western Sydney in many ways, so it was hard for him to deal with the hype. 'I'm so young,' he says. 'And all of a sudden I was in that position, so I guess I have to just learn as I go.' Mick went on to win that event too, capping off an almost-perfect Aussie leg.

Back at home in Coolangatta, Mick's surfboard sponsor was doing some calculations. In the previous month, their number-one star had banked just short of US$50 000 in prizemoney. It was a complete whitewash.

'Yeah, there were times when I did sort of feel unstoppable, I guess,' says Mick with his customary shyness. 'I was just concentrating on my own surfing, you know. I didn't care about money or results. I didn't even care if I won or lost. When I went for a turn I was just thinking about the turn.'

Mick took the zone along with him. He had slept with it, eaten with it, he took it wherever he went. By the time he got to Hawaii at the end of the season, he was almost a superhero, animated by his characteristic white top. Shapers from all around the world were throwing boards at him for feedback. At last count, he had about 36 with him on the North Shore, which kept every surf fresh, but he still wanted to win.

He explains his competitiveness: 'Sometimes I am so competitive, but other times I can be in a heat and I don't even want to be there, I'm just over it. If I get last, I get last. If I get through, I get through. I couldn't give a fuck.' It's almost like he's saying 'fuck you' to all our expectations — that he'll win and lose at his leisure, not ours. 'Sometimes it actually depends who I'm up against, though,' he says. 'That gets me going sometimes.'

In Hawaii, it was Andy Irons, one of the world's highest-paid surfers, and Mick and Andy put on a display at 10-foot Haleiwa that had all who saw it scratching their heads. They took on the infamous 12-foot rip bowl like they were surfing a two-foot shore break. They went crazy, some spectators admitting it was the best surfing they'd ever seen. Mick then went on to place third at the Rip Curl World Cup at Sunset in the next event, smashing eight-time triple-crown winner Sunny Garcia along the way.

If there was anything left for Mick to conquer, Hawaii was it. 'I was a little disappointed when I didn't qualify [for the WCT] the year before, but I had talks with guys like Nathan Hedge, and he explained the WQS was like doing your apprenticeship. I hadn't had much experience in Hawaii at all, so I just wanted to go there and get used to the waves so I was ready for it. I was just having a really good trip because the waves were so good.'

By the end of the year, Mick had won just about everything. He claimed US76 775 in prizemoney and qualified easily for the top 46 for 2002. He won the WQS ratings and also a car when he was voted *Surfer* magazine's surfer of the year. For someone yet to start on the WCT, it was probably the best performance in WQS history. Inevitably, Mick had sponsors chasing him everywhere, wanting a piece of him. At the time of our interview he was debating whether to go to America the following day after being nominated for ESPN's Young Sportsman of the Year.

Mick now owns two properties — a house and a unit. He drives a Commodore wagon and owns a brand-new wave runner, given to him by his sponsor, Red Bull energy drinks. With a bank account that's getting more deposits than withdrawals, it must be hard to handle at times. 'It's weird,' he says. 'I don't know what they expect from me. I just want to do my own thing.'

One thing Mick is going to have to learn is how to handle his money. So the 20-year-old has done what any young man would do and has brought in the big guns to take care of his financial affairs:

MICK FANNING

Mum. 'I just trust her, ya know. I'd rather give my money to her than anyone else.'

Newcastle, March 2002. I sat down on the footpath at Newcastle Beach with Ed Fanning and watched Mick paddle out for his quarter-final heat in the Mark Richards Newcastle City Pro. Ed had so much pride in his eyes. 'It was always a dream for at least one of us to make it,' he said, looking over the scene with a beer in his hand. 'I'm glad one of us has.'

Mick was flying across the small waves, doing figure-eight carves only inches out of the pocket. Ed was laughing. No matter how much he watches his brother surf, he is still blown away by his ability to improve. When Mick came in, it took him about 10 to 15 minutes to reach us. In that time he had signed at least 50 autographs, posed for 10 photos, spoken to news crews, radio announcers, the singlet marshall and thanked everyone for telling him how good he was. I watched him walk up to us, his cartoon-like white hair highlighted by his slight, still-developing frame. Sometimes you forget how young he really is. 'Well surfed,' I said, joining the list of fans. 'Yeah, good job Michael,' said Ed, looking at him proudly, but with the unspoken authority of an older brother. About an hour later Mick won the event, kickstarting his 2002 season. That day in Newcastle, he had a message for anyone aspiring to the same dream: 'Sometimes you win, sometimes you lose. As long as you enjoy yourself it doesn't matter.' He grabbed a sip of his brother's stubbie. 'Just believe in yourself. A lot of teachers and stuff at school told me there is no future in surfing. It just goes to show that you shouldn't put anyone down.'

Mick is more than a professional surfer, he is a *surfer*, and he carries that message in its purest form. That's how he handles the hype. 'Life's short, ya know. I started surfing because I enjoy it, just like anything. People become lawyers and they forget about the little things that make life enjoyable. They don't want to be there because it's not fun. With surfing it's all fun, so you may as well try and keep it that way.'

MICK FANNING

Neco
PADARATZ

Occasionally the emotion gets too much for Neco Padaratz and he snarls like an animal. I was in Argentina for a WQS event at possibly the world's worst beach, Mar del Plata, when it happened. I was sitting in a room playing cards with Will Lewis (a WQS surfer) when this incredible noise erupted from somewhere in the hotel. It was Neco Padaratz in the suite above, psyching up for the final of the event with Silverchair's 'Cemetery' playing at ear-splitting volume. The whole city of Mar del Plata was shaking as Padaratz paced back and forth above us, his footsteps as heavy as a giant. Will and I freaked.

Then he started jumping, the pressure shaking free the textured cement on the ceiling, almost triggering a seismic reaction in the old hotel. I could even hear his deep breaths. The snarls were in Portuguese, I guessed, and very intimidating. Then the music stopped, a door slammed and Padaratz's footsteps got closer. Will and I hid behind the curtains and peered through them nervously. 'Aargh!'

We saw the green nose of Neco's surfboard, followed by his familiar tattoo-covered body. The *loco* in Neco had become a locomotive. He was walking down the beach like he was marching into war. Will and I thought we should go down and watch. He absolutely ripped, but in the last minute got an interference against Victor Ribas, clearly overpsyched. He still placed second, despite only counting two waves instead of three. He didn't look happy. Will and I walked back to the hotel, a little disappointed as well.

Just before we walked through the front door we were brushed aside and almost knocked over by Neco. He stormed past us and slammed the door to his room, screaming and punching the wall. I heard his board get thrown across the room. About two minutes later, he walked past our room again for the presentation. His head and eyes were still red and his fists bleeding from punching the wall. It was terrifying.

Neco Padaratz doesn't like coming second. Not many people do, but Brazilians take their competitive intensity to another level. Neco, one of the best performers — if not *the* best performer — from Brazil, takes it even further.

'We have a lot of people working hard here in Brazil to try and make something of themselves,' says Neco, number 25 surfer in the world in 2002. His English is good and he looks you in the eye when he speaks. 'You have to go, and if you don't go, watch out! Because someone will knock you over.'

Surfing in Brazil is intense. It's not like Australia where you take your turn and relax with the ocean. Brazilians are incredibly full-on. If someone gets the inside of you, it's their wave — and they'll go, yelling and screaming all the way. Intensity is in their blood. It's not just the way they live, but also the way they survive.

'When everybody thinks of Brazil, they think of Carnival, they think of the women, they think of the party, it's all they see. But there's the other side. There is tragedy, there is violence. It's unknown, and it's sad that people can make such a beautiful land become such a horrible place.'

To make something of yourself in Brazil, you've got to do it by being more passionate and more competitive than anyone else. Adversity is common to almost everybody in Brazil, and to rise above it takes incredible determination. 'When you live in Brazil, you are subject to everything,' says Neco. 'You really need the money and you need to work, but there is so much corruption.'

In a country where you are either rich or poor, the Padaratz family was among the lucky ones. He grew up inland at a place called Blumenau before moving to Florianopolis, a wealthy cosmopolitan island in the south of Brazil. 'We just went down to see the ocean one day, for whatever reason, and we never went back,' says Neco.

He learnt to surf on the many beach breaks around Florianopolis. It was a good training ground. He also had the advantage of having as an older brother Flavio Padaratz, the most successful surfer ever to come out of Brazil, and as a friend Fabio

NECO PADARATZ

Gouviea, along with Flavio one of the first Brazilians to take on the world at the top level.

The main criticism of Brazilian surfers is that they are supreme small-wave surfers, but lack the power and technique to surf properly when the waves are perfect. This is because of the waves, or lack of waves, that they have in their homeland, which means that their technique favours short, flat turns. But it's not just the waves that make professional surfing on the world stage hard for Brazilians. It's cultural differences.

That's where Neco had an advantage over his brother and Gouviea. In 1994, he moved to Australia to learn English and to compete in the National Junior Series. It worked. He went back to Brazil a better and worldlier surfer. But when he returned, he realised how difficult it would be to turn professional.

'It's really hard to be respected as a surfer today in Brazil,' says Neco. 'It's not easy to get money and when you find it, you need to prove that you are determined and that you want to fight. In Brazil our money is really low and we have really big economic problems. A lot of the surfers don't speak English because we are such a poor country and it's difficult to get educated. To send them out to the world and say, "Be a pro surfer", is really tough.' Despite these problems, Neco has an upbeat message to deliver: 'We need to stick together, and the more Brazilians that travel together the more powerful we can be.'

The thought of that brings a shiver down the spine. Anyone who has travelled and come across Brazilians is frustrated by their lack of etiquette in the water. They are intensely competitive everywhere they go. They are loud and dominate line-ups. But these are just the rich idiots of Brazil who are used to looking down on people and have no respect. The surfers who compete are not as bad.

NECO PADARATZ

They are trying to learn their sport and are much more respectful. Unfortunately, to some extent they do carry their culture of 'run over, or be run over' around the world. In Brazil, every sport has rules and you use them to be the best. It's why their soccer players collapse theatrically when they're tackled and their surfers snake you. They are not just trying to be better, they are doing what's inculcated in them: survival.

Brazilian people show their emotions like no other people on Earth. The first time I went to Brazil was in '94. It was for the World Amateur Titles in Rio and we arrived to see a country draped in black. It was the day Ayrton Senna died and the Brazilian president had declared a national day of mourning. I vividly remember arriving at my hotel and seeing a 17-year-old Neco Padaratz crying in the lift.

It was a typical example of Neco's passion for his country. 'I carry my flag with me on everything. My bags, my board covers. Not just because I'm Brazilian and it's in my blood, but also to say, "Look, I'm from far away, man — and I fought all my life to try and be something." Whether I win or not, I need to carry that message.'

Though surfing is growing in Brazil, it doesn't touch car racing and football. On every street corner kids are playing soccer; on a fresh pitch in a rich suburb, or a dirt paddock in a *favela* (slum). These are people tying to make something of themselves, trying to break out of the *favelas* and make a life. It has been proven by people before them that it is possible with hard work. People who play with more passion and intensity than the next person so they can rise above their squalor. On the soccer pitch and in the surf, everybody can be a winner, a local boy once told me. But there is a huge distinction between surfing and football in Brazil.

NECO PADARATZ

'If the soccer players come back from a game they get a car, they get a house, the President comes around and they have a big dinner. Surfing is so far down there.

'If you are a professional surfer in Australia or in the US, people go "Wow", you know,' says Neco, looking me in the eye, and I can feel his emotion. 'If you say you're a professional surfer in Brazil, people go, "Oh yeah, whatever." We don't have the communications to show that we are someone. We don't have the support from the magazines or the TV.

'I want to go to the President, just once, and say, "Could I have five minutes with you? Can I talk to you just as a normal guy? Not as an appointment?" I want to at least try and show him that we go out there and we try hard. I train hard every day and sweat every day to make something of my life.'

At perhaps the height of Neco's career, he mysteriously vanished from the pro tour. He was kicking arse, winning events — and then left. There were rumours of some strange things going down. At the time, his wife had just given birth to their first son, and his mother-in-law, who is apparently skilled in some kind of witchcraft, was allegedly casting spells on Neco to make him stay at home in Florianopolis with his family. In any case, Neco dropped off the tour when he was at his highest ranking. He had surpassed his brother and was taking Brazilian surfing into the top 10 in the world, and then he disappeared. When I asked him the reason behind him leaving, it took him a long time to answer. He was clearly emotional about the issue.

'Ummm, my health was really bad. I had a chronic inflammation on my oesophagus. If I didn't get out and look after myself, maybe I get the cancer. Maybe I couldn't surf any more, maybe I couldn't do anything any more ... maybe I lose my life. So I had to get healthy. At that stage I didn't really know what I wanted to do with my life. Then after all of that, I realised something.' He paused. 'If I spend every energy inside me to surf, people can respect that. You have to do something for the will, and to never give up.'

Through all of this, Neco became even more determined, more passionate and more intense. He requalified easily when he came back, winning perhaps the most difficult event to win along the way, the US Open. He is looking to push himself even more.

'I train really hard and the results might not come straight away but I am changing a lot of things. Once I get that together, I will be something really good. It's the first time in 16 years that I've got my mind together and my body together.

'I'm helping my kid a lot more too. He is getting big and is surfing already.' He had the proudest expression on his face as we looked towards his arm, on which he has a tattoo of his son. From the look on his face, it is clear his son is now the most important thing to him.

'I want him to know that when I come back from overseas, I come back as a professional surfer and that he can respect that because I trained so hard to be where I am now. I do this now because I have a kid who depends on my dream of being something. People need to know why I scream and why I go crazy. Every time I win a heat, it's another bottle of milk that I buy for him, so there is a lot of reason for that. I'm real passionate for the sport that I do. It is my everything, it is my breathing. That will give him some direction, so I cannot surrender. I will be something so that he can be something too.'

NECO PADARATN

Kieren

PERROW

K ieren Perrow's idea of crazy is putting an extra dollop of chocolate fudge on his ice cream. His attention to detail is always intense, occasionally unsettling, but there are times when he seems totally free. Like now, in Hawaii, 2000, as he spoons a generous portion of Ben & Jerry's ice cream down his gullet. He has momentarily forgotten about the seven poems he has half written, the contract proposals he is compulsively readying for 2005, the soy milk he will need for his organic cereal in two mornings' time. It is all about the ice cream.

SARGE

Just five hours earlier we were sitting out the back at Waimea Bay on the North Shore of Oahu, one of the world's best-known big-wave locations. It was around 20-foot, with bigger sets. Kieren's small 68-kilogram frame sat barely wet on top of his borrowed 10-foot long gun, like a small child on his dad's surfboard. The intelligent young man from Suffolk Park on the far north coast of New South Wales looked out of place. He always does. It was crowded that day, as usual, and North Shore aggression mingled with the sea spray that blew thick where even birds wouldn't dare fly. Egos were finding their place in the line-up. A set usually decides what you are out there for. When this one came through it looked huge, about 25-foot and seemed to be harbouring thoughts of closing out the island's deepest bay. The line-up revealed itself and some surfers bolted for the channel, to the horizon. Others waited in the spot to catch it. Kieren was one of them. He paddled deeper towards the danger of the impact zone, towards a steeper take-off. He paddled into the wave with the same look with which he beheld the ice cream, pure freedom and excitement, like a small kid about to go down a slippery dip for the first time. It sounds crazy, but that's exactly what he looked like. He had the wild-eyed concentration of a toddler, pure and innocent, blissfully unaware of consequence. Three people took off on that wave, but Kieren was the only one with a smile on his face.

'I never really surfed big waves when I was growing up,' says Kieren. 'There kind of weren't any around in Byron [Bay]. But I always loved barrels ... and the energy you get out of a big barrel just quadruples.'

Kieren doesn't just flirt with danger, he launches himself at it. It's almost the only thing in his life he doesn't administer his intellect to. He gets lost in the moment. 'I think growing up in a place that doesn't get big waves, you don't get jaded from it. Hawaiians just seem to take it in their stride when it gets big because they are so used to it. I don't often get the chance, so I go crazy.'

Back in Australia, we looked up at his place at Tugun, on the Gold Coast. Sitting at his table, which was covered in books, notes, receipts, and things-to-do lists, I remembered when we were in England a few years earlier, staying at a friend's house. Every morning we'd be out the front waiting in the car for him before we went surfing. Kieren would be the last person ready for anything, so much so that my Pommy mate started calling him 'Karen'.

Life's pretty good for Kieren now. Two years ago, we would have still been sitting in a friend's or sponsor's house with grovel boards dominating his quiver and his beloved '68 Corolla out the front. Now, we were sitting in a nice house he had rented overlooking Tugun, with a cupboard full of ice cream and a brand new Subaru Outback 4WD sitting out the front. Soon it will be sitting out the front of the new house he has just bought in front of Tallow Beach at Suffolk Park.

Kieren is now in the top 46 of the world, a dream for every competitive surfer. Not just because you get to surf against the best in the world at the best breaks, but also because you finally get to make some good money out of a sport you love. 'I missed out by one spot in 2000. But I think if I had've made it I wouldn't have been ready mentally,' says Kieren. 'It's a big jump you know. My goal in 2001 if I had've qualified would have been to just stay in the top 46. Now I want to win contests.'

Kieren was not that good when he was a junior. He charged, had a good forehand re-entry, but was slow and boring. He placed second in the Hot Buttered/Ocean & Earth Pro Junior in '98, and after another final at Bells, was leading the most prestigious Junior Series in

KIEREN PERROW

the world from Taj Burrow. I had first noticed him the year before when he smashed an eight-foot lip at Rottnest Island. It was huge and messy, with thick south swells bumped up by the 'Fremantle Doctor'. He was so committed to this bottom turn that I thought he was going to pull through the back of the wave, but that doesn't happen much. He dug in as if it was his backhand and went straight through the roof vertically, smashing through it and freefalling down. 'I love that feeling of weightlessness,' he says, with a hint of that crazy look coming back. Kieren may not have been the best surfer that year, but he did the most committed turns. It was like he conceptualised a bigger weapon, created it from the brink of oblivion, and then beat the fuck out of his opponents with it. Most juniors didn't want to fight him when it was over six-foot. They still don't. He is one of the true masters of challenging waves like Teahupoo. 'I always knew he charged,' says Taj Burrow. 'But I didn't know he surfed so good.'

'I think I figured out when I was young that I wasn't the most naturally talented person there, so I had to be smart and beat them tactically,' says Kieren. 'It's a hard thing to do — admit to yourself that you're not good at something, or not the best. I grew up really thinking and dissecting the dynamics of heat strategies and now that my surfing has caught up to everyone else, I'm a lot more confident.'

Kieren's surfing evolved on the point breaks of Broken Head and Lennox Head. It's smooth and relaxed. Like most surfers that grow up on point breaks, nothing's forced. He waits for sections to come and finds his rhythm, never forcing sections out of nothing. But unlike most point-break surfers, he surfs incredibly vertical. That's where he has something better — he hits the lip harder than most. 'It's easy to surf horizontal when you grow up on a point break, but I really tried hard to keep my surfing critical, even when it was small.'

Kieren scored a 95.7 TER for his HSC and has since clashed minds, mingled wits and debated global economics with the best of them. He has an ability to think for himself and a passion for learning. There is also a spiritual side to his personality. But he doesn't speak about it unless people ask.

'I like to feel like I'm continually evolving in life. It was hard there for a while on tour. I had done it for three years and said to myself, if I don't qualify this year [2000], I'm going to walk away. No trips, nothing. I was going to study environmental science and engineering. It's still something that I'd like to do. But because I was so close, I couldn't throw it away.

'My main motivation for qualifying was to surf big Pipeline or Tahiti with just one or two other people out. No doubt! I couldn't stand another year of WQS beach breaks. I wanted to test myself at Hawaii. You can't push yourself enough at Pipe when you are free surfing. You've got to take what you can, and it's not always pretty. Sometimes you get lucky, sometimes you don't.'

Kieren is not a delicate genius when it comes to surfing big waves; he is absolutely and insanely stupid. It's as if there is one part of his brain that doesn't work. He hunts big Pipe, especially Backdoor, with unrivalled gusto. Most of the waves he catches there are speculators. He gets a chance, he swings, he goes — that's his routine. The constant punishment, the stitches, the 50 boards he has left there in a hundred pieces, don't deter him from going back to Hawaii every year, twice a year.

'I remember the first time I went to Hawaii in '96. There was this energy in the air from the ocean. This raw potential energy and it's so exciting. I've been there twice a year since, broken at least five boards per

KIEREN PERROW

trip. But the experience I've had can't be bought. Boardwise, bodywise. It's all worth it.'

'He's fuckin' mad,' says Koby Abberton. 'I've seen him do the craziest shit. You wouldn't pick it though. He looks so … normal.' When Kieren got the cover of *Tracks* in the 'Australia's Heaviest Wave' issue last year, it was a trip Koby actually went on too, but Koby flew back to the Goldy because he caught wind of a swell at Kirra (reckon he's kicking himself now?). When I told him at Margaret River about the scary new wave, he said, 'Fuck yeah, get me there.' When I told him that Kieren was going too, he paused, suddenly apprehensive. 'Oh fuck!' It wasn't the first time their competitive madness got together.

The Gotcha Pro, Tahiti, 1997. It wasn't the first time Kieren went mad in big waves either, but it was the first time he was noticed. It was also the time when Teahupoo made its first big statement to the world. Teahupoo, which means 'skull's pass', has been justifiably labelled the gnarliest wave in the world and the waves there were like nothing we had seen before. We sat waiting for our heats on the final day, not knowing what to do or expect. Contest director Steve Robertson was telling us — Brad Gerlach, Sasha Stocker, Kieren Perrow and myself, who were in the next heat (the round before the quarters) — that if we didn't want to, we didn't have to go out. 'It's too dangerous,' he said. 'I'm gunna call it off.'

But then there'd be someone's voice from the channel, usually Nathan Hedge's or Koby Abberton's, that would spark a bit of the cowboy in everyone. 'Just go!' We knew this was going to be a monumental day. Sasha and 'Gerr' got a couple of medium-sized ones straight off the bat; the big ones were unrideable and nobody had attempted one yet. The reef at Teahupoo sucks you in when it's big and leaves you out of position when a set comes in, so you've really got to be aware of your spot in the line-up. We had anticipated it and the wave approached. It was huge, sucking us toward it like a river rapid. 'Are you going?' asked Kieren. I hadn't even contemplated it. The sets weren't rideable, I confided to myself. I looked too deep anyway. Excuses. Kieren swung late and I had a view looking down at him taking off on the vertical slab. The entire Pacific Ocean seemed to be behind him. The view as you paddle over the wave is intense at Teahupoo. Even the reef seems to get dragged with the water up the face. The crowd was cheering the big set and then went suddenly quiet at the thought of someone riding it. Their silence turned to amazement when they saw he had a huge smile on his face. The wave cracked thunderously out of view, filling the silent void. The noise that wave makes is deafening. It spat out into the channel and I thought Kieren was dead for sure, until I heard the excited screams. Surfing with Kieren can be both inspiring and demoralising.

I was a spectator after that heat. I watched Kieren's semi — yet another 10. He then got smashed and washed over the reef into the shallow lagoon after a crazy wipeout. It was scary stuff and the crowd was running out of winces. With 10 minutes remaining, he waved off jet-ski assistance that would have meant disqualification and powered out the back into the take-off zone. We thought it was his ghost, as he should have been dead. Red-faced and bleeding from the impact, he'd swapped the three pieces of surfboard he had added to the growing list of fibreglass casualties and paddled out on his 7'6", still excited, like there was still enough time to almost die again. With one minute to go he got another 10 and made the final. 'It was the most exhilarating and the most humbling experience of my surfing life,' says Kieren. 'But I still love the place.'

KIEREN PERROW

When Kieren goes to a foreign country, he doesn't just get dropped off at the surf, do his job, and complain about how people don't speak his language and make his food — like so many other pro surfers. He wants to learn and experience it all. 'It's the most accelerated learning experience you'll ever get. It's all there: culture, languages, different people just doing different things. That's where you learn about life . . . and everything,' he says.

'I went to school stoned pretty much every day of my high school life. The day I left school, I knew I just had to give up. I did well at school but it's not the type of learning you should be doing. It's such a closed little world and I knew it. School doesn't open your mind, it closes your mind in specifics when you should be learning about the world. When I finished school, I knew I just couldn't face the world stoned. I haven't smoked since.'

Kieren's dad is South African and carries a worldly air, as does his mother, and Kieren even spent two years in South Africa as a toddler. I went to J-Bay with Kieren and Andy King (a WQS surfer) in '98 and it was cool watching him reacquaint himself with his roots. He met his babysitter who hadn't seen him since he was in nappies, and they talked of old times. 'It felt strange to go back to J-Bay. My last memories of there were being up to my four-year-old knees in seashells! The beach is amazing, and now the wave will draw me back. It feels like home to me, my first memories of life.'

Later in life, Kieren once again became a traveller and was enjoying his new healthy lifestyle and that he'd chosen the right path in life, but old emotions shut out by clouds of endless marijuana were flooding back. 'Around the same time as giving up smoking I began to write a lot, mostly poetry. I never realised what a powerful tool writing can be. It gets it all out rather than keeping it all bottled up inside. Bottling things up is very dangerous. It's also a creative outlet as well as an emotional one. So I put down the bong and picked up a pen. It helped me with so many things. It breaks down barriers.

'Sometimes it's harder to break down barriers that you have with people when they're the ones you love. I used to write my mum a poem and then we'd talk. I used it to release unhappiness or issues I had, depression. Lately I haven't been doing much writing at all and I think it coincides with my happiness. I've been really happy lately with qualifying and stuff. But in saying that, it was always a dream of mine to get a house, which also coincides with me qualifying. It's a strange feeling that I have now, with all of this new material wealth. But I think the anticipation was almost better.'

We agreed that the better your life gets, the higher your expectations are. 'I still have my day-to-day frustrations, like everyone. It's never constant bliss.'

'But you're in the top 46 now, life's got to be all good. You're on a roll,' I offer, as I once shared the dream.

'Of course, but it's all relative. I heard a saying once: "Be humble for your fortunate life." I think anyone living outside a Third World country can claim a fortunate life. It all just comes back to having perspective. Get out of your realm that you live in day to day and appreciate just what's out there. It's a constant battle because there is so much negativity and anger out there and it can really play on you.'

Kieren is awaiting the first event of his WCT career. He is excited and looks very happy. Nine surfboards sit next to the table. Kieren knows what he wants. All these boards are brand new and I am so familiar with his routine that I don't even have to ask. I know that by the end of the week three of those boards will work perfectly for every

KIEREN PERROW

possible condition at every possible venue on the Gold Coast. The rest will go back to the shapers with an essay and perhaps a poem about what minute detail went wrong.

'He really know his boards,' says Tony Cerf, one of Kieren's first shapers. 'He gives me so much information, sometimes you just have to say, "Hey Kieren, go out and just ride it".'

Cerf isn't the only one who's noticed Kieren's perfectionist nature. 'He's such a bitch,' chuckles Andy King. 'He fluffs like nobody I know. He seems so busy all the time, but I don't even know what he is doing. That's why he is so good at everything, he doesn't leave a stone unturned. He's good to travel with too because he does everything for you.'

There are many who have benefited from Kieren's intellectual services. In the Hawaii season of '98–'99, I accompanied Kieren, along with a few other WQS surfers, to the Annual General Meeting of the ASP at the Turtle Bay Hilton on the North Shore. We wanted to voice our opinions about a few things, but with all our heroes in the room we were a little shy. Then, all of a sudden we hear: 'That's ridiculous!' KP jumped at an argument in the same way he jumps out of a line-up of the top 46 surfers at Teahupoo, putting his hand up for the biggest wave nobody wants. 'Go KP!' we muttered to ourselves. This little WQS surfer from Suffolk Park was clashing wits with the sport's governing body, industry heads, surfer reps, including Luke Egan and Sunny Garcia, and had them back-pedalling. When he started using smaller words they realised they had perhaps the best surfers' rep the sport has ever seen.

'He's got to be one of the most marketable surfers out there,' says Greville Mitchell, Chairman of the ASP. 'For long-term value, you've got not only someone that charges big waves, rips and could possibly come close to winning a world title, but also someone who has the brains to take himself and a company wherever he wants. Companies would have to be stupid if they didn't see that. He's really been one of the key figures in the growth of the ASP lately too.'

'I got into the ASP as a surfers' rep,' says Kieren. 'I got involved during a real changing period. The surfers were getting a lot more involved and I didn't know what I was up against. I hadn't done much public speaking since I left high school, and back then I was the stoned school kid. At the first meeting I was saying that the ASP should own the events and license out the sponsorship to the companies like in tennis. I didn't realise it at the time, but it was in front of Gordon Merchant [the boss of Billabong], Doug Warbrick [the boss of Rip Curl] and Alan Green [the boss of Quiksilver]. It was pretty intimidating. I didn't know what the repercussions would be, but at the time, the companies owned the sport, and that was just ridiculous.'

Kieren is an intensely passionate and intelligent man, but he has also possesses a perverse and creatively entertaining sense of humour which unleashes toward anyone equipped to handle it. It's his release from the day-to-day intellectual transactions he withdraws and deposits in copious amounts. Sitting in the *Tracks* office one afternoon, I had a press release from Hawaii. It's the only place I miss from the tour and I usually sweat on these results. This one came back saying that Kieren had broken five boards in one day on his way to the quarters. Yeah, yeah, heard it all before, I thought to myself. Could be any day for Kieren Perrow.

But this one was heavy. He apparently broke a board in three bits, and his leg rope entangled around the bottom and kept him underwater for a two-wave hold down. They were making out that he was seriously injured or had almost died. I had to get the scoop, so I emailed Kieren to see if he was eating ice cream through a straw. His reply came back in typical KP style. I could imagine him laughing to himself as he wrote it.

Here's the unedited version that appeared in *Tracks*: 'Thanks for the concern, but good old Kieren is still alive and well. Never would I let death stand in the face of a thrilling ride. Well maybe when I've got kids or something. BUT NOT NOW GRIGGS. KP IS STILL A LUNATIC. A STUPID ONE AT THAT. BUT I LOVE IT. Help me, what can I do??? They probably talked it up a little bit anyway. I did come the closest I've come in Hawaii to the ethereal light, to the mysterious dark, to the blown out candle, to the truth, to the secret life of us, to the world of eternal orgasm (smothered in chocolate), to the end. But I didn't. I lived to see another empty tub of Ben and Jerry's. And I'm happy. Also had some very tasty barrels in the meantime. On the wipeout front, had some very good ones too. That one in particular was exceptional. Was very frustrated at the end of heat, had no waves (literally, my total score was 2.4!!!!!!!!) and this big set had just come through and closed out across to avalanches so I had even less waves after duck-diving all the foamy 15-foot beasts. Then this sneaky inside one came at the end, a 12-footer, and though I was way too deep, I went anyway. Got licked at the bottom, hit a wet foamy patch and went head over heels. Proceeded to get grounded into the reefy bottom (out the back! it was about bloody 20-feet deep) so I could lose some more skin to the ocean. It was very dark down there, and wet. Lots of water actually, all over me like a King Neptune's stacks-on. Then I tapped out, but it wouldn't get off, so I had to use my huge bulging feet muscles to start kicking for the surface (where was it??). All the turbulence was very annoying, like a mob of teenage girls at a French contest ... wouldn't let me up! Or was I going down? By this stage I couldn't tell. All I knew was my lungs needed water, without hydrogen preferably. I kept thinking that I was going to pop up and get mowed straight over by the next one, but the boys told me it had already passed. I'd been down for the count of two!! It would have been nice if they had told me then, rather than when the information was useless and I was safe(r). Anyway, I was almost there when my leg jerked back and I stopped nearly dead in my tracks!! It's funny how your body always fights life to the death. But this time it was my board, broken and still stuck somewhere down there connected to my leggie bone that was connected to my anklebone. Damn. OK, now I was a bit worried, but as you can see there was no reason. I'd be dead if I wasn't writing this so I must have made it (or did I? Is this just a parallel universe? No because Kylie's not licking chocolate off my body, yet.). Yes, lucky for me the water had to end somewhere and the air begin otherwise I'd probably still be swimming. So I yanked on my leg(gie) and thought about ripping it off — my leg that is. I really needed to breathe. It gave up the fight and I gasped out into the froth, inhaling mostly that, but air too. I thought to myself right then, as losing the heat seemed so inconsequential, it's moments like these you need Minties. Or very good sex, one of the two.'

Don't let Kieren confuse you with his writing style or his surfing. Just sit back and enjoy his surfing — maybe with a tub of ice cream.

KIEREN PERROW

Luke

EGAN

'Why has everyone always called me big?' Luke Egan asked me, as a coconut fell with a crashing thud to our right. I freaked, entertaining thoughts of a crashing commando-dive out of the impact zone. Luke didn't even flinch as he watched the line-up. 'Isn't there another word for it?'

We were checking the surf at G-Land and I cleaned my pants as Luke predicted a high-tide pulse. 'It's gunna be on,' he said, pre-occupied with the wave and slightly frustrated that the surfing minds of today couldn't come up with something more intelligent than 'Big L.E.' The fact is, in over two decades of surfing Luke Egan has always been the big guy doing the big turns on big waves.

I asked Luke to sum himself up in one word. He seemed surprised at my question. Yet he was relaxed as ever. I thought how great it must be to be so good at something that you don't ever have to talk.

'Another word?' His mind ticked in rhythm with the palm trees that swayed like a pendulum over our heads. I guess big would have to do for now. At 5'11" and a lean 90 kilograms I wasn't going to argue.

'When we were surfing G-Land the other day,' he continued, 'somebody came up to me and said, "Don't you wish you were a little whippersnapper so you could surf these waves." I went, "Actually, no." Because once I've got speed, I've got the weight and the build to do damage, and I enjoy doing damage. I enjoy being a big person riding little waves, because I can do things where people can't even fathom how I could move so much water on such a small wave. I dig it.'

In the true Aussie way, other competitors dish it up to him, with a small taste of sarcasm as a defence mechanism. Luke doesn't fall for that shit. He usually lets his surfing do the talking. 'It's always small people that come up to me and go, "Gee your boards look big," or "Gee you're huge." I think it's a complex and they wish they were as big as me. I get it every day, people picking up my boards and going, "Gee this looks big." I go "Yeah! This is made for a man, not a boy." Usually it shuts them up.'

Since joining the pro tour in the mid-'80s Luke had developed a massive following because of his style, power and creativity — the three weapons on every surfer's Christmas wish list. He scored the best sponsorship deals too. 'When we all first started doing the tour,' former top-10 surfer and friend Richard 'Dog' Marsh told me, 'we were all doing it tough. Nobody had any money. We were going to Japan or whatever and sleeping in board bags on the streets or beaches.' He laughed. 'Luke would always rock up in a hire car and check in to a hotel on the beach. We hated it.'

Luke was just about everyone's favourite surfer, though he remained something of an enigma to all his followers: 'I'm a pretty humble person, and not outspoken unless I know something is wrong. I just wouldn't take a punt like that. I'm a bit reserved. There is not much hoo-ha in the media about me and I've always wanted it like that. I don't want to be involved in the rumours or the gossip or whatever. My focus has always been to just surf good and let it all happen riding waves. I just want to say nothing and go surfing.'

And that's the way it was at G-Land too. He was either in the barrel, looking for the barrel, or thinking about the barrel. To get on Luke's wavelength you have to almost think like him. As contagious as that might sound, it ain't easy. He has both a diploma in advanced thinking and the attention of a cheetah at the mere hint of a surfing conversation that borders on the technical.

He also comes from a proud surfing heritage. Luke's family (mum, dad and sister) have been in the surfing industry since the early '60s. Clothes, surfboards, any money his family has ever made has come from surfing. His family set the precedent; Luke just took it to another level.

Luke's dad, Sam Egan, still one of the most respected shapers around, made boards for Luke like most parents made their kids toast. Spoilt? Probably, but all Luke wanted to do was surf. During our interview, Luke's posture would slip and his face would frown when I

LUKE EGAN

asked questions about himself or others. But as soon as we talked about surfing he would snap to attention as if, after 24 years of doing it, he was still uncovering its secrets. 'I'm 34 and I still get up for the early every morning at first light! I'm so excited because I'm going surfing. Every day is like Christmas Day when I'm going surfing.'

He talked about his school days at Merewether. Of how he wasn't so competitive when he was younger. It was all about surfing and surf time. Of how all of a sudden, like most people, the word 'career' hit him like a freight train of responsibility. 'My parents and my teachers were going, "School's over. You've got to get out there and do something." I thought...' The pause was for dramatic effect as he rose to an upright position once again. '"I'm a surfer!" Once I made that decision everything sort of fell into place.'

Technically, his own surfing blossomed, and for good reason. Growing up in Merewether, he was among some of Australian surfing's greats, including four-time world champion Mark Richards. I could imagine Luke watching him in his formative years, probing and banking the secrets of MR's act. Luke doesn't just watch and appreciate, he watches and learns. 'When a guy keeps coming home with world titles it shows you how it is done,' he said. 'It shows you that you can make a living out of pro surfing; that you can enjoy the lifestyle that we [surfers] love on a full-time basis so it sort of becomes your base plan. We saw it for years and discovered what it was all about and developed a base plan from that. Merewether and MR made us; in a sense it otherwise could have gone either way.'

Luke is continually analysing things. He breaks down his craft in every conceivable way to develop a deeper understanding of what he does — and take it to another level. He's always thinking and I could tell his mind had been ticking for an alternative to 'big'. 'I grew up really quick when I was a kid,' he told me. 'Then I just stopped. I think if I'd spurted later it might have upset my balance as a surfer.' It's amazing how talented people always seem to find the positives in everything. Straight away I looked at my own lanky frame and theorised my next ride. 'I'm kinda stoked that I grew so quick because I've been able to practice at the same size, riding the same boards for so long.'

Growing up with his dad as a shaper has allowed him to develop his understanding of surfboard designs. 'Luke is so on it with his boards,' his current shaper Jason Stephenson told me. 'He has a board shaped for every location around the world, and just about every variance in conditions as well.'

'I hang out in shaping factories every day,' admitted Luke. 'I've just grown up with it, with my dad shaping and stuff. He's always been cool with letting me ride whatever I want to. I never had to just ride his boards all the time. He kinda goes through stages too. Like right now, he's into making my guns and they go mad. I've always had to be heavily associated with a shaper though.'

You can see Luke gets a kick out of his deeper understanding and actually loves sharing it with just about anyone; it's his life. 'When Kelly came along in the early '90s and pushed everyone's boards narrower with a lot of curve...' He started slouching again. 'People are still obsessed if their boards are too big and it's just a load of fucking crap. If I've got a board that's wider and thicker, but I can still fit it in the pocket, I'll ride it. Thicker boards mean more speed and if I can hit something with more speed that's functional, it's better than having a little board that's pretty hard to ride. My dimensions are six foot five, by 19 and a quarter and always around two and a half.' Big! Even if a perfect barrel came through, he wouldn't have noticed it.

LUKE EGAN

The tutorial then shifted to barrel riding, and he had my undivided attention. 'When I started riding the flowrider, I learnt a new technique for riding the barrel.' The flowrider is a mechanical mobile wave and Luke rode it at Fox Studios in Sydney for the Siemens Mobile Wave Tour. Luke sat in the barrel for literally minutes, maintaining the style and grace he is famous for while tonnes of water gushed at him from jet-like machines. 'I was just looking at the nose of my board and where the barrel was hitting the water, instead of just looking out to the face for an exit. When I tried it in the ocean I was more in tune with what the wave was doing and getting deeper and longer barrels.'

This is when Luke is in his element. He doesn't care for the bullshit. He just wants to surf and talk about surfing. But where does he get this motivation from? 'Kids keep me motivated,' he said. 'I love surfing with younger guys because they are just new minds and they keep coming up with new stuff which I want to do.'

Right now surfing is breaking up into factions: big-wave riding, aerial surfing, and a valiant attempt at all-round surfing by the top 46 in the WCT, where Luke currently resides with A-1 views. Surfing is at its most progressive stage — and to stay afloat, you have to be an all-rounder. 'I've always just accepted everything,' he said. 'You hear people going, "Orr, fucking aerials", but I really loved surfing with Ozzie Wright. I really respect him and I love exploring and going surfing with people who have a different perspective. That's what fuels my fire — just to be a surfer.'

Luke moved to the Gold Coast about four years ago, leaving his beloved Merewether behind, for the same reason he gets out of bed so early ... to surf. And the Gold Coast has some of the best waves in the world: Kirra, Burleigh, Snapper Heads, D-Bah. 'There's something about having your own house up there and waking up every morning knowing that today you could get the best wave of your life,' he said.

Luke places himself where he can learn more, catch better waves and evolve his surfing. He has perfect waves on the Goldy, the young brigade of Mick Fanning, Dean Morrison and Joel Parkinson to push his surfing, and of course his number-one sparring partner, who has also made his home the Gold Coast in the last six years, 1999 world champ Mark Occhilupo. And Occy is another who knows a lot more about surfing than he lets on. 'We talk about boards and everything else as if we are not competitors,' said Luke. 'We've got our own little team. It's pretty rad that I looked up to his surfing when I was a kid; I was obsessed with it. He's so fluent and flamboyant. To be able to progress to the same level as him and then travel the world as sparring partners was unbelievable for me. Occy helped me a lot last year when I came runner-up. He was saying to me "Hey, you know you can win this." That was one of the reasons I think I had a good year.'

A good year indeed. Luke won his first WCT event back in '97, a long-overdue victory made sweeter by the perfect waves he won it in. He won his second event at Cloudbreak in 2000, setting up a world title race with long-time rival Sunny Garcia. Luke beat Sunny in the most prestigious pro junior in the world early in their careers, the Hot Buttered/Ocean and Earth Pro Junior. They have been rivals ever since. Sunny had never actually beaten Luke in over 10 years and, ironically, the pair didn't even meet in the world title showdown.

'I love Sunny,' said Luke. 'He's like a brother to me and he deserved to win the world title that year. There's nobody that kept as much focus through events. I was feeling good, but Sunny was always there. I take my hat off to him.'

LUKE EGAN

What about the intimidation? Sunny is well known for abusing judges and some feel it was what got him through some of the tough heats. 'Yeah, I actually spat the dummy about that in Tahiti last year. But Sunny can't do anything about it. It's the way he is, it's where he's from and you've just got to accept that. But sometimes I think it does get a bit out of hand when he loses a heat fairly and still blows up at the judges.'

Attitude is probably the only weapon Luke lacks in his quest for a world title. You get the feeling that not too many things get to him and that, perhaps, this is the knife he needs to sharpen more than anything else. 'Yeah, I think I've got to be more greedy to win a world title. But I would love to go against that, be myself and win a world title by not being greedy.'

The palm trees swayed overhead and I asked him why he hadn't won a world title. 'I'm sort of a slow learner, I never really grabbed something and ran away with it like Kelly or Pottz did that year. I've always just gone along with what's happening and I think that's my problem. That's sort of what I've been focusing on at the moment.' I could tell he was talking about karma, letting it all unfold. 'If it's time for my experiences to pay off, then it will happen. If 2000 was the best year I'm going to have, then that's the best year I'm going to have. I'm not going to change my attitude on surfing and I'm not going to change my attitude on competing. There's plenty of guys who haven't won a world title; Machado, Dorian. You've got to remember that every year there can only be one champ, and so many things have to come together to make it happen.'

In a world of winning and losing by 0.1s, it was so refreshing to hear a surfer not blame anyone else for their own shortcomings. Luke

Egan is just enjoying the journey, stoked that he can still get up every morning and surf: 'I was talking to Kelly about it recently, actually. We were on a boat trip in the Mentawis and we said to each other, "Do you think we'll still be doing this when we are 50 ... surfing and doing trips with each other, looking for waves?" I Hope so, I told him.'

LUKE EGAN

PARKO

Joel Parkinson had just got out of the surf at D-Bah with Mick Fanning and was dropping a couple of grommets home when I called. 'Just hang on a sec, Griggsy,' he said after half-answering a few questions with yes and no.

'You sure you want to talk now?' I asked.

'Ummm...' He was struggling to make himself heard above the muffler of his SS ClubSport, which roared like a young lion. He was trying to concentrate, but I could hear the grommets in the background stealing

SARGE

his attention — and I could sense they were trying to crack him up. 'I can't say anything bad, hang on.'

Maybe he was just trying to shelter them from the tales of debauchery from his four or five extra years travelling around the world as a young professional surfer. 'Oh shit, I just ran a red light … hang on, just give me a minute and I'll drop these grommets off.' Another long pause.

'Who are they?' I asked.

'The Harrington boys; good surfers too. I hang out with 'em all the time. They're my little mates.' The car stopped. 'Righto, get outta here ya little smartarses,' said Parko as the door of his sports car opened and closed. I could hear the grommets grabbing their boards and getting out of their hero's machine, still laughing. 'I'll pick you up tomorrow.'

About five years ago, when Parko was a 16-year-old grommet, he was that exact same smartarse — an energetic little clown who spent most of his time in the water and with friends looking for a laugh. A lot has changed since then. At 21, he is now perhaps the most marketable surfer today, commanding six-figure contracts and winning events against his idols like Kelly Slater. But despite the new SS ClubSport, the new property on the top of the hill at Kirra with 360-degree views, the exposure, the hype and the money, Parko has not changed at all. He is still that little smartarse who just wants to go surfing all day every day with his mates.

'My life has changed so much in the last few years,' he admitted. 'But I'm just trying to not take it so seriously. All I ever want to do is surf and hang out with my mates. I have to adapt to what is happening now but everyone is adapting to a new job or something at my age. I won't complain. Unless I get injured or something, cause then I can't surf.'

PARKO

The vehicle was running smoothly now on the Gold Coast Highway, with only the captain onboard. 'I just went for a surf with Mick [Fanning] this morning,' he said. 'And I'm going to go hang out with Deano [Morrison] this arvo. They're just your mates. We've got heaps of mates up here and you just hang out with whoever's around. Like right now, I was just hanging out with these groms.'

Though he'd only just got out of the water an hour before, he was on his way back to D-Bah for his second surf of the day, with Deano. It's an incredible relationship these guys share. 'It gets better all the time surfing with Mick and Deano. I love it. It's so healthy. We are definitely competitive with each other, but we are always there for each other as well.'

It's a formidable relationship that has the whole world talking right now. The three most exciting surfers today grew up together, went to school together and have surfed together since they first met as teenagers when Parko moved down from Nambour, on Queensland's Sunshine Coast. His father Brian and cousin Darryl Parkinson were Coolangatta legends, producing some of the best surfing in the '70s and '80s. Joel was always going to surf. He was born into the lifestyle and first stood up on a board when he was three. But their move to the Gold Coast was crucial in Joel's development as a surfer. 'I always wanted to live there. My sister lived there and I used to stay with her on the weekends and stuff, but the waves were so good, I never wanted to leave.' But in trying to keep up with each other, the rivalry between Joel, Deano and Mick hasn't always been healthy.

On a boat trip in '99, the 18-year-olds were going crazy in the Mentawis in Indonesia. It obviously wasn't the first trip they'd done together, but their hunger for the waves and their competitive nature spilled over at night when the Bintang beers came out. The crew on the

PARKO

boat went through the 10-day supply of alcohol in the first few days. They were playing drinking games and basically trying to keep up with each other. They were typical 18-year-olds talking up their ability to down a drink and keep it down. Though a few quiet trips to the back of the vessel were in order.

The games continued when they got off the boat in Nias for the O'Neill Deep Jungle Open — a four-star WQS event. They kept it up during the event too, staying up until they all passed out simultaneously from exhaustion as much as alcohol poisoning, heads down in a pack of cards and mozzie repellent. The only thing that stopped them in the end was when they went their separate ways. Because they simply wouldn't give up. Mick went back out to sea on a Rip Curl Search trip while Dean and Joel went home to D-Bah, where they could get back to the business of pushing each other in the surf.

Though he claims Kirra is his favourite wave, Joel does most of his practicing at D-Bah. You could rock up to D-Bah any day of the week and see the likes of Mark Occhilupo, Luke Egan, Beau Emerton, Jay Phillips, Mick, Dean or Joel there. If you want to be a good surfer, it's a good place to practice. If you want to be a freak, you practice all day every day like Joel. But Joel doesn't see it as practice. He just wants to surf — and through this enthusiasm to surf four times a day, he has carved out a unique style.

His surfing looks more suited to point breaks when you see him out at Snapper or Kirra. When you see him surf at these places it's as though they are the only waves he surfs, such is his affinity with a point break. He surfs so relaxed and playfully that it becomes hypnotic. But where he is unique is that he also applies this lack of urgency to his beach-break surfing. He can take off on a closeout and fit three turns in quick succession, but they will flow together as if it they were one. This is because he simply concentrates on one turn at a time. He will have an eye on the next section to help him with manoeuvre choice, and how he wants to flow out of it. But after that choice is made, he concentrates on the turn. And by completing that turn fluently and smoothly, he can flow into the next section, and so on.

His uniqueness was lost on judges when he was growing up. Or at least they couldn't understand it because they hadn't seen it before. On a pro junior panel in '98, the year he won the Junior Series to become Australia's best junior surfer, he had second grade judges scratching their heads and looking over their shoulders for answers. He was so smooth and in control that the judges suspected a lack of criticalness in his surfing. No 17-year-olds surf with that kind of maturity.

'I don't think my surfing evolved in any specific way,' he said. 'I never thought too much about style either. I always just wanted to do certain turns. To do turns like the rest of the guys, but in my own way.'

He was miles ahead and though he won just about every contest, it seemed he wasn't completely appreciated until he got his first shot at the big guns on the WCT.

J-Bay, 1999. Parko went into his first WCT event as a wildcard after a clean sweep of the Junior Series and disposed of the best surfers in the world in the same fashion as the little kids he made look silly back in Australia. He played with the J-Bay walls like a new toy. Unlike his peers, he wasn't under pressure to boost his WCT rating; he was just an 18-year-old kid there to surf J-Bay. In doing so, he became the youngest-ever surfer to win a WCT event — and it was obvious there would be more.

He went straight to Durban on a high for the Gunston 500, a six-star event on the WQS. From round one, first wave, Parko scored a 9.0

PARKO

with a massive carve on a closeout section that would normally have seen a floater or re-entry. But that's Parko. He lost the next round, but didn't click out. He never seems to care too much if he wins or loses, he just went straight back out in the surf and surfed all day. Then went on a bit of a drinking binge that lasted the rest of the year with his good mate David Rastovich.

'We were going crazy that year,' says Rasta. 'It was our first year away and we were just going, "Oh my God, look at all these girls, look at all these parties."'

Parko still managed to fit in a couple more wins in WQS events, which was unprecedented for an 18-year-old. He also won the Billabong World Junior at the end of the year in Hawaii. 'The competitive freak that he is, he just won everything,' says Rasta. It had been a very long year for Parko, who had barely been home since his win at J-Bay in July — and it was now December. Though he was surfing all day every day somewhere on the North Shore with Rasta, you could tell his heart craved Coolangatta. 'I didn't give a fuck about the contests then. I just wanted to go home. Nothing else mattered. I was supposed to stay around for the ASP banquet to collect the World Junior Title, but fuck . . .'

It was an early lesson in responsibility for Parko. He had won contests, won lots of money, been introduced to the party scene and been away for the better part of the year through South Africa, Indonesia, Europe, Brazil and Hawaii. The hype that surrounded him would soon grow stronger. In his first year he handled it well.

'My life's changed a lot,' he said. 'That's just life. I've got to adapt to the situation I'm in and keep myself the same. I was just surfing lots through it all, ya know, and giving it a go. I wasn't taking it too seriously. That was the key I think. Just surfing heaps, going hard and if it's meant to be it's meant to be.'

If ever it was meant to be, it was at Snapper Rocks for the first event of the WCT in 2002, the Quiksilver Kirra Pro. It was Joel's second year on the WCT after qualifying easily in 2000. 'I have a soft spot for Snapper,' he confided. It was apparent one of the three Coolangatta kids would win that event, but after Mick and Deano lost in the third and fourth round, all eyes were on Parko, especially when he advanced to set up the match of the event versus Kelly Slater.

Kelly, the six-time world champ, was back from retirement and had just wiped the floor with the reigning champ, CJ Hobgood, in the previous heat. The super heat was on at Burleigh, and despite pumping waves at Kirra, it seemed the whole coast had turned up to support Joel against the champ, or at least witness perhaps the best heat in history.

'He's surfing better than Kelly, I reckon,' said Luke Egan upon arrival. 'I reckon he's going to kick his arse. And you watch, it's going to be like the old days. Whoever beats Kelly will go on to win the contest.' As he was talking, Joel ran around the point for his heat. He looked focused and determined. The cheers were acknowledged as he ran, but he didn't get caught up in it.

When Parko ran around that point, he looked like he knew he was destined to win it. Slater panicked while Joel picked off his waves. It was uncharacteristic of Kelly, like he knew he had to pull off something special, and desperation showed in his wave choice. Joel sealed it with his last wave, another effortless barrel riding and carving display of playful trickery. He really is a delicate genius. He emerged from a barrel on his last wave, looked out the back, and the ocean and Kelly were lifeless. He knew he had done it. He

PARKO

directed himself to shore and raised his arms to the crowd. At that moment, about half the population of the Gold Coast had their hands in the air. Two days later, he re-enacted it, this time at his beloved Snapper Rocks where he crushed Corey Lopez like a stinkbug. He did exactly what Luke Egan predicted and did a couple of victory laps on the back of his shaper Darren Handley's ski to thank the crowd that had been so good to him all week.

Like a true down-to-earth Aussie, Parko thanked his family, his friends and invited everyone on the beach to come and have a few beers with him in the car park. They were all there, like they are every Friday afternoon in Coolangatta, a bunch of mates celebrating the end of the working week, the end of a good surfing day and probably the most special day in their young friend's life. The party was long and hard. He was number one in the world.

Just a week later he was at the top of his favourite hill above Coolangatta. It boasts views over Snapper, Fingal, Surfers Paradise, Currumbin and Burleigh. With an extra $60 000 in his back pocket, Parko slapped down a deposit on perhaps the best bit of property on the coast.

'It's bizarre,' he said. 'I used to live in that street and used to always go up there and just watch the coast. I can see all the way up to Surfers from here. It's pretty funny that now I own it.'

A week later he celebrated his 21st birthday. It was a good week for the young kid. If things go according to plan, it's going to be an extraordinary career.

PARKO

RABBIT

W ho wouldn't be nervous? we were in Bali for the World Grommet Titles in '94 and to fuel our competitive desires we had two of the sport's greats — Mark Warren and Wayne 'Rabbit' Bartholomew — as our coaches. Mark was cool, calm and collected. Stoked to be around some young energy again and excited about being coach for the Australian team. For Rabbit, it seemed much more personal, as though a loss here could undo all the good work he and his peers did representing our country in the '70s and '80s, establishing

Australia as the best surfing nation in the world. He looked determined. Focused. Strategies were in place and we'd been set straight about the traditions we had to uphold. We hadn't even got off the plane yet.

Rabbit is one of the most determined people you'll ever come across. A pioneer, he first nursed the dream of professional surfing whilst watching his local heroes at Rainbow Bay in the early '70s, mimicking their moves on a playground swing. 'I inflicted a nasty head gash on a bodysurfer on my first attempt,' says Rabbit. We had hooked up via email to do my interview, and Rabbit loves any opportunity to write, having a real gift with words. 'So I spent a year surfing the swing. It was great, I developed style, coordination and balance, all the while remaining landlocked, thus keeping safe those surfers that actually entered the water. Looking back, my sense of balance and timing acquired on the swing served me well, because one fall would have resulted in horrific injury. I'm pretty sure in this litigious age that the swing has been outlawed.'

Within minutes of meeting Rabbit, you become aware of his sharp wit, sense of humour, talent for turning a few words into a piece of art. But behind his skill for public speaking is an ambitious will to succeed, whether it's the telling of a story, surfing a heat, a friendly game of tug-of-war or a meeting with the ASP, it's 100 per cent focus.

When Rabbit worked up the courage to get back in the water, he gave it his all. He also began competing, with much success to his great surprise, and this in turn spawned a dream. He looks over the Gold Coast now like a photo album, a twinkle in his eye as he remembers his roots. 'I used to walk five kilometres to and from school, and it was during those walks that my vision of pro surfing came alive. I dreamed of going from country to country competing in a grand prix style circuit, culminating in Hawaii with big events at Waimea, Pipeline and Sunset Beach. I actually had a board stashed at a halfway house, and that certainly kept the vision nice and fresh on the return march.'

Small brushstrokes at a time, Rabbit's dream, like his character, was starting to take a colourful shape. As a teenager, he began winning contests and as a beneficiary of an intense rivalry with Michael Peterson, emerged from the Gold Coast as one of the most competitive and intimidating guys around, ready to take on the world.

'I was always competitive,' recalls Rabbit. 'I once registered to represent my school in high jump, only to learn on the day, much to my humiliation, that I couldn't even clear the first level. So I wasn't short on ambition, only talent. When I realised I had a gift for surfing, I attacked every opportunity like Attila the Hun. I also had an axe to grind with people who stigmatised surfers as no-good, dropout bums. I would also add that growing up with Michael Peterson and Peter Townend drove me competitively.'

But it wasn't just who he was with, but where he was that formed his personality. A place that would soon be tagged 'Surfer's Paradise'. 'Growing up in Coolangatta in the '60s was magical,' says Rabbit. 'Surfing perfect D-Bah, Snapper and Kirra with a couple of hardcore mates was ridiculous fun, and we knew it! Plus Cooly was a super fun town, especially if you were into playing pinball and shooting pool. I would have to say that the surfing lifestyle on the Goldy in the '60s and '70s was a golden era. I guess it was far too good to keep it a secret, but we sure did get more than our fair share of empty barrels.'

With the perfect training ground, it was now time to get serious and bring to fruition his vision for pro surfing, and Rabbit put all his energy into being the best. There was no such thing as a pro circuit yet

RABBIT

and though Rabbit fared well in one-off events and Australian titles, the surfing world, in terms of events and exposure, was concentrated on three small beaches on Oahu's North Shore in Hawaii — Sunset Beach, Pipeline and Waimea Bay. Anyone worth their weight in salt with a point to prove would have to do it in Hawaii, or fall into professional obscurity. Hawaii could either make you look really good, or really bad, but just getting the opportunity to compete would prove harder than hurdling the high jump back at school.

'In Hawaii, invitations to big events were rare as hens' teeth,' recalls Rabbit. 'For example, there were 24 invitees to the Duke Kahanamoku Classic, and 20 of them were Hawaiian legends. The rest of the world scrapped over the four other spots. Guys like Ian Cairns, Terry Fitzgerald, Paul Neilsen, Peter Townend and Michael Peterson were ahead of me, not to mention Californians, Floridians and national champions of Australia, Great Britain, New Zealand, Japan, USA and Brazil. It was like threading the eye of a needle, and I would write to event promoters Fred Hemmings and George Downing pretty much begging for a start. When no invitations materialised in the mailbox, I took a different path. My new strategy involved a kamikaze attack on Pipe. I reckoned that one good season of sacrifice at Big Pipe would work its magic, and while it took two assaults I had figured right.'

This gung-ho, strategic approach set him apart in a world of people trying to be individuals. He had found his niche and his reputation as a big-wave maniac was growing. But he still hadn't received a start in the events. 'In one comical, yet nerve-wracking situation,' recalls Rabbit, 'there was MR, Shaun Thomson, Mark Warren and myself lined up on the beach in anticipation of the British champion withdrawing on this huge day at Sunset in the '74 Smirnoff.

By virtue of a more ass-licking letter, plus a superior national record, MR got the nod. I loaned him the entry fee, and after winning his heat he had to compete in 25–30-foot Waimea the next day. It was so awesome! Even though I was shattered, when I saw a 35-foot set close the bay out early the next morning, I thought, "Well, maybe better him than me."'

With pro surfing still a pipe dream Rabbit persisted with empty pockets, surviving on adrenaline and keeping that focused determination and vision of where he wanted to be.

'I survived by the seat of my pants, both in the line-up and on the beach. I was very committed to making the big time, and without a national title behind me I figured I'd go harder than everyone on the North Shore. It paid dividends, but boy did I get some people pissed off at me. I had the blinkers on and I went for it at every opportunity. I lived with Ian Cairns [top-five surfer and member of the soon-to-be "Bronzed Aussies", four Australians who banded together to promote themselves], who was not only my mentor at Sunset, but got me in more hot water with the locals than a Hollywood scriptwriter could dream up.

'At Pipe, I ran my own race, developing an insane rivalry with Shaun Thomson ['77 world champ from South Africa] for backside honours. Shaun had the polish and I had the *cojones*, and together we pushed the envelope pretty hard. There were amazing sessions where we knew we'd gone where no one had gone before, but the price was some horrific wipeouts, hold-downs, reef plants, free-falls and stuffings. It was a whole lot of fun, something that will remain with me forever. The good thing about getting old is not getting caught inside at third reef Pipe.'

Rabbit, though, was beginning to make enemies in high places and came down to earth with a big hard thud. At the time, the 'Sultan of

RABBIT

Speed' and fellow wordsmith Terry Fitzgerald had warned him: 'If you're going to play the bad guy, you better be the best.' Rabbit, who had just written an article for *Surfer* — the biggest surfing magazine in the world, published in America — called 'Bustin' Down The Door', where he gloated about the new Aussie push and dominance over the Americans, didn't listen. His brashness and go-for-it attitude had started to put him in hot water — and where it really mattered, in Hawaii. And so began his banishment from the North Shore.

'God, I was in deep shit there for a while,' says Rabbit. 'Luckily I was so naive and stupid that I didn't quite realise how much trouble I was in. For a whole season, as the case mounted on me beach by beach, I was totally oblivious to the danger. I was the surfing equivalent of Mr Magoo, blindly driving through life-threatening situations as though [I were on] a theme park rollercoaster. I was banished from the North Shore from October 3, 1976, until November 21, the day before the Smirnoff [the biggest surfing event at Sunset Beach]. I holed up at Turtle Bay, which with its golf courses, condos and security, lulled me into a false sense of security. I was actually no safer, plus they knew where I was, so when the periodic rabbit hunt took place, I was easily found, but as it transpired, not as easy to catch.' Over a period of weeks Rabbit was beaten to a pulp by the ultra-territorial locals, losing teeth and constantly looking through black eyes. It was in these dark times that his true spirit shone through.

'Only once did I consider running for the airport,' he admits. 'But I couldn't find anyone ready to run the gauntlet with public enemy number one on board, so I hung tough, or at least I hung. There was really nowhere to run. I instinctively knew that if I bolted for Oz I would be running forever, and the North Shore still figured big time in my dreams. So I copped my lickings, developing quite a survival mechanism in the process. There was definitely fear and trepidation on my arrival back on the North Shore (in '77), and suffice it to say I had learned my lesson. Looking back, the whole episode taught me respect, and it was kind of like a ritual of manhood, setting me up mentally for my next level.'

The next level, of course, was world champion and as close as he'd been in previous years, Bugs knew it was within his reach. He chased it with a passion and competitive approach that, in the softening of world sport in general, would leave most sportsmen of today quivering. He would play mind games and get incredibly physical in the water. They were hardcore days and Rabbit won the title by being the hardest.

'Being crowned world champion was the realisation of a dream, a feeling akin to making the final ascent on my personal Everest. It's one thing to build notoriety for a brand of surfing and achieving great heights — for me, Pipeline — but to officially arrive at the number one spot is the stamp that one really needs to establish a credible image.'

Rabbit was now a household name and had done a lot to help create a healthy image for the sport, challenging the lazy stereotype of surfers as 'dropout bums'. But in dedicating his life to winning the world title, he had, in his own words, 'missed out on being a teenager'. At this time, Bugs was hanging out with a hot young crew of surfers like Gary 'Kong' Elkerton and Chappy Jennings; guys that partied pretty hard. He took them under his wing and recaptured a lot of his youth. But there was a price. His relationship with his wife was suffering, and so was his ranking.

'I partied hard partly to mask my personal devastation in losing the title race to Tom Carroll in '84, and partly to mask my deep sense of

RABBIT

failure after the breakdown of my marriage in '83. It was very self-indulgent, very hard-paced and sometimes got very messy. I lost interest in performance surfing, and watched indifferently while, after a decade in the top five, I slipped firstly out of the top 10, then tumbled out of the top 16, sometimes pulling out of events to hit a rock concert on the other side of the country.'

They say you can't keep a good man down and Rabbit is no exception. Though he stalled in between tour life and what's known to the rest of the population and feared by professional surfers as 'the real world', Bugs soon found his niche and began to attack his new goals with the same voracity as his world title bid. It always came back to his passion for surfing and the dream he had so long ago. 'I went back to my grass roots,' he says. 'Coaching kids, staging pro-am surf contests and putting a lot of time into the Snapper Rocks Junior Development Program. It was a blast. I really needed to do it for my personal development, and things began evolving all over again. I basically dedicated my life work to surfing, plus I was doing a fair bit of environmental work, but when I took on the national coaching directorship I consolidated my resources and focused my energies on developing champions.'

With the passion and dedication that Rabbit possesses, anything he sets his mind to has panned out the gold. The focus was back and as Australia's coach in amateur world titles, he did make champions. He was also contest director for the Billabong Kirra Pro for a few years and, somehow, one of the world's most fickle waves turned to perfection for the event, gaining media exposure all over the world. People were saying he had a direct line to Huey the surf god. Others put his success down to his positive energy and incredible self-belief. From there he became more involved with the ASP. And his resurrection couldn't have come at a better time.

'It wasn't long before I sat on the ASP board of directors as a regional rep,' says Rabbit. 'I do remember walking into a surfers' meeting some years earlier in Hawaii. In attendance were the champions of the day, including Curren, Carroll, Pottz, Elko, Macauley. As I walked up the stairs they asked me when I was going to take over this thing and fix it up. I laughed it off, but I had already considered this career move, and that fateful walk up the stairs seeded a thought in me that I figured I'd activate some day, when the time was right. That day came in early '99, and I knew the timing had presented the biggest challenge for both myself and the ASP itself.

'I took it on fully knowing of the level of unrest and disillusionment in the ranks. I do believe it has been part of my destiny to reach this cycle at this time, but at least the ASP has a leader who loves the sport as much or more passionately than anyone on earth. I've always felt comfortable working in an environment where one is forced to overachieve just to keep your head above water. It has been an extremely tumultuous couple of years, but there is something to show for all the toil.'

Indeed there is. I remember sitting in a room at Sunset Beach one Hawaiian winter when all the WQS competitors had called for a meeting. The faint smell of mutiny was in the air and there was talk about leaving the ASP whose administration was far from adequate at the time. When the world champ walked through the doors just after sunset, and began one of his legendary motivation talks about the future of the ASP, everyone listened. We knew we were heading into a positive era with a leader whose dedication to the cause and motivation for the sport eclipsed all who had come before him. He has since helped surfers double their prizemoney, increased the good wave venues on the tour and recently helped seal a multimillion-dollar deal with International Management Group (IMG) and subsidiary Transworld International (TWI) that will take surfing to the world via the production and distribution of TV news feeds from the WCT and dedicated WCT television programs.

'I suppose I'm a bit of a dreamer,' Rabbit says, 'and by a fortunate set of circumstances have been able to work on fulfilling most of my dreams. To that end, I am a fairly driven individual. I tend to keep plugging away at projects until they are completed with a satisfactory result. When I commit to something I have an unfaltering belief in coming through with the goods. By compartmentalising each process, I can more accept setbacks and, after working through the problems, forge ahead toward a favourable outcome. I have always appreciated the simple pleasures, such as a good surf session, and with that as my foundation stone, can tackle some pretty hefty challenges.'

Back in Kuta in '94, the World Grommet Titles had been stitched up the Rabbit-coached Australian team. But Rabbit wasn't finished. He took us all out to Tubes, a surfers' café, to celebrate. In the café there was a horizontal bungee jump in which participants, strapped to the bungee cord, have to run across the room and try to grab a beer positioned on a seat. Of course, it's designed to be out of reach, and we all had a go but fell short of grabbing it. However, Rabbit stepped up and against all odds, against all the laws of physics, crawled along the floor, with grazes from his nails to his knees, and grabbed the beer to thunderous applause. It may have taken 25 minutes, but he was determined to make it. Which said a lot about Rabbit — for him it's not over 'til it's over.

RABBIT

Maz

QUINN

The *haka* is a potent symbol of New Zealand, a dance traditionally done by Maoris before going into war. It is meant to send fear into their opponents before the battle. But when I saw Maz Quinn do it for the first time in '94, it was not very convincing. He was the shy boy up the back with the confused choreography and an embarrassed step. The little green kiwi necklace around his neck danced with more intimidating rhythm. And I mean no disrespect.

I'll never forget what happened 14 hours later. It was his first heat in the

FRANK

'94 World Junior Titles and in one wave he put more fear into his competitors than a haka danced on land mines in a closed room. Maz may not be the most convincing exponent of the haka, but he is definitely proud of where he is from. He still wears that kiwi, but it's a little more fixed now. 'I lost my necklace,' he says, showing me a small flightless bird etched in ink on his bicep. 'So I got a tattoo instead. I can't lose that.'

Maz's shyness on land is in stark contrast to his intensity when he is on a wave. The boy from Gisborne on the east side of New Zealand's North Island picks it up another level when he is in the water. It's obvious he learnt how to dance with the ocean first and last.

To anyone who has seen Maz's explosive surfing, he is a true entertainer whether he is coming first or last. 'At the end of the day, I just wanted to go for a surf and for people to take notice,' he says. 'I didn't want to be seen as a shit surfer. One of my main goals was just to be known as a good surfer. If I can do that, I'll be happy.'

Right now, Maz is pretty happy. Not just because he has qualified for the top 46, the first New Zealander ever to do so, but because he's back at home and having a break from his gruelling schedule. And what a place to break. The air in New Zealand is fresh and the hills are an electric green, bisected by flowing rivers and creeks. It's almost like Australia, but with a condensed topography, and often the country's inhabitants argue they fit more sports stars in their two small islands than Australia does as the biggest island on earth. They definitely hold their own — and Maz is one of their finest.

The beach next to Maz's house is up there with the best. It is long and riddled with deep channels and rip-banks. 'I grew up here,' says Maz proudly. 'Right in front of Wainui Beach. It's like a little surf city.

Everything here sort of revolves around the beaches. An hour or so either side is just endless reefs and points too, so you just need the right swell direction and we have perfect waves.'

Not only is Wainui Maz's favourite beach, but he's the beach's favourite surfer. He is a local hero. He even has a burger named after him in the main street — the 'Maz Burger'.

Despite his love for his home beach, Maz likes nothing better than jumping in a car and travelling. The landscape in New Zealand surprises you at every corner and, as the jokes you hear in Australia will confirm, there are sheep everywhere. So many, in fact, that across the country they indent the steep hills like the steps of a pyramid with their hooves as they forage higher for food.

'Dunedin is one of my favourite spots,' says Maz of the southernmost city in the South Island. 'They have the best waves. It's just really cold. I spend a lot of time down there in summer. You can get away with a short arm steamer and there are so many crazy places if you know where to go.'

When Maz got to a certain age, he realised that if he wanted to get to the next level, he had to move across the Tasman and subject himself to the best Australian talent. Of course he copped the best Australian jokes too. 'Yeah, I copped a bit. It's just the Aussie sense of humour though, so I didn't let it worry me.'

Despite having the core of New Zealand's surfing talent in his main street at Gisborne, with guys like Blair Stewart and Damon Gunness as neighbours, he realised the value of contesting the Australian Junior Series — without doubt the most competitive junior circuit in the world. Every winner of the series has gone on to the top 20 in the world, and that was something Maz quietly had his eye on.

MAN QUINN

'I'd won a couple of Cadets and a few open titles I think,' he says of his New Zealand career. His vague memory makes you realise that from an early age Maz placed all his competitive importance on a world scale — starting with Australia.

'They've got a pretty good circuit there in New Zealand, eight or 10 contests a year,' he says. 'The boardriding clubs in Gisborne are real active as well, which helped a lot. But I knew if I wanted to get anywhere, I had to come to Australia and do well on the Junior Series. So I lived in Sydney for eight months and did the series full-on for about three years.'

Maz developed very close friendships with a lot of Australians who played on his shy character and fed off his explosive talent. Guys like Jake Patterson, Ozzie Wright and Sam Carrier all spent a lot of time with him. Maz also came at a time when the Junior Series was incredibly competitive. Danny Wills, Will Lewis, Jay Phillips, Chris Davidson and Luke Hitchings were a few. Maz worked hard to beat these guys and in his last year, all his hard work paid off. He won. 'It was my last year so I was pretty stoked,' he said.

When I say hard work, Maz is not someone who trains like a demon; he just puts in about 24 hours' surfing a day, rain, hail or shine. He's the keenest surfer you'll ever come across. I remember one day in France he went surfing at about 8 o'clock in the morning and it was pumping. He stayed out without food or a break until 6 o'clock that night. He does it all the time.

'I've always been like that since I was a grommy. When the surf's really good I'll just stay out all day. Sometimes when you get in a rhythm of getting good waves it's hard to come in. I figure, what else am I going to do, so I just stay out there until that rhythm goes away.'

But it never seems to, unless he goes to Hawaii, but he still finds an excuse to stay out all day. 'In places like Hawaii I do stay out for a while because it takes longer to get the waves. There are also so many guys out there who are ripping. Every single pro surfer is there, so you can't waste it.'

At that stage of his career Maz was spending a lot of his time in Oz competing. 'Just being in Australia was so good,' he says, 'because you can go to any beach and there will be at least 10 standouts, where at home there are only one or two.' But once he started on the WQS he started going home again more often; the fresh air, surrounding mountains and endless rip banks called for him. So did the 'Maz Burger'.

Although he'd steadily improved thanks to his trans-Tasman commitment, for years Maz was the king of inconsistency.

In focusing on his free surfing, his competition act became stale. His surfing was so hot and cold, the kid really did struggle, despite his ability, and he needed attention. The best way to describe Maz's surfing is explosive. He doesn't pull out of turns, like some surfers do. It's pure 100 per cent commitment. Hard and fast off the bottom and often sliding out of top turns — such is his intensity. When he finds his feet and his rhythm with the wave, he can get on a devastating roll, using his last turn as the basis for his next turn which he'll always push a little harder. When he gets going, he gets going. The only thing that stops him is when he falls off — which does come with the slippery territory. 'I didn't have much confidence in heats and I seemed to give up really easily,' he says. 'If I took off on a wave and bogged on my second or third turn, I'd just flick off, so pissed off. I'm a bit of a perfectionist like that. If I don't start a wave really well it's hard for me to finish it really well. But now I've got a bit more experience and I've learnt more about heats. Before now, every year I was making a final and that was pretty much it, I'd

MAZ QUINN

blow out. So I just worked on getting three waves. I sat down with a really good friend of mine at home and he said to me, "Look, you're surfing good enough, you've just got to get the three waves." It just seemed to click after that and I made the heats I needed to make. Looking back at it now it seems so easy.'

After what felt like an eternity of close calls and should-have-beens, Maz finally qualified for the WCT in 2001, cementing himself as a professional competitor, not just another free surfing talent like a Brenden Margieson. Maz wanted to take it to that next level and he also loves competing. 'The beating people and getting beaten doesn't do that much for me, but just having something to work for keeps me motivated in the surf every day. You know when you get a new board or something, you just want to surf all day. Surfing with good guys, whether it be free surfing or competing, it's the same thing for me. It just makes me want to be surfing every day.'

Of course qualifying made Maz a national hero. All of a sudden the shy boy had to talk. He's getting better at it, but I imagine it's improved about as much as his haka. 'Yeah, they were sort of picking up on it [the fact that Maz was going to qualify] after each result I got. I was getting emails and phone calls from everyone at home, especially the media. Then when I made it, it was crazy. Every TV show, radio station ... It was good. I've sort of learnt how to deal with it. It can only boost your career so ...'

More than anything though, it was a boost for New Zealand surfing. The small country in the South Pacific had another export beyond the woolly beasts that graze on the pastures that surround his home. 'Yeah, hopefully it can show any NZ grommy that they can make it. I hope that me making it pushes the other guys. I'm sure I won't be the last New Zealander to qualify. I'm sure Bobby Hansen and my brother will qualify and do it for NZ as well.'

I'm sure his younger brother will too. Jay, his name is. And with a World Junior Title under his belt already, a residential stint in Australia and a certain inconsistency, it looks like he is well on the way to following in Maz's footsteps. His time will come. We know that now.

'Yeah, he sort of is like me,' says Maz. 'As soon as he switches his free surfing to contest surfing he'll take off.'

'Are you worried that Jay will be a threat?'

'Yeah, I'll be worried when he makes the WCT.'

The Kiwis now boast another hero in their proud sporting heritage. If the surfers coming through are half as good as Maz, perhaps they will have another sport to embrace like rugby. Maybe it will inspire a whole new generation of Kiwi surfers to come out of the land of the long white cloud. I just hope they do the haka better than Maz.

MAZ QUINN

Peter

TROY

I was nervous when I arrived at Peter Troy's house, but excited too. I drove a borrowed '83 Falcon up a windy hill above Coolum Beach on the Sunshine Coast, where rosellas, cockatoos and kookaburras could be heard amongst the sanctuary of eucalypt trees. The northeast trade wind brought further comfort to his hidden oasis. He laughed when I had to climb out the window because of broken door handles. 'Yep, common problem that,' he said as I extended my hand. 'What is it? An '83?'

Peter's wife offered me a drink and

I sat down opposite him, about to hear just about the best story ever. At 63, Troy was inducted into the Australian Surfing Hall of Fame for an extraordinary life in surfing: the first to surf Bells, the first to surf a shortboard in Australia, the man who started the Bells Beach Easter Classic, the person who introduced surfing to Brazil, and discovered Nias. He hitchhiked to all these places; from Peru through the Amazon to Brazil, through the Arctic Circle, across the Sahara and to Mount Everest on a motorbike. It is an incredible story that started in the chilled southern waters of Bells Beach, where in 1949 an 11-year-old Troy surfed there for the very first time.

'We blew up these surf mats — and just went surfing,' he recalled. 'In those days after the surf mats we were riding the clubby-type hollow boards because the introduction of Malibus in Australia didn't happen until 1956 (since Malibus had first arrived in Australia in 1915, they had transformed into a longer, surf rescue-style board). I think the events in my life were lucky — [as they were] for all of those who were surfing in earlier times. Because I just happened to grow up in Torquay, I just happened to be 18 years old in 1956, and was selected in the Olympics to represent surf lifesaving and in surfboard-riding demonstrations at the Olympic Games at my home beach at Torquay. The Hawaiian lifeguards were there and they had full Malibus — famous names like Tom Zahn, Greg Noll, Bob Burnside and Mike Bright. It was on that day on 26 November 1956 on my home beach that I had the opportunity of walking down the beach and saying, "Hey can I have a ride on one of those?" So, indirectly, I was there on the first day that we rode shortboards in Australia, and this happened before they went to Sydney and the surfing revolution started.'

PETER TROY

And so began the life of a dedicated surfer: 'We were left in Victoria with only a memory of one day, and we had to try and think of what the boards looked like so we could try and copy them, and we could only do this with marine plywood and hardwood sides, and hollow insides. That was sort of the first year of the Malibu.

'There was a little group of surfers in Victoria, and primarily at Torquay, who wanted to shape boards and who had that rebellious attitude of wanting to break away from white shirts and suits and going to work in a bank. Rock'n'roll was just starting and the Beatles hadn't even been heard of. We were there not knowing what we were doing. But we were wanting to break away from having to turn up at seven o'clock for surf lifesaving and do a patrol on the beach, paint the clubhouse, stand to attention when the whistle blew. We found that very difficult, in an abstract way — to break away. So we thought, "Well there's one place we can hide, we can go to Bells Beach and they won't know we're there." And so we actually went to Bells to escape doing patrols and being in the surf club, and so 30 of us formed the Bells Beach Boardriders in 1958.'

A year earlier Troy had left school. 'I didn't want to work in an insurance office or a bank, but I had that dream that I could hire out deck chairs or rubber surf mats on the beach or I suppose in today's vernacular, coach surfing or be a professional surfer, but there was no way you could do that. There were no shops, no surfboard factories. There was just no industry yet.

'Some guys who were capable might have made us a couple of boards in their garage of a weekend, but they only made it for the cost of the materials, and maybe their labour time. Another man called Vic Tantau and I started making surfboards under the name of "T Boards", and for some strange reason the idea was that maybe we

PETER TROY

could sell more boards if we ran a surfing contest; and so he and I ran the first Bells event at the end of January 1962. Two surfers were down there from Sydney, Robbie Lane and Glen Ritchie, and they had a great contest. They went back to Sydney and they said, "Hey, we've been in Victoria and there's surf at a place called Bells Beach."

'Different people were ringing me up and saying, "Are you going to hold a contest next year?" And I said, "Yes", and they said "Well can you shift it to Easter, so we can get the Easter vacation and not have to take our holidays and we can drive down on the Friday, surf the contest on Saturday and Sunday and drive back on Monday?" So in 1963 the first Easter event at Bells was born.'

The Bells Beach Easter Classic is now in its 31st year (it went pro in 1971) and is probably the most successful surfing event of all time. By bringing surfers down to Bells, Troy was indirectly treading a path into the new world of travel.

'Towards the end of 1962, Bob Evans, who had taken some surfers to Hawaii in the year previous, was ringing me up and saying, "Can I come down? I just started a surf magazine called *Surfing World*, and I want to bring down a young surfer so I can take some photos." He wasn't interested in the local surfers because our standard of surfing wasn't suitable in selling the image. The young guy he brought down was a teenaged Midget Farrelly [who would later become Australia's first world champion in '64]. He and Bob Evans stayed at my home and we went down to Bells. The story was written, the photographs taken, and the second issue of *Surfing World* magazine in Australia had Bells Beach on the cover and a whole story inside showing Midget and local surfers. Of course that was when the whole of New South Wales and Queensland and everyone knew that there was surf down there.

PETER TROY

'It was also during 1962 that Bruce Brown was travelling around the world with Mike Hynson and Robert August with the idea of making a movie on surfing in all different countries around the world in their summer, which eventually went on to become *The Endless Summer*. But when he came through Australia from South Africa, every place that he actually touched on, or visited, the surf was terrible. In Sydney he met Bob Evans who had some movie film of surf carnivals and some early surfing of Midget with different people and he gave some film to Bruce Brown. Bruce took it to America and said "That was really nice of that guy," and so he sent out to Australia a surf movie that he'd made a year earlier called *Surfing Hollow Days*. So Bob Evans had in his hands the first-ever surf movie that was going to be shown in Australia.

'When the kids, who'd never seen surfing, said the movie was absolutely sensational, Evans realised the potential that everyone in Australia might like to see this surfing of big waves in Hawaii. It also opened up the idea of travel, and here is the word, this "travel", because no one had done it. So he rang me up and said, "Would you like to show a surf movie in Victoria?" Of course, I said, "yeah," and so I was the first person to show a surf movie in Victoria and that turned out to be in I think, February, March 1963, before the Easter '63 contest. It was very, very successful financially. I had no idea what money I made, but I was able to buy a block of land and build a shop, I was able to buy a sports car and I was able to quit my job. I had money in my pocket and with the rest of the money that I made from showing those movies I was able to travel for three years around the world without working. That was all done in three weeks showing a surf movie.'

He got comfortable while I was wearing the edge of my seat. It was that word 'travel:' this was what I'd come for.

PETER TROY

'I was very paranoid about travelling at first because I couldn't speak any language and I was absolutely petrified about where I would be able to eat my food, where I would sleep. The obvious answer at that time was that there was a lot of migration into Australia after the war and there were boats bringing out migrants, and ships were all going back to Europe empty. They were offering concession travel, so I got on a ship in Melbourne and went to England.

'The idea was to compete in France and see if I could win one of their early European titles. That would have given me entry into the semi-finals at Makaha in Hawaii which was, in those days, the only real surfing contest where you could make a name for yourself. So I won the European Title and had a lot of travel between May 1963 and December 1963 to actually get to Hawaii. I had to sail on a yacht across the Atlantic, and on a stopover in America I ended up sleeping in a hearse with "Murph the Surf", a Californian surfer/shaper who was later involved in a massive jewel robbery.

'At that time I was unique, and the ticket was having a surfboard under my arm and an Australian accent. I mean even today you might be an oddity on a suburban train in Bombay in India with a surfboard, but you were an oddity anywhere in the world with a surfboard back then. Most people didn't even know what a surfboard was. People would stop and look and that's how you met people. You're carrying this 10-foot thing under your arm and everyone's going, "Wow!" It's like travelling around the world with a grand piano.'

Troy arrived in Hawaii in December 1963, at a time when the infamous Pipeline had only been surfed for two months. 'Butch Van Artsdalen was one of the pioneers there and there were cameras on the beach filming a bodysurfer called Larry Lumbek who was doing spinners in the tube at Pipeline. Because photographers were there we thought we'd better go out and surf. So we paddled out and I didn't know how big it was, probably about eight foot or something, but it was really the wrong size, it was breaking on the inside reef, not big enough to be safe, and I didn't know anything about the right take-off points. I was really wanting to get exposure in these magazines and become known worldwide and that was my downfall because I actually had a very bad accident. I went face-first into the bottom, broke my board, ended up with severe lacerations and pieces of reef stuck in my face, and when I came out of the water that's what they captured on the cameras. They thought that was fantastic because I became the first person seriously hurt at Pipeline, and ended up in the magazines for that reason. Because of that I couldn't actually surf in Makaha, but everyone knew who I was because I had this black eye and stitches all over my face and everyone was going, "Well, that's the guy that got hurt at Pipeline".

'At that time the Peruvians were trying to organise an international contest, which would arguably mark the beginning of world surfing. Felipe Pomar [the Peruvian world champion] had been asked to invite one surfer from each major surfing country in the world to have their expenses paid and travel to Peru. He asked me if I would go, and I accepted, of course. I went down there with Phil Edwards from California, Fred Hemmings from Hawaii, Joel de Rosnay from France and a guy called Max We Heland from South Africa. We were the international core of surfing in Peru.

'I suppose that was the exact moment I became a traveller and an adventurer, instead of a surfer. I had a year to kill in Peru before the World Titles, and after being there for six months and living the life and experiencing the culture there, I wanted to see more. So I was taken

PETER TROY

up into the mountains [the Andes] and put on the top of a truck of Gaucho Indians and I said, "I'm going round South America and I'll be back in six months' time for the world championships."'

Troy decided he'd hitchhike through the biggest rainforest in the world and come out the other side in Brazil. 'I was taken to these mountain villages, and in the end I was sleeping in dirt-floored cabins with smoke stains all over the walls, eating out of a communal bowl with a whole family and sleeping on mats on the floor. I ended up [speaking] a horrible language that was a mixture of eight different countries and dialects.

'Later I was living with headshrinking Indians in the Amazon, and using blow darts to kill and eat animals. You go through all these adventures and you come out the end and you tell people. They go, "Wow, that's impossible!" and you go, "well, that's just the way it worked."

'So anyway, I arrived after walking, paddling canoes, and floating on driftwood to the mouth of the Amazon, which is 220 kilometres wide, so that was an experience in itself. I arrived halfway through '64. I came out of the Amazon jungle and out to the coastline and I thought, "Well, I'm here now. What do I do?" I decided to travel all the way down the coast of Brazil, just to see if there might be surf. But, because I'd been in the jungles and everything, I didn't actually have a surfboard with me. I'd left those in Peru because I was going back in nine months' time, and it just seemed totally foolhardy to try and travel across the Amazon with a surfboard under my arm.

'As it was I had had to get rid of my watch and I had to just become like the peasants were because if I carried any books or I was seen to be educated, they weren't going to take me along as one of them. So I really had to use the same sort of hammock that they would sleep in, stay in the same place, eat the same food and sleep with them, a very primitive type of lifestyle. When I came out the other end I wasn't really a European at all. My weight had gone from maybe 90 kilos down to about 60, and I had amoeba type things inside of me that I'd got out of the Amazon somewhere that were chewing up all my food vitamins, and you know, quite a lot of bugs, parasites and illnesses from things in my feet and toes, and from not washing.'

Peter ended up going all the way to Rio de Janeiro, where a chance encounter led to him introducing surfing to Brazil. 'I was walking along the famous beach called Copacabana and in the distance in front of me on the footpath I could see a guy carrying a surfboard. That was the first surfboard I'd seen since leaving Peru. He was a 15-year-old French boy and I asked him, "Is this your board?" He said, "Yes, I just got it today from my father." He said his father was the Ambassador here from France, and he'd just bought a surfboard for him in New York, although he'd never surfed in his life. And this boy was walking along with this board under his arm not knowing where to go or how to even surf. So I said, "Well, if we can see somewhere where there's some waves I'll show you how to ride it." We reached the end of Copacabana and we walked through these couple of streets up over a headland. There was a left-hand wave breaking off this rock reef onto the beach. So I got out there and caught some waves and sort of ran up and hung five over the nose and did a couple of laybacks, cutbacks and things and was having a good time. Then I looked towards the beach and there were five hundred to a thousand people standing there, looking at this guy doing something that they'd never seen before.

'They'd seen me doing things that they just couldn't comprehend. Two of them came forward, and took me back to their house because they wanted to be the person to put me up — just like I wanted to be

PETER TROY

the guy to put Midget up. I drew a template of a board for them on the floor of the house on brown paper and we tried to find a way to buy materials to make a board. Other guys came around as well and wanted to know about this sport of surfing.'

Troy became a local hero and made the papers for introducing surfing to Brazil. People were dying to meet him, and through this he had more opportunity to travel. 'There was a guy there from Argentina who was studying medicine and he said, "If you come down to Argentina you can stay with me." When I did reach Buenos Aires, my story of creating surfing in Brazil had gone ahead of me, and this guy let me stay in his apartment. He had a 15-year-old friend whose father happened to be the Minister of Health in the Argentine Government. So I had dinner with him one night. At the dinner table the Minister of Health found out I'd been in a surf club in Australia and that I knew about resuscitation and Australian lifesaving methods, and it turned out that Argentina desperately wanted to know about that. He thought, "Well this is good for me," so he mentioned this to the President of Argentina, and I was taken along and had a 20-minute interview with the President. The President asked me where I was going, and what I was doing. I said, "I'm trying to see your country and I want to go down to the very south in Tierra del Fuego." He must have mentioned it to the Minister of Health. "Well, when the Health plane goes off next time, put your guest on there, he can use it to go down to the tip of South America." So I was actually given a plane by the President of Argentina. It was beautiful, because that sort of thing really can't happen today. It's not going to happen that way ever again.'

Troy commands a lot of respect when he talks. He is confident and intelligent, an incredible storyteller with an amazing tale to tell. But he was only warming up.

'So I got to Tierra del Fuego and then I got bitten by a new bug. I was in a place called Puerto Williams which was the southernmost community of people living in the world. I thought, "Well, I've made it here, why don't I hitchhike to the northernmost town of the world?" That turned out to be quite a long adventure.' But there were no time restrictions on Troy. He didn't have to be home for dinner at six o'clock. 'In the next eight months, I travelled from the tip of South America to nine degrees from the North Pole, hitchhiking.'

And of course there were plenty more adventures along the way. 'I'd been told that there was a Chilean cargo boat that operated up through all the fjords in southern Chile and met up with the southern tip of the Pan-American Highway [the longest highway in the world that stretches along the western coast of both American continents]. I thought, "Well, that's obviously the way for me to go." And so I got on one of these boats that left once every seven weeks. I bought the cheapest ticket which put me right down in the bottom. I was sleeping on bare steel — it was freezing — and each day I had one bowl of soup and stale bread as food.

'We docked in this harbour one day and were told to be back at three o'clock. I came over the hill of this town just after two o'clock, and the ship was starting to turn around in the bay to go. I became hysterical because I wasn't going to get out of this place. I ran down and asked someone to row me out to the ship. As we got alongside the ship he got frightened that he was going to be pulled into the propellers. The crew knew that I was there but they couldn't find a ladder to put over the side. So one guy threw a rope over the bow, and I grabbed hold of the rope frantically and started to try and climb up onto the ship. But I got up under the bow and in the end I just had to hang there and wrap the rope around my feet. The guy on the rowing boat had left and the ship's starting to go out into the ocean, and they've got this foreigner hanging off the bow! In the end someone told the captain but he said he couldn't stop the ship because of the currents and everything, so they eventually got me on board on one of the rope ladders. I got taken up to the captain and he said, "Where did you come from? I didn't know I had you on this ship." I said, "I live down on the bottom." He told me, "Oh, you can't stay down there."'

Securing better accommodation on the boat, Troy found his way to Chile, and then on to some obscure islands called Isla Juan Fernandez, where he stayed in the cave where Alexander Selkirk, the character who Robinson Crusoe was based on, had lived. Then his massive northward journey continued all the way to the edge of the North Pole, hitchhiking by boat, plane, car ...

'I worked with two guys in a little freight boat in the north of Norway out in all those little fishing islands, living in the hull, and ended up on this place called Spitsbergen, nine degrees from the North Pole, with polar bear hunters. I came back down and travelled for three days with a man in Finland who drove a road grader. I couldn't speak a word to him! Those sort of things just kept on happening.'

Troy decided that Africa should be his next port of call, but how would he get there? He met someone who told him he could get paid to carry passports into Israel. The plan went wrong, though, when he got picked up by the police in Syria and was banned from all Arab countries in the world.

Having survived that setback eventually he made it to Windhoek, the capital of South West Africa (Namibia). 'I met these German guys there and they said that they were going to try and drive a Land Rover, a four-wheel drive, from Windhoek across the southern part of Africa

PETER TROY

and come out in Kenya. I looked on the map and I went, "Oh yeah, sounds good. I could probably hitchhike that". So I just started to hitchhike. It happened to be the weekend, the day before the Easter school holidays, and a guy was driving along in a truck, and he stopped to pick me up. In the back of the truck were a lot of school children from isolated farmlands and farmhouses. This guy was one of the farmers and he'd gone into the main city to take all the children from all these farms back. So when he got to the last farm he said, "Well ... this is it," and I'm the last guy. He said, "If you're going to Kenya you go straight up that road over there", and that was like saying "Well if you're going to Alice Springs from Brisbane, you just keep going past Birdsville over that road out there". I was in the middle of the Kalahari Desert. I had something like 492 kilometres between where this guy dropped me off and this town called Meru.'

Troy was dropped off at five o'clock in the afternoon, and after a few hours walking, it got dark. No vehicle had come that day and he was in the middle of the Kalahari. 'I just lay down and tried to sleep. Maybe I slept from eight o'clock to one in the morning, and then I'm awake, and I'm going, "Oh yeah, what'll I do, sit here, throw a few stones? I might as well get up and walk". So I got up and walked. I walked all that day and not one vehicle passed until I went to sleep that night. And this went on for four days. In four days and four nights I didn't see a vehicle, and I had to keep going, I couldn't go back. I don't know how far I went. I think I actually walked two hundred and something kilometres.

'Then someone came along. Of course he just couldn't believe it, that there's a guy up there walking. So he picked me up and told everyone that he'd found this guy walking, and he gave me a room in his house. That's how it happened. People would find me and want to hear my story, probably so they could tell their friends how they found this crazy white guy in the middle of the desert, or wherever I was. Then I went off with him a few days later and we went right out across the other side of the Kalahari. We went through the area where the famous film *Born Free* was shot. We went through there and we came out on the Zambezi where Victoria Falls is. And so I'd crossed the Kalahari!'

It was three years since Troy had left his Torquay home. The final leg of his epic trek was in South Africa, where he surfed Jeffreys Bay in '66. 'There were surfers there, a lot of guys going down from Port Elizabeth, and it was really on the South Africans' map, but it wasn't known worldwide. Cape St Francis had been in Bruce Brown's movie [*The Endless Summer*], but Cape St Francis wasn't Jeffreys.'

From there, Troy decided he'd had enough and looked for a way to get home. He found a ship that was going from Durban to Perth, then simply hitchhiked across the Nullarbor and arrived in his hometown of Torquay.

'I walked into the kitchen at home and said hello to my mother and she didn't know who I was. I was just totally different, she didn't recognise me, not at all — and it took me three hours to convince her I was her son. I had hair hanging down the middle of my back, I had a beard, I was absolutely black from being chewed up in the sun and my clothes were ratshit. She'd seen a young man go away with a tie and a suit on, and this freak came home!'

Back in Australia, Troy became partners with famous moviemaker Paul Witzig and together they bought the Manly Silver Screen, a cinema. As well as showing films — including surf movies — they also put on rock'n'roll concerts and stage shows.

PETER TROY

They were crazy times. 'We had transvestites coming over from Oxford Street on the ferry and staying in our picture theatre all night, doing all sorts of stage acts. Then the next day we'd clean the cinema out and we'd be doing *Snow White and the Seven Dwarfs* for Manly High School. Then that'd become a surf movie at five o'clock and then another movie at eight o'clock. Then at 11 p.m. it'd be rock'n'roll, and then at two o'clock we'd sleep on the couch.'

With the money he'd made from the cinema, Troy decided to take another trip, this time to Indonesia. The first guys to surf Indo had done so in 1970 and '71, but Troy wasn't far behind. Once again, though, injury stuck. 'I got a surfboard embedded in my back at Uluwatu and nearly lost my life there, stuck in Balinese hospitals that were really dirty. But I got through that, then I thought I could sail an Indonesian boat back to Australia and that sunk. I could have virtually gone over and maybe discovered G-Land, but didn't really know there was surf there. I got on a yacht and went north around Timor and ended up in Darwin.'

Back in Australia, Troy and his girlfriend decided in 1974 to travel through Southeast Asia by motorbike. The plan? To ride their motorbikes from Torquay to Tibet and, ultimately, Mount Everest. Along the way Cyclone Tracy hit, which grounded them in Darwin for a while, but they got back on track and found themselves in unusual company, on a *Women's Weekly* cruise with a boat full of 60-, 70- and 80-year-old holiday makers. It was bound for Hong Kong, but the ship stopped in Bali.

'They put our motorbikes on the life raft, put the life raft over the ship and dropped us down the side without passing any Immigration or Customs. We just got on the motorbikes and started riding, and eight months later after riding through the jungles and up mountains

PETER TROY

and carrying the bikes up the sides of cargo boats and everything, I discovered Nias.'

Troy discovered this tiny island off Sumatra, with Kevin Lovett and John Geisel, who he'd come across on his travels. At the time malaria was rife, as was cannibalism and witchcraft. But they were blinded by a perfect wave at a place called Lagundri Bay, and that's where they camped.

Recently, Lovett was asked to go back to Nias for an SBS television documentary, 30 years after their discovery. When he got there, he looked up and found the people who had given him food during the '74 trip. It had been a hair-raising experiences at times. At one point, a witch doctor had been told to kill them. 'They thought that we'd come from another planet,' said Troy, 'and that when we were sitting on our surfboards we were actually fishermen taking away their food. They had no idea that we were surfing, so they went to their witch doctor and he put potions into the food that was being taken out to us at the camp and so they were slowly poisoning us, and we were to be sacrificed on the point [where there were] skulls already there from the tribes. In actual fact, Kevin's girlfriend, when they went back the second time, became extremely ill and nearly lost her life. John lost his life a few months later, in Afghanistan.

'It's frightening in a way because that's the innocence that you travel throughout the world with and that's the same for everywhere. It doesn't matter if you're in the jungles of the Amazon. I mean they can take your life just like that. You might think it's a great adventure to be using a blow dart to get the monkey and seeing shrunken human heads. Actually doing it and seeing them in the hut that you're living in, and going, "Oh well, that's five shrunken heads", you don't think that perhaps you might be one of them. And you don't know that you actually might be doing something wrong in their culture to the point that they want to take your life. You wouldn't know.

'So this is really a realisation for all of us who surf, whether we're just going to one of the islands in the Seychelles now or we're going to go to the Nicobar or Andaman Islands and we just walk in there as very naïve travellers. Innocent people could end up in a jail in Bangkok for the rest of their lives, or a jail in Turkey like [in] *Midnight Express*. You could be up in the north of Sumatra and you go into a northern province and the Muslims don't want you ... life's *very* cheap. In the end, you've just got to do the natural things right. Try to be pleasant; you're not out there to rip people off or take their girls or anything. You behave and you try to be a smart person.'

After Nias, Troy and his girlfriend travelled extensively through Asia and Africa, on the way reaching Camp Two at 18 000 feet on Mount Everest. With this expedition under his belt, though, and now on the verge of turning 40, he was starting to feel the magnet of responsibility.

'I didn't have a block of land or a car or a job, I had nothing. I was just a vagabond. It hit me very strongly at 40 that I had to do something, and the surf industry in a way had gone past me. There were successful stories all around me. So I grabbed the opportunity of going into business with a guy called Mick Court, and we started a clothing company. We became successful for a while, but went broke because we just got too big too quick and we just didn't have money.'

It was then that Troy returned to the surfboards business. 'I went back into surfboards and surf shops and ended up owning Mooloolaba surf shop. I owned a shop in Noosa, and I remained a surf retailer until two years ago. So, the whole circle back again.'

PETER TROY

In early 2002, Peter Troy was inducted into the Australian Surfing Hall of Fame, for his overall contribution to surfing. After having been to 140 countries, in which 10 years of his life was spent on the road getting from one place to the next, Peter made an incredible speech about life. He called it 'Holding Out Your Hand'.

'What I was trying to say in that speech was that when I was 10, someone, an Olympic sportsman, held out his hand and I actually was taught to surf, and that somehow, eight years later, Americans held out their hand and said, "Ride this board." Then I go all around the world and someone in a magazine office says, "Start a museum," and hold out your hand to all the surfers in Australia. And now today, after being a surfer for 54 years or something, I'm in the surfing museum. I walk through the door, I'm on the wall, but I've got to hold out my hand, so that just one kid out of 30 walks through those doors, becomes captivated and he says to himself, "I want to be a surfer."

'In a way, our interview is exactly that, and hopefully the guy who reads it will get a paragraph, or picture, or a vision that changes him. It's still out there to be had. People who I talk to and who I try to give a new style of life to, what I actually say to them, in a metaphoric way, is "Walk across that road, go down to the beach, take your clothes off, and swim towards South America." If you have conviction, someone out there will take you to Atlantis, or a dolphin will come up and give you a ride, or a yacht will come past and go "What's that guy doing swimming?" And you'll be taken to New Zealand or Tokyo, or wherever you want to go, or don't want to go. You didn't go there with that vision, you just took off to swim. And something else came along, and realised your conviction and your faith in what you were going to do, and took you somewhere else. And on that journey you

PETER TROY

learned to dive, you learned to navigate, you learned to fix motors, you learned another language, you come back into your own culture and you've got everyone else beaten. You're worldly, you know languages, you know experiences, you know hunger, you know wealth, you know poverty. You can walk down the street and hold your head high, because . . . you are a surfer.'

I walked past a 1914 American hardwood surfboard owned by the legendary Duke Kahanamokn, the only one in a private collection, and out to my borrowed '83 Falcon. Peter Troy held out his hand to me, then guided me out of his driveway with a smile. 'Good luck,' he said.

PETER TROY

Luke

MUNRO

WILLIAMS

Luke Munro has a story no one of an envious disposition wants to hear. He is good-looking, comes from a very rich family, and is Australia's most successful junior surfer right now. He has the world at his feet, but he doesn't want it yet. It started in '99 when he won the World Grommet Titles in Bali. Then his competitive career lulled for a year or two — but it was calculated, anticipated. The slow transition to the next level came in 2002, when he won three pro junior events on the trot. In the same year he won a wildcard into the Quiksilver

Kirra Pro, on the Gold Coast, the first event on the WCT. During the event, he had six-time world champion Kelly Slater staying at his house, nurturing his talent. You might think the shy 18-year-old has a future whenever he wants it, with qualification for the WCT just around the corner. You'd be right. Judging by his recent performances you may think he's going to make it happen straight away. You'd be wrong.

Newcastle, March 2002. It was an incredibly fast turn for a junior. Tight and quick, he swept through the thick section like a shimmy. I sat on the beach watching, about to enter a line-up crowded with youngsters. They were all practising for the Billabong Pro Junior that was in its second day at Newcastle Beach. Luke Munro was going for his fourth victory in a row and looked in form in the fading light, a professional unit amongst uncertain kids. He was almost out of place.

A couple of rocks popped up menancingly at the end, destroying a chance for the near-perfect completion to Luke's ride. A crowded line-up also boiled over on the beach, as the top seeds and other competitors and locals marched like army ants to the surf. It wasn't an inviting time to be in the water. Luke, the current leader of the Billabong Junior Series, decided one wave was enough. His heat wasn't until the next day and the standard warm-up session for event number five was discarded. He was clearly above that now. 'I was going to have a practise heat, but I couldn't get any,' he said, pulling his leg rope off and walking up the beach. 'They can have it. I'll be right.'

Luke picked me up in his car about 30 minutes later. I hadn't lasted long either. He greeted me outside his five-star hotel on the beach at Newcastle. Despite his tender years, he makes good money — he had made about $12 000 in prizemoney alone in the preceding few weeks. 'It was an exceptional couple of months,' he admitted.

LUKE MUNRO

Kirk Flintoff and Clint Kimmons, two more of the country's best juniors were passengers. The car was Kirk's, a brand-new Holden Barina with mag wheels and a boom box that took up half of his boot. It sent vibrations through my whole body, my heart beating to the sound of the bass distortion. It was clear that the days of Australian juniors struggling to make enough money to get to the next event are long gone.

We drove to the Great Northern, Newcastle's most famous pub, and while Kirk and Clint played the pokies, Luke and I sat with a beer and talked about his new life as a superstar in the making. His surfing is relaxed, yet tight and fast. He has that beautiful combination of technique and innovation. When you look at him — his pretty hair, piercing eyes, brown skin and Quiksilver logos — you can't help but think of Kelly Slater 10 years ago. It was ironic that Kelly was there at the start of Luke's career, at the Quiksilver Pro, to give him a hand.

'He's incredible, that guy,' said Luke. 'Just how much time he spends with everyone.' Barely having swapped nappies for boardshorts, the 18-year-old had found himself being tutored by the sport's best-ever performer. It's something every young surfer dreams of. 'He's so patient,' he continued. 'Answers everyone's questions and deals with everyone so well. Just having him come around to my house, surfing with me, spending time with me, it was so good.'

'So what did you learn from him?' I asked.

'He's a freak! We went surfing one day at South Straddie and did some tow-ins behind my jet-ski. I'd launch him into a wave and he was pulling off these crazy back flips. It was incredible, he'd pull a back flip and just keep going along the wave without losing his speed. I was a bit rattled surfing with him at first — I was all stiff and nervous — but after a few days I loosened up.'

LUKE MUNRO

Slater was also hanging out at Luke's house. But often, question time was monopolised by Luke's mates. 'There was so much I wanted to ask him, but I was a little shy. Then my mates came around and were just asking him anything. They were going crazy. It was heavy. One of my mates goes, "So what about those two twins you were hanging out with the other night — did you fuck 'em?"' I was mid-sip and just about covered Luke in beer. I leaned over and asked an old couple for a serviette, wondering if we'd made or spoiled their evening.

We were in the pokie room now, a focal point of a lot of these juniors' spare time. Colours, jingles and games. It's pretty full-on, but when you are making good money and still living with your parents, you've got to spend it on something. Luke threw in his second $20. 'Fuck, I blew $2000 at the casino one night on the Goldy,' he admitted. 'I was just betting big. Kelly was betting these massive amounts.'

'How much?' I asked, trying not to make eye contact with the pokies.

'Thousand-dollar bets in the top room. I had won US$1500 that day in the MSF Expression Session of the Kirra Pro, so I thought I could mix it up with him. The money I won was in traveller's cheques and I cashed them into chips straight away. So it was never money,' he laughed, then stopped. 'I lost most of it.'

Luke fingered the notes in his wallet before exiting for some fresh beers. 'Fuck, I've got to start watching my money now,' he admitted. 'I know what it's like for everyone now who has a loan. Those banks make so much money, it's heavy.'

'Loan? What do you mean?' I asked. Had he got the new PlayStation, or a new pushbike?

'I just bought a house,' he said nonchalantly. 'If it takes me 25 years to pay it off, I'll give the bank $600 000!' Impressive sum. Impressive too is the fact that these grommets are making that kind of money. But even more impressive is the fact that they are having a go at life at such an early age. They might be making money, but aside from the odd gambling habit, they're very smart with their finances.

The house Luke bought is on top of Tugun Hill, just around the corner from his home break on the Gold Coast, The Alley at Currumbin, a place where he's spent the better part of his life. We settled back down in our seats with our second beer. I watched him put his ID back in his pocket.

'I lived in Brisbane until I was five,' he said. 'Then I moved to the coast with my family. We had a house just a couple of blocks back from the beach, so it was awesome. Dad was involved with the surf club a lot so I was in the surf early with Nippers and stuff.'

This early introduction to the surf also gave him confidence to have a crack at surfing at a young age: 'I first stood on the front of a clubby board with my dad when I was six. Then I was just hooked. I found an old board at the dump and starting surfing every day. But between Nippers and surfing, there was a conflict of interest.'

A spell in the Nippers is something every Goldy grommet goes through. Nowhere is this iconic Aussie ritual more apparent than on the Gold Coast. 'Every single beach on the Gold Coast has a surf club. It's just tradition. When you have kids you put them through the Nippers to learn surf skills and not drown when you are at the beach. It's almost compulsory here. So I did that until I was 15 and then...' The conflict of interest. He was doing well in the surf carnivals, but he was also doing well in surfing, which was way more fun.

LUKE MUNRO

'I won a couple of Australian Surf Club titles, which was good. Dad was President [of the local surf club] and was really proud. I'd also won Queensland titles in different club events other than surfing, so I had a career there if I kept it up. But my motivation swung to surfing. I lost the discipline, and when you lose that, it's over. I just didn't love it like surfing.'

With his energies devoted to surfing, Luke's career began to blossom and the long point breaks of the Gold Coast made a perfect practice ground. 'It's good,' he admitted. 'But it's also a disadvantage, because sometimes I won't go left for weeks. Like right now, the waves have been pumping and I can't remember the last time I went left. It's not good for contests, so I go down to D-Bah a lot now that I'm aware of it and practice there.'

A young girl walked past. She was incredibly attractive. About a minute later she walked past again and stopped, fluttering her eyelashes. Then frustrated by Luke's lack of response, she stormed off. She didn't look used to getting the cold shoulder. Luke looked used to giving it, though: the kid is smooth as silk. When I next went up to the bar the girl who had been snubbed came up to me and asked, 'Is that Luke Munro?' I confirmed it. 'Oh he is *soooo* hot,' she said.

Luke is one of those guys who seems to feel totally comfortable in being a champion. He gets awesome results and rips the shit out of it. His surfing style is very polished. It's smooth and fast. He goes for the big turns in the big sections, but instead of trying to force turns, he just gets his board in the right spot and uses his technique. Power and intensity will come with age and he knows that. He hangs with the top 46 a lot too, so his surfing has the right type of influence. Though he isn't in the top 46 league yet, you get the feeling it is a matter of time. But like his surfing, he is not rushing it, or forcing it when it's not there. He is relaxed and focused. He knows the section is coming. But he has settled himself and is waiting patiently, building the venom, and waiting to strike. This is where he's smart. This is where his transitions are made perfectly. At a time when Australia has just produced a surplus of champions, Luke is going to kick back and wait his turn. Wait until his surfing is at the top level and then put his hand up. He doesn't want to be another number. He is almost too cool for that.

'Quiky want me to get straight onto the WQS and qualify,' he said. 'But I don't want to yet. To me there is a bit of a traffic jam there at the moment. Australia doesn't need another superstar yet. I reckon my surfing will be so much better in three years, so I want to wait until then. I don't want to just do it because I should or can. I don't want to just jump on the WQS tour half-ready and see what happens. I want to wait until I'm ready to win the thing. I want to make an impact.'

This is the difference between the best and the people that make up the numbers. Luke Munro is smart — but more importantly, he's patient. He didn't win the Pro Junior that week, only making the semis. Additionally, he didn't wait to contest the Mark Richards Newcastle City Pro the next week. He was leaving for some remote part of Africa with Kelly Slater on a Quiksilver promo trip — avoiding the traffic, nurturing his skills. Luke's time will come, I guarantee it.

LUKE MUNRO

Other great surfing titles from Harper*Sports*

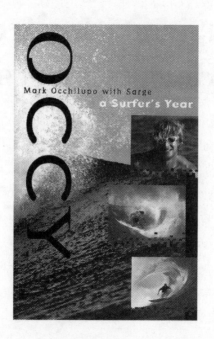

OCCY

Mark Occhilupo with Sarge

a Surfer's Year

OCCY
A Surfer's Year

Mark Occhilupo with Sarge

If there was one story that enthralled and captivated the surfing world in the 1990s, it was the resurrection of Mark Occhilupo, the one-time grommet from Kurnell who launched himself onto the world tour in 1983 and over the subsequent decade steadily rose through the ranks to a high of #3. But then, in the early 1990s, Occy dropped off the face of Planet Surf and, in his own words, 'hibernated'. Three years spent in the surfing wilderness saw his ranking plummet to a low in 1994 of #490 and his weight balloon from 75 kg to 111 kg.

Then, in spectacular fashion, Occy made a comeback. He got into top shape and returned to his spiritual home — the waves. In 1997, he finished runner-up in the world title race behind six-time world champion Kelly Slater, and over the next two years bagged a swag of tour victories. In 1999, at Barra Beach in Brazil, in the second last of the season's 13 scheduled ASP events, he finally clinched the elusive crown he had worked so hard for, becoming the last surfing world champion of the twentieth century.

A Surfer's Year picks up where Occy left off in Rio, following the day-by-day highs and lows of life on the World Championship Tour and Occy's all-out effort to successfully defend his title. From his 1999 triumph in Brazil to the 2000 Billabong Pro in Anglet/Mundaka in Europe, Occy has recorded, in his own words, a wry, honest and vivid account of what it takes to get to the top — and to stay there. With superb action and behind-the-scenes images of Occy in and out of the water, it's the hottest sports book of the summer.

ISBN 0 7322 6855 9

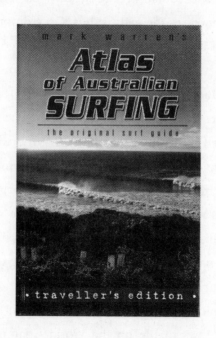

ATLAS OF
AUSTRALIAN SURFING:
TRAVELLER'S EDITION

Mark Warren

From the warm, clear water and unforgettable waves of far north Queensland to the cold and unforgiving swells of eastern Tasmania, *Atlas of Australian Surfing: Traveller's Edition* provides the most complete state-by-state guide to all the great surf breaks around Australia's coastline.

A former world and Australian champion, Mark Warren has been surfing the great Australian breaks since he was a grommet growing up in Sydney. Now his 30 years of experience and knowledge have been distilled into the new traveller's edition of his bestselling guide to the Australian surfing scene.

Atlas of Australian Surfing: Traveller's Edition offers a whole new range of surfing possibilities for those prepared to travel a little further than their local break.

It's much more than an adventure. It's an odyssey.

ISBN 0 7322 6731 5

new edition of the cult classic

'articulate, personable
calculating & stylish.
rabbit defines an era of
innovation and individualism.'
— kelly slater

wayne **rabbit** bartholomew

bustin'
down the
door

with sim baker

BUSTIN' DOWN THE DOOR

Wayne 'Rabbit' Bartholomew with Tim Baker

From street urchin to world surfing champion to boardroom heavyweight, this new and revised edition of the bestselling cult classic captures all the intrigue and adventure of Wayne 'Rabbit' Bartholomew's remarkable personal journey.

World Champion in 1978, World Masters Champion in 1999, and currently CEO/President of the ASP, Rabbit's charisma, flamboyance and warrior spirit have helped define surfing over three decades.